# Kidfree

## & LOVIN' IT!

**Whether by Choice, Chance or Circumstance**

D0890713

# Kidfree

## & LOVIN' IT!

### Whether by Choice, Chance or Circumstance

—The complete guide to living as a non-parent—

## Kaye D. Walters

SERENA BAY PUBLISHING

Kidfree & Lovin' It!
Whether by Choice, Chance or Circumstance

Published by
Serena Bay Publishing
Post Office Box 1331
Summerland, California 93067

ISBN: 978-0-9860014-2-0

Edited by
Denise Iest, Be Write
deniseiest@hotmail.com

Cover design
Dave Walters, Walters Group
www.waltersgroup.com

Cover photograph
Yuri Arcurs/Shutterstock.com

Back cover design
Sean Kirkpatrick, 4-Hour World Productions
www.4hourworld.com

Printed in the United States of America

## DEDICATION

This book is dedicated to my soul mate, Brian,
who makes it a joy to be kidfree!

# CONTENTS

INTRODUCTION.................................................................................................... 9

## —PART I—
### WHY WE ARE KIDFREE
#### The "Who, What & Why" of Non-Parenting

**CHAPTER 1**
KIDFREE? CHILDFREE?—*Who Are We?* ................................................15

**CHAPTER 2**
WHY PEOPLE HAVE KIDS *(Not all Reasons are Altruistic)* ...............................29

**CHAPTER 3**
WHY WE DON'T WANT KIDS—*101 Reasons Not to Parent* .............................45

**CHAPTER 4**
"I HAVE NO URGE OR DRIVE TO PARENT"—*And Dabbling Doesn't Do It!* ........53

**CHAPTER 5**
"I LIKE MY LIFESTYLE"—*Why Change It?* ..........................................61

**CHAPTER 6**
IT IS FINANCIALLY RESTRICTING *(To Put It Mildly)* ....................................73

**CHAPTER 7**
EARTH DOESN'T NEED MORE HUMANS ...............................................81

**CHAPTER 8**
"I DON'T PARTICULARLY LIKE KIDS" ....................................................89

**CHAPTER 9**
PARENTING: THE GOOD, THE BAD AND THE INEPT ...............................97

**CHAPTER 10**
"I FEAR CHILDBIRTH"—*(And What it Might Do to My Body)* ........................109

**CHAPTER 11**
"I DON'T WANT TO BRING THEM INTO THIS WORLD" .........................117

**CHAPTER 12**
"I WOULD HAVE TO GIVE UP MY CAREER" *(Or Alter it Greatly)* ...................129

**CHAPTER 13**
"WE LIKE OUR RELATIONSHIP" *(And Having Kids Could Ruin It)* ..................139

**CHAPTER 14**
PETS & SURROGATES ARE MORE FUN *(Even Better Than the Real Thing!)* ....151

## —PART II—
### ISSUES WE FACE
#### THE "NOT-SO-LOVIN' IT" SIDE OF NON-PARENTING

**CHAPTER 15**
OUR FOUR BIGGEST FEARS—*OF NOT HAVING CHILDREN* ......................................161

**CHAPTER 16**
PRESSURES TO PROCREATE—*AND FOLLOW THE NORM* .........................................175

**CHAPTER 17**
"BREEDER BINGO"—*AND CREATIVE COMEBACKS*...............................................185

**CHAPTER 18**
"STUNTED SOULS"—*AND OTHER CHILDFREE MYTHS* ...........................................195

**CHAPTER 19**
STIGMA AND STATUS—*IN A KID-CENTRIC WORLD*................................................205

**CHAPTER 20**
BREEDER ENTITLEMENT—*AND THE UNFAIR BABY BONUS* ....................................221

**CHAPTER 21**
SINGLE & KIDFREE *(FOR BETTER OR WORSE)* ........................................................233

**CHAPTER 22**
WHAT IF WE DON'T AGREE?—*WHEN ONE WANTS AND ONE DOESN'T* ................247

## —PART III—
### THE GOOD STUFF
#### PURPOSE, HAPPINESS AND KIDFREE RESOURCES

**CHAPTER 23**
FINDING PURPOSE—*BEYOND PROCREATION* ........................................................259

**CHAPTER 24**
ARE WE HAPPY BEING KIDFREE?—*YOU DECIDE!* ...............................................269

**CHAPTER 25**
YOU ARE NOT ALONE—*PROMINENT PEOPLE WHO PASSED ON PROCREATING* .....281

**KIDFREE RESOURCES**
A POTPOURRI FOR NON-PARENTS ........................................................................299

**AFTERWORD** ........................................................................................................303

**ACKNOWLEDGEMENTS** .......................................................................................305

**ABOUT THE AUTHOR** ..........................................................................................307

**NOTES**..................................................................................................................311

## INTRODUCTION

What compelled you to pick up this book? Are you considering bucking the trend and not having children? Are you not sure where you stand? Or, have you always known you didn't want kids and are experiencing issues with or without a partner? Perhaps you always thought you would someday, but circumstances were never just right.

Whatever your reasons, you are probably part of the growing group who will not be joining the ranks of parenthood in this lifetime.

I was driven to write this book for the same reasons many of you decided to read it. I was grappling with my decision not to have kids and the consequences that might incur. Once awakened to the fact that I would not be a parent, I was faced with questions. What would people say? Could I be fulfilled without having kids? Would I regret not having them?

It was as if I stood beside a carousel with everyone on it, and was choosing not to get on. Was I the only one who felt this way? I had to find out. I turned to my friend Google and typed in "don't want kids" and—to my surprise—found millions of results. After exploring a plethora of blogs and websites, I found I was not alone and that there are even terms for us like "childless by choice" and "childfree."

Why aren't we having children? Is there something different about us, something we all have in common? What are the downsides of not being a parent? I bought a few insightful books on the subject, but they didn't answer all my questions. There needed to be a study done on us—a comprehensive survey that questioned not just hundreds, but *thousands* of adults without children, whether they were childless by choice or by chance. So, I set out to do it myself, and to write the book I could not find.

## The Surveys

I needed to find answers about the group I was about to join for life—the non-parents. I wanted to know it all—the good, the bad and the ugly—including their opinions, fears, reasons for not having children, and issues they contend with in this kid-centric world.

What better way to find out than to ask these questions directly to adults without children? Not just hundreds of non-parents, but thousands; and not just in my own backyard, but around the world. I created the Kidfree Survey and administered it both online and by hard copy. I presented this survey for five years to any and all adults without children. Some were friends and folks I'd met, but the bulk of my respondents came via websites, blogs and online networks for the *childless by choice* and the *childfree*—and even from my own website: www.kidfreeandlovinit.com

With my 22-question Kidfree Survey, I queried more than 3,800 adults without children, aged 18 to 80, from 55 countries around the world. My respondents average 37 years of age; about 80% are female and 20% male; and as a group they possess a higher than average level of education.

Through their responses, I found answers to questions I didn't even know I had, and that I wish I had included in the survey. This prompted me to launch a second survey: the Childfree Dating Survey.

In my online discussion groups, I learned that to be *single and childfree* carries with it a whole different set of issues, not the least of which is trying to find a childfree mate. The Childfree Dating Survey was designed to explore these issues and ask questions I had missed on the Kidfree Survey. This survey garnered more than 600 responses, and was closer to a 70/30 female-to-male ratio. Over 60% of these respondents were single (as compared to 22% on the Kidfree Survey), and they shared with me their techniques for finding a mate as well as their opinions on when to tell that certain someone you "don't want kids." Likewise, those respondents who are now in a relationship shared their success stories (and horror stories) on finding a like-minded childfree mate.

Sample copies of both the Kidfree Survey and the Childfree Dating Survey can be viewed on my website: www.kidfreeandlovinit.com.

All in all, among the nearly 4,500 responses to both surveys, I found much witty—and sometimes humorous—advice on how to deal with the issues we face for not jumping on the parenthood bandwagon.

### Exploring Non-Parenthood

With my study findings and over five years of research, I have put together a complete and in-depth look at why people choose not to parent and the issues they face for not doing so. Besides research, I draw on decades of observation of those around me to learn truths about parenting. I share several true stories and anecdotes throughout this book, and when I do I often change the names to protect the innocent (and the *not so innocent!*).

It should be stated that I am biased to a degree, and to claim this is a completely objective discourse on the pros and cons of non-parenting would be misleading. Clearly, this book is filtered through the eyes of a non-parent who—for various reasons—is pleased to be free of offspring.

I do, however, back up my bias with stats. In fact, it was the plethora of research, studies and facts included herein (because I'm admittedly a statistic junkie) that in the end made me even more relieved I'm not a parent. I was so surprised with the wealth of information I accrued that *Kidfree* kept increasing in size and took triple the time to complete!

A note regarding quotes: All quotes in this book that are from my survey respondents are distinguished by an em-dash (—) followed by a name or gender, age and/or location. All other quotes are accompanied by a squiggly line (~) known as a tilde, the author's name and/or a reference. Quotes with no credit are my own quotes.

The first part of this book looks at parenting vs. non-parenting. It defines the different groups of *adults without children* and their reasons for not procreating, and also takes a look as the various reasons people *do*.

Part II examines the issues we face for living in a kid-centric world and not following the norm, while dispelling several myths about the childfree. Part III explores whether we are happy and/or can find purpose in life being a non-parent, and concludes with an exclusive list of prominent people over the ages who did not procreate.

\*   \*   \*

Just as I did by writing it, I hope you—by reading it—will find the knowledge and answers you seek about living the life of a non-parent. You may find sections herein you relate to, and others you want to skip over. With quotes from thousands of non-parents around the globe, you are bound to find yourself—or a kindred spirit—among these pages. Enjoy…

# —PART I—

## WHY WE ARE KIDFREE
### *The "Who, What & Why" of Non-Parenting*

# CHAPTER 1

## Kidfree? Childfree?
### *Who Are We?*

*When I came across the term "childfree" a year ago, I felt liberated.
Suddenly there was a real definition for how I felt, and how I am,
and an entire group of people who were like me and didn't require
an explanation of why I don't have kids!*
—Mandi B, 31, Austin, TX

*It's "girl's night out" since Sandy's back in town, and we're all sipping various beverages that have as little in common as we do with each other. We are an eclectic group of friends ranging in age from our late 30s to early 60s, but are all happy and successful. As I look around the table, I realize we run the gamut of marital statuses: one married, two divorced, and two never married. What's even odder is that the majority of us—three out of five—do not have children, nor will we ever.*

While our group may be odd, the number of people who are not procreating—referred to as the "childless" by governments and census bureaus—has doubled in the past thirty years in the United States and is increasing in most countries worldwide. But, while there are childless among us, most of us don't call ourselves that.

"Childless" connotes a lack of something, which those of us who have quite full lives without kids feel misses the mark. Just as we would not label a parent "freedomless," we do not expect to be labeled "childless" if we are happy. We have developed, instead, terms that better describe most non-parents—"childfree" and "kidfree"—which we will define herein as we take a look at just who, where and why we are.

## The Universe of Non-Parents

All non-parents are adults without children that fit into one of the following categories at any given time in their life. Those who...

- **Want children in the future**
- **Are currently trying to conceive**
- **Wish they had children, but feel the choice was taken from them**
- **Are content to accept that circumstances did not suit their intent to have kids**
- **Are certain they don't want children**
- **Are undecided about having children**

Put a star next to the category you fit into above, and see if it changes by the end of this book. *Kidfree & Lovin' It!* speaks to the last four categories of non-parents above, but parents and wannabe parents who wish to read this book in order to understand a friend or relative who has chosen the path of non-parenting are certainly welcome.

It should be noted that those who desire to parent and those who don't cannot be lumped into two categories of "yes" and "no," but rather fall somewhere along the following parenting continuum:

| No Desire to Parent | | — | | Neutral / Unsure | | + | | Strong Desire to Parent | |
|---|---|---|---|---|---|---|---|---|---|
| **10** | 9 8 7 6 5 4 3 2 1 | **0** | 1 2 3 4 5 6 7 8 9 | **10** |

Where do you stand on the scale? Many people move one way or the other on the continuum during their lifetime as they learn about themselves and what parenting entails. Others are steadfast from a young age and never change.

My Kidfree Survey found that many start out wanting kids when they're young, and then move to the left on the scale as they grow older, like this Floridian:

> I wanted them 'til I was about 14 or 15, then I was a fence-sitter 'til about 37, now I'm 100% positive I don't want any. —Female, 42, South Florida

The one thing we *do* know is that the desire to parent is waning throughout the world, especially in countries where women are well-educated and strong in the workforce. You might be surprised to find which countries are leading the way in non-parenting.

## Leading Non-Parent Nations
*Trends Around the World*

The management of fertility is one of the most
important functions of adulthood.
~Germaine Greer, Australian writer, feminist

While the birth rate is still growing in undeveloped countries like Niger where women give birth to an average of nearly eight offspring each, the overall fertility rate (number of children born per woman) of the world is actually declining. This decrease in fertility rate—from 2.8 in 2000 to 2.47 in 2012[1]—can be attributed to two simple factors: women having fewer children, and fewer women having children.

You needn't worry about human extinction, however, as we are still about 20% above the replacement rate of two births per woman.

It's interesting to note which countries are the leaders in low fertility rates and childlessness. In a report put out by the U.S. Census Bureau, the number of women ages 40 to 44 in the United States who have remained childless doubled from 10.2% in 1976 to 20.4% in 2006.[2]

That means one in five women in the U.S. are not having children! The study also found that those who had children averaged *one child fewer* in 2006 than did thirty years before.

Despite these numbers—and despite the fact that the very term "childfree" started here—the United States does not lead the world in the childless trend, not even by a long shot.

The chart on the following page shows a partial list of countries with below average fertility rates—all of which were well represented by respondents to the Kidfree Survey.

Note that countries like India, Israel, Malaysia and the Philippines—which were also well represented by survey respondents—do not appear on the list, because they are above the world average fertility rate of 2.47. However, upon checking the last few years' statistics from the Central Intelligence Agency (CIA) World Factbook, we find that these countries' fertility rates are indeed falling.

You can look up the total fertility rate (TFR) for each country in the world on the CIA's following website featuring the World Factbook, which they claim to update weekly:

www.cia.gov/library/publications/the-world-factbook/fields/print_2127.html

| Countries with Below-Average Fertility Rate (partial list) | Fertility Rate 2012 est.[3] (# children per female) |
|---|---|
| World Average | 2.47 |
| Argentina | 2.29 |
| South Africa | 2.28 |
| Mexico | 2.27 |
| Brazil | 2.16 |
| France | 2.08 |
| New Zealand | 2.07 |
| United States | 2.06 |
| Ireland | 2.01 |
| Costa Rica | 1.92 |
| United Kingdom | 1.91 |
| Netherlands (Holland) | 1.78 |
| Australia | 1.77 |
| Norway | 1.77 |
| Denmark | 1.74 |
| Finland | 1.73 |
| Sweden | 1.67 |
| Belgium | 1.65 |
| Canada | 1.59 |
| China | 1.55 |
| Spain | 1.48 |
| Switzerland | 1.47 |
| Russia | 1.43 |
| Germany | 1.41 |
| Hungary | 1.41 |
| Austria | 1.41 |
| Italy | 1.40 |
| Japan | 1.39 |
| Poland | 1.31 |
| Czech Republic | 1.27 |
| Lithuania | 1.27 |
| South Korea | 1.23 |
| Taiwan | 1.16 |
| Hong Kong | 1.09 |
| Macau | 0.92 |
| Singapore | 0.78 |

Surprised? I was equally intrigued when discovering these numbers, having been of the belief that the Western world would be leading the pack in non-parenting. In fact, it is the Eastern world that holds the five most childless countries in the world.

What is most fascinating is the "birth dearth" that's occurring around the globe. Whether you see this as good, bad or indifferent, there are sources at work here making humans less willing or able to procreate. Let's explore four types of non-parents in relation to their choice in the matter.

### Childless by Circumstance
*Infertility or Dearth of Opportunity*
Never found a man worthy of fathering my children!
—Jules, 41, Telford, England

Perhaps you always wanted to have kids—or assumed you would someday—but your situation just never allowed it. There are a variety of circumstances we may find ourselves in that are not ideal for bearing or raising children, the most obvious of which include: inability to conceive, an unwilling partner, or not finding a willing partner in time. We've all seen people who have ignored these barriers and reproduced anyway (i.e. the single woman who chooses to become a lone parent, or the hitched woman who chooses to—oops—procreate against her partner's wishes). The conscientious childless does not see these as smart options, and opts instead to refrain from parenting.

What about the infertile couple that wants kids but can't conceive? About 12% of women aged 15 to 44 have difficulty getting pregnant or carrying a baby to term.[4] But, for the record, fertility is not just a female issue, as it is just as likely to be a male potency problem. With the proper means and motivation these couples can choose to adopt. But some would rather remain childless than raise someone else's child:

If I can't have them naturally, and it appears that I cannot, then I do not want to raise someone else's child. And no matter what people tell me, I believe that adoption and sperm/egg donation amounts to raising someone else's child. —Cori, 39, New York, NY

Fortunately (for millions of orphans) there are couples with such a strong urge to parent, they don't mind raising "someone else's child," and thus adopt. Others see their infertility as a sign that they weren't meant to parent children.

Nearly 6% of respondents (both male and female) to the Kidfree Survey answered that they are "unable to conceive." One of them—who we can classify as "childless" rather than "childfree"—is a 46-year-old woman from Littleton, Colorado. She rated her love for kids as an "eight" on a scale of one to ten, and when asked if she was happy being kidfree, answered, "No, but it wasn't like I had a choice. It was just the way it was supposed to be." One reason she says she's not happy is, "because I think I would have been a good mom and I'll never know what it's like." Since she is currently single, adoption for her is not a viable option.

Another childless survey respondent—a 56-year-old writer from Oregon—is unhappy that she does not have children, although her spouse didn't want them anyway (which could be why they didn't adopt). She feels "neutral" about kids in general, but still regrets not having them and fears "growing old with no one to care for me."

Other "childless" are perfectly able to conceive, but have not found a partner with whom to procreate. More than 22% of my survey respondents are single, and about 4% of these wish they had children. One 43-year-old single male from Santa Barbara, California said he would have liked to have children if he had found a spouse in time. This is a common reason people don't procreate today, and partly why non-parenting is on the rise.

Many women these days forgo early motherhood to focus on careers, which takes them into their thirties before they may (or may not) start looking for a partner to have children with. Those who do look may not find a partner so quickly, and wake up in their late thirties or early forties single and childless, as the following woman explains:

> There are many singles out there who are not in a position to have children. It's hard enough just trying to find someone to share your life with anymore. Are these people supposed to do it alone or settle for someone for the sole purpose of having children? And if it takes until your 40s to find that person and have a child, there are many health issues to consider. With a 50% divorce rate, many people aren't rushing into having children only to find themselves childless and divorced in their mid to late 30s. This doesn't leave much time for finding a mate...and mating.
> —"Ran Outa Time," 41, Florida

This woman may have run out of time, but she has also crossed over from childless to "kidfree" in that she once wanted children, but is happy now because, as she says, "I can feel like a grown up kid. And now that I am established in my career, I am able to travel and see the world."

The concern that, "if I can't parent correctly I will not parent at all," was voiced by many respondents, and is nothing short of unselfish. One female who is "not sure" if she wants kids, says she has both her age and her job to consider. Like many, she does not believe she should have kids if she is working outside the home:

> I don't have a spouse (or a significant other) now. I am getting older and therefore there is an increased risk of having a child with a disability. If I find a spouse, I would only have kids if I did NOT have to work outside the home. —Female, 37, Phoenix, AZ

Many women these days get used to having a career, money and independence, and wind up changing their mind about having children altogether. I estimate that about half of all non-parents remain childless due to circumstances not being ideal, rather than an early choice not to parent.

A "Childfree by Choice" study in Canada found that almost one in ten people aged 20 to 24 do not *want* to have children, yet twice as many—one in five—are not having children in Canada today.[5] One might infer, then, that *half* of these non-parents are not procreating due to *circumstances*.

Besides being infertile, too old or partnerless, other circumstances might include simply not having the money or means to provide for a child, or not having the physical or mental wherewithal. And thank goodness these people have the foresight to not bring a child into the world under circumstances that are not ideal for raising him.

## Childfree by Choice
*Without a Doubt*

I'm not Childless, I'm Childfree!
—Jenn, 35, McAllen, TX

The antithesis of one who desperately wants kids but can't have them—hence "childless"—is one who *can* have them but chooses not to. Like Jenn above, these are the "childfree." Or, as Suzy Q (47) from Kansas who has never wanted kids puts it: "Childfree by choice, not by chance."

The hyphenated term "child-free" can be found in use as early as 1913 in a piece by the American Journal of Sociology exploring mothers' envy of women without children.[6] The word "childfree" gained popularity in the 1970s with the inception of the National Organization for Non-Parents (NON). Now widely used in English-speaking countries, "childfree" ("CF") is preferred over "childless" which implies a *lack* of something.

One by-product of coining a term to make non-parents feel better about their choice is that it unintentionally makes some parents feel worse about theirs. Over the past several years, as the term childfree gains momentum on the Internet, I've seen many parents voicing their disdain for its negative connotation. In their view—like the term "flea-free"—"child-free" is anti-child. This is an unfortunate misconception, as many childfree love kids, but just don't want their own. Rather than a jab at parents, *childfree* is intended to be a positive label for those who have chosen to take the less-trodden path of non-parenting.

One can become childfree at any time in their childbearing years. Over half the non-parents who took my survey said they have *never* wanted to have children. These are the confirmed childfree, some of whom knew—like Brenda—as early as preschool where they stood on the issue:

I knew as a preschooler that I was childfree, and being childfree was one of the things on my "list" of things I wanted in a husband. He had never wanted children either. We both enjoyed his nieces and nephews and friends' children. I did not expect to find a soul mate that fit my list as soon as I did or where I did. —Brenda, Childfree Network member

Other CFs—like those below—remember a point in their childhood when they realized they didn't want children:

When I was about 5, I was shopping with my grandmother and I saw a mannequin wearing a wedding dress. I told my grandmother I wanted to get married but NO BABIES! Apparently, even at 5, I was adamantly childfree! —Jess Davis, 27, Cincinnati, OH

When I was 14, I announced to my parents that I did not want to have kids. My mom laughed it off and told me I would change my mind later in life. Well, when I hit 30 and there was still no talk of children, she finally realized I was not kidding. —Cosmo (female), 35, Jackson, WY

The childfree networks are chock-full of people who, at an age before many of us even thought about parenthood, knew they weren't interested in it. Many felt indifferent to children even as a child, and preferred the company of adults. Although I wasn't a confirmed childfree, I recall getting bored playing with the kids at family parties and sneaking away to listen in on adult conversations, which seemed more interesting to me.

I also remember how other girls loved mothering the younger kids— picking them up and carrying them around like babies, feeding them, dressing them, etc. No interest here! I just didn't have that "maternal thing." The difference is, I didn't know back then that I didn't want to parent. I just assumed I would like everyone else. This puts me in the 47% of childfree who didn't always know they didn't want kids, but figured it out later in life, like Anne from Kentucky:

When I was younger (teens/early college) I assumed I would have kids, because that's what people do. I eventually realized that that wasn't the same as *wanting* to have kids...then realized I'd never had that maternal feeling/instinct. So I didn't exactly want them, but I hadn't fully decided not to have them. —Anne, 27, Louisville, KY

In fact, nearly half of all respondents who "don't want children now" or "aren't sure," had actually *wanted* children when they were young.

I wanted children when I was younger and believed that it was just what you did when you were an adult. As I grew, examined the issue more, and became more in touch with myself, my feelings about the issue changed.
—Female, 20, Fredonia, NY

The beauty of becoming "childfree" is that there is a feeling of weight lifted off you when you make your decision. Although there are issues to face for not following the norm, there is a feeling of peace when you find your truth and make the choice that is right for you.

Perhaps you will find—like 37-year-old "Smiley" from Sublimity, Oregon—that "Happiness is being childfree."

## The "Fence-Sitters"
### *To Parent or Not to Parent, That is the Question*

I am a definite fence-sitter. I have moments of wanting them,
but always come back to the negatives of it
and can't find a compelling reason to do it.
—Camille, 34, Utah

In addition to those who pine for children and those who are glad they are free of them, there is a substantial group of people in limbo. These are the fence-sitters. Now, more than in our parents' era, men and women everywhere are realizing we have a choice: to become a parent or a non-parent. And, although it sometimes complicates matters, choice is a good thing.

Over 13% of Kidfree Survey respondents say they are "Not Sure" if they want to have children. This indecision usually reflects a conscientious person who does not take the job of parenting lightly, and who is weighing the options carefully before making a choice that will change the rest of his or her life. Isn't it ironic that age and wisdom often bring with them ambivalence and uncertainty? Or is it just that we learn to question more?

When I was a teenager and younger I did want kids. At this point I am completely on the fence and leaning more to the "no" side.
—Chriss Sheehan, 35, Landenberg, PA

It is often ambivalence that leads to introspection, which in turn brings clarity. Many of you may be leaning one way or the other or waffling back and forth about the prospect of parenting. Perhaps this book will help you find the answers within yourself. If only more people would take pause before procreating, there might be a lot fewer unhappy parents and children in the world.

## Kidfree & Lovin' It
*By Choice or By Chance*

Being "kidfree" is more than a choice; it's a positive mindset.

There's a new term I coined for the gray-area group of non-parents who don't fit neatly into "childless" or "childfree." It is a broader term that includes both those who are non-parents by choice as well as those who are non-parents by chance. The term is "kidfree."

Before I started publicizing the term, I noticed that the only two times it appeared on the Internet, it was used by parents—once to describe a "kid-free zone around the stove" and once by a mom relishing "a quiet kid-free moment." (Perhaps this means parents won't take offense to the term?) Either way, I am tickled to say the term "kidfree" (without the hyphen) is starting to bloom on the Internet, and is now used as a nom de plume by many a proud non-parent and blogger.

Anyone without kids can be "kidfree" if they choose to be. A woman who—for physical reasons—cannot bear children, can be kidfree. A couple that—after years of trying to conceive a child—comes up empty can be kidfree. A single man or woman who simply never found the right mate to procreate with before time ran out, can be kidfree. Any non-parent who wanted to have children, or at least assumed they'd have children, but circumstances did not fall into place, can—in fact—be kidfree.

But why aren't they labeled "childless" if they wanted kids and couldn't have them? Because they have not only accepted this fact, but have *embraced* their new life path. They are not complaining or cursing or whining or pining over the reality that they will not be having children.

Rather, they may—at the least—be making the most of their life as a "non-encumbered non-parent," or—at the most—be rejoicing at the opportunities life without human dependents has brought them. Here are three examples of true "kidfrees," all of whom were unable to conceive:

> Most of my stories have to do with being childfree due to infertility. Some people have no clue that it's not necessary to go through all the invasive procedures (IUI, IVF, surrogacy, adoption) when it is just as fulfilling to lead a life without children.
> —Jennifer, 29, Dallas, TX

> At this point and time in my life I am very happy being kid-free. I am able to continue my education and become a lawyer without the extra stress of children. Also, I can do whatever I want to do, whenever I want to do it.
> —Redhead, 26, Selma, AL

Infertility brought us to this lifestyle. We did not originally plan a childfree life when we got married, but through the years of trying to become parents, we realized that we were already happy with our life the way it was. Kids would mess that up. Even though we cannot become parents of our biological child, there are other options toward parenthood, but we no longer wish to become parents. All that time to think about our true, deep reasons for wanting kids changed our life plans completely. We are happy this way. —Female, 33, Michigan

Perhaps you didn't *intentionally* choose not to have children, but circumstances have brought you here. You are "childless" if you are upset by this and feel life has dealt you an unfair hand. You are "kidfree" if, in hindsight, you are glad about this, and rejoice at the freedom and experiences not having kids has brought you. Even "fence-sitters" are kidfree, if they recognize the good fortune of their situation.

### Truisms and Diversities
#### *Non-Parents Revealed*

The kidfree are as diverse as their reasons for not procreating (of which there are dozens we will soon explore!). Yet there are some common threads running through our colorful circles.

Overall, those who have elected not to be parents tend to be more highly educated and possess more professional and managerial occupations.

Researchers have also found childfree couples to have higher incomes, to live in urban areas, to be less religious, to subscribe to less traditional gender roles, and—no surprise here—to be less conventional.[7] But they're leaving something out...

When I announced to a childed friend of mine that I was writing this book, she asked, "Have you found any truisms about the childfree?" The first thing that popped into my mind was all the online chatting in my childfree group about cats, dogs, birds, rabbits, horses and other beloved or exotic pets. As I came to discover, the kidfree tend to be animal lovers more than the general public. A preponderance of animal rescuers and veterinarians also live among our ranks.

This prompted me to ask about pet ownership on the Kidfree Survey. My survey results found the percentage of non-parents who own pets (71%) to be substantially higher than the national averages in the U.S., Australia or the UK (52%-63%).

What really sets the childfree apart, however, is their level of education. World-renowned demographic expert David K. Foot of the University of Toronto concluded that a female's education is the most important determinant of the likelihood of her reproducing. The higher her education, the less likely she is to bear children.[8] This explains why developed countries are leading the way in childlessness.

My survey reached the same conclusion about the unchilded being more highly educated. In fact, respondents to the Kidfree Survey were *more than twice as likely* to be well educated than the general U.S. population over 18 years of age.

The chart below (comparing Kidfree Survey respondents with U.S. Census numbers for age 18+) shows that more than 40% of non-parents have attained a Bachelor's degree compared to 17% of the general population of the U.S.; 19% have attained a Master's degree compared to 6%; and 5.4% have attained a Doctoral Degree compared to 1.1%: [9]

**Higher Education Attainment**

■ U.S. 18+  ▨ Non-Parents 18+

The reasons non-parents tend to be more educated than the general populace may be twofold:

1) The more educated the female, the higher her career opportunities and the longer she puts off motherhood, often indefinitely.

2) Those who have chosen *not* to have children have more time and money to devote to higher education and/or to go back to school.

While non-parents could be labeled "well-educated, professional, unconventional, progressive and pet-loving," there are exceptions to the rule. We are a diverse crowd with personalities as varied as the masses. We range from atheists to deeply devout, introverts to social animals, and homebodies to world travelers. And, while many of us welcome having fewer responsibilities as non-parents, others seek out charity work, mentoring jobs, and volunteer rescue work because they have the free time.

More importantly, while some unchilded truly dislike children, most of us are neutral to fond of them.

Politically, those who choose not to procreate tend to be more socially liberal as a whole, but non-parents do not share a unified political or economic philosophy. We run the gamut from the religious right to the liberal left, with a slew of independents and libertarians in between. This is why most childfree groups tend to be *social* rather than political in nature (although we do partake in political sparring now and then!).

*　　*　　*

*As the waiter brings our tab to conclude girls' night out, I realize that all three of us non-mothers are "kidfree" to different degrees. But then I think about my one absent friend—Lori—who is "childless." She is not happy with her situation and wishes she had found a man in time to have children. She often glamorizes motherhood and what could have been.*

What is it that draws people to parenthood? Before we examine the many reasons people don't have children, let's take a look at the possible reasons people *do*…

# CHAPTER 2

## Why People Have Kids
### *(Not all Reasons are Altruistic)*

When people ask me why I don't want children, I ask them why they
do/did. They never can seem to come up with a convincing reason.
—Jez, 37, Ohio

The pitter-pat of little feet; unconditional love; the miracle milestones; creating a "mini-me;" carrying on the family name; someone to care for me when I'm older… These are a few things a parent looks forward to when bringing home his or her bundle of joy.

But there are many more reasons people procreate—some altruistic and others just plain self-serving. So, before we examine the reasons people opt *not* to have kids, let us take a look at the reasons people *do*.

When asked, "What are the reasons your friends and family had kids?" a non-parent named Tilly Smith from Australia replied, "This question is hard to answer, because how often do people actually discuss why they decided to have children?" True! People find no shame in asking us why we don't want kids, but can you imagine how politically incorrect it would be to ask, "Why did you have kids?" No, this is something we have to determine through observation, because even a parent may not have thought through their reasoning before they reproduced.

This chapter reveals what we non-parents speculate were the reasons our childed friends and relatives had children, and they range from the saintly to the simply sinful. We'll start by examining the most predominate reasons people have kids, and end with a laundry list of all the reasons imaginable that people procreate.

## It's The Norm
### AKA "Part of the Script"

You go to college, you get married, and then...babies!
That is what you do.
—Sara, 33, Alma, CO

Remember the childhood rhyme: "First comes love...then comes marriage...then comes baby in the baby carriage?" Little girls chanted it like a mantra. One of the main reasons humans have children—or, more accurately, the main reason they *don't refrain from having them*—is simply because "it's the norm." More than 85% of respondents to my survey checked this as a reason their friends or family members had kids.

Like most animals, humans are largely followers. And, because it's part of the script and everyone's doing it, people think they should follow suit, as Anne surmises:

I think the rest of my family and friends are following a script that is pre-written. They think they HAVE TO get married and have babies.
—Anne, 34, Cincinnati, OH

What is the script? It usually goes like this: 1) go to college, 2) get married, 3) have babies, and 4) live happily ever after. Right? It's what we (in the U.S.) call "the American Dream," although that might also include the proverbial house with a white picket fence.

In fulfilling the script, many folks skip number one, increasing numbers are skipping number two, and it's debatable how many people actually achieve number four! Every country has its version, but the script always includes number three—having children. After all, it takes courage "to live beyond the mold," as this CF puts it:

Most people have children because they believe it's "what people do once they get married." For some reason, many can't see their lives being fulfilled without reproducing. Some even go so far as to think it's their reason for living. I believe humans have reached a point where we can exist beyond our primal needs to mate and carry on the species. There's so much more to experience, but people can't get away from the belief that having children is not negotiable and never even try to live beyond the mold. —M. E., 20, Sunland, CA

The following female with her Masters Degree, believes that lack of education compels people to follow the norm and procreate:

I do not mean this to sound rude, but (especially when I lived in Virginia) having a family is the "norm" for people who have no education and feel like their only option of "doing something with their lives" is to have kids.
—Dawn S., 28, New Jersey

## They Want to Live the Family Lifestyle

*Some just really wanted to have a family. They saw parenthood as a source of joy, and who am I to argue with them as long as they don't argue with me? I view it as a very personal decision, just like religion and diet.*
—Max Barons, 36, Austin, TX

Let's face it, having kids is about wanting to be a parent and live the family lifestyle, right? Well, hopefully. Lifestyle encompasses what you eat, think and do on a daily basis, and you better like what you design for yourself, or you may not live happily ever after. For some that means being a soccer mom with a van full of kids on her way to Chuck E. Cheese, and for others it means anything but.

The good news is, some 70% of my survey respondents said they thought their friends and family had kids because "they wanted to be parents and live the family lifestyle." This is key, because it is unfair to yourself and your kids to have them in spite of the fact that you don't really relish the job description. "Checking out" of parenting once you find you don't enjoy it, is not a good option.

The purported perks that come with parenting persuade many prospective parents to procreate. Besides fun-filled family holidays, they may look forward to the unconditional love of a child, the joy of watching them grow, the challenge of being a parent, teaching them good values, and an increased sense of purpose and worth.

## They Love Kids

*Many friends and family members just plain love kids.*
—Julie, 29, Dallas, TX

Loving kids and wanting to have your own is a good reason to have children. In fact, it should be a prerequisite. Children need love and attention. If one does not truly like spending time around kids for long periods, one should not intentionally reproduce. It's as simple as that.

Many survey respondents said their friends and family members had children because "they genuinely love kids, and parenting comes naturally to them." (Kate, 40, Los Angeles) In fact, over 56% thought people have kids "because they like/love kids." Both my brother and sister—who love the family lifestyle—fall into this category, as this non-parent describes:

They truly love children and family is their highest priority—they simply want to be surrounded by them. —Susanne, 37, Sydney, Australia

As Judy (32) from San Diego says, "They simply like and want children, in a way I don't." And this is why they make good parents, because they simply want them so badly that it is worth the hard work and sacrifice to raise children. When your heart is into something, it's worth the challenge.

"Loving kids" on it's own is not a good enough reason to have them, however, if one does not have the means to raise them. Take for example Nadya Suleman, the woman who had enough embryos artificially implanted in her womb to give birth to eight children (in addition to her six), in spite of being jobless, on food stamps, living with her parents, unable to pay her hospital bills, and no father for the children. When asked "why," she told the media she loves kids. She may love them, but she is a good example of someone who does not have the tools to raise them.

Many non-parents who love children have refrained from having their own. They may choose to teach or work with kids, but they do not feel equipped—for a variety of reasons—to raise a child from infancy to adult.

## Biological Urge vs. Instinctive Drive

*The biological urge has been by far the dominant factor in my friends' decisions to have kids, often leading them to have children while in unhealthy marriages and relationships.*
—Tiara Lynn Agresta, 30, Chicago, IL

Much ado has been made about biological urge in regard to procreation. Whether its prevalence in men is as strong as in women is a subject of many blogs and books. Women's biological urge seems to manifest through thoughts of babies, partnering and reproducing. The urge often overpowers any rational life plans that had been made up to that point, as in this woman's case:

> I was totally 100% sure I didn't want children until about 8 months ago when it hit. First it was an inkling that maybe I could be a good mum, which transformed to the realization that I would want to have kids one day, which swiftly descended into an all consuming desire to have kids RIGHT NOW! I don't think all women get the urge, but I certainly did.
> —curlylib (post on naturallycurly.com)[1]

It's true, not all women experience this urge, but I did in my early thirties. I remember being touched by baby ads on TV and considering men for their potential "fathering" qualities. The difference is, I didn't act upon it, and actually ran from a few opportunities, only to find the urge dissipate over the years. Most female humans still succumb to the "urge" and that is why we will not be going extinct any time soon.

Biological urge is a raw compulsion without regard to reason. Some say it is tantamount to sexual urges, and it's no coincidence that our sexual desires peak in our best childbearing years. Although humans were given the unique ability to reason and plan ahead before acting on our impulses, some yield to this "biological imperative"—the perpetuation of the species—and then justify the reason later:

> The stated reason [they procreate] is irrelevant, it's a biological imperative—they "want" kids...They make up reasons to rationalize the compulsion. —Jose Fritz, 32, King of Prussia, PA

"Instinctive drive" is a slightly different animal that applies to both men and women. It is more of a gut feeling. About 44% of my survey respondents felt friends and family had children due to their "instinctive drive to be a parent." This is good, because if one instinctively feels they are meant to be a mother or father, they probably are. It is a lack of this instinctive drive that compels many of us to stay unchilded.

## To Keep Their Marriage/Relationship Together
### *AKA: "Band-Aid Baby"*

> Their marriage was failing and they thought
> a child would magically cure it.
> —Julie Ann, 28, Colorado Springs, CO

When structuring my survey, the thought never occurred to me to add a very prevalent reason to my multiple-choice question of why people have children: To Keep their Relationship Together and/or To Strengthen a Weak Relationship. Since this is one of the last reasons I would have a child, I failed to include it in my list of answers.

Well, it turns out to be a biggie. Thankfully, I offered a space for "Other" reasons to procreate, which hundreds of respondents utilized. Dozens of non-parents wrote of relationship reasons for couples reproducing, ranging from the mild "To try to make their relationship stronger" (Lexy, 23, Mastic Beach, NY) to the robust "Two different couples who are friends of ours told us it was either DIVORCE OR KIDS!" (Barron, 32, Denver, CO), and plenty of reasons in between:

> To hold the relationship together. —Miss P, 37, South Hampton, England

> "Keep" the significant other. —Mandy, 23, Scottsboro, AL

> To save a failing marriage, but that never works!
> —Gaynor, 53, Canberra, Australia

> Some women have children to hold their relationship with their partner together, thinking the man will be more committed if they have a child or two together. —Darlene, 46, Alberta, Canada

So, in effect, there are people procreating to "solidify" a (perhaps shaky) relationship and to ensure "commitment" from a (non-committed) partner, as well as those who try to "strengthen" a weak relationship, "keep" a significant other, or "save" a failing marriage. Can one child do all this? Or will it spell disaster for the family? I'd put my money on the latter, and don't think it's a gamble one should take.

Robbie gave me the Band-Aid Baby analogy when revealing two bad reasons he thinks some have kids:

> I truly believe this: 1. Band-Aid Baby: Some couples will have a child to distract from, or heal a troubled marriage. It doesn't work. 2. Badge of Legitimacy: Some women (more common in teenage girls, I think) will have a child as proof, to self and others, that they are desirable. The offspring being proof that they have had sex.
> —Robbie Thwart, 41, Maryland

### To Carry On The Family Name, Genes or Legacy

> To make a male heir to the family estate and name.
> —"Spurlgurl," 35, St. Michaels, MD

Twenty-seven-year-old Cypress from Berlin, Wisconsin, reports that—in addition to loving kids and/or wanting to keep their marriage together—some people she knows had kids because they "wanted to carry on the family name." There's not much to say about this reason other than, "Huh?" Is the family name really that important?

I admit I'm glad my brother had a son to carry on the Walters name, but it's a lousy reason to procreate (and certainly not why *he* did). First of all, what if you don't have a son? I know a woman with five sisters and no brothers who told me her parents finally quit trying. Secondly, if your son becomes a disgrace to the family, you'll wish he never bore your name!

One of my survey respondents, when asked what her fears were about not having children replied that she wished she had somebody to leave her things to when she passed. Okay, leaving a legacy behind is important to some. But wouldn't it be nice at the end of your life to be able to pick and choose what special treasures go to which special friends or relatives rather than having to divide it among your offspring who are expecting—sometimes waiting for—it all?

Linda Kay (below) seems to have had her share of misguided boyfriends who wanted to procreate for these reasons:

> My ex-boyfriend told me once that he wanted some kids to "pass his legacy on to," to which I replied, "Give it to your nephews or your niece." He also couldn't tell me *why* he wanted a kid, he just "felt" it. I actually had one ex-boyfriend who wanted to literally "present" his child (a boy, no less) to his mom along with a huge arm flourish and say "A SON!" Needless to say, we didn't last too long... —Linda Kay Marshall, 43, Slater, IA

The desire to "carry on the family genes"—which 39% checked as a reason—is no less vain than wanting to carry on one's name, and can prove equally disappointing, as we shall see below.

### They Wanted a "Mini-Me"

I've often heard they like the "science experiment" of finding out what "a little bit of me and a little bit of my husband" will make!
—Phoena from happilychildfree.com, Texas

We've all fantasized of what a mini-me or a mixture of the two of us would look or act like, haven't we? Her looks and his brains, his body with her eyes, and so on. Not only is this an egotistical reason to reproduce, but sometimes it's best left to fantasy. Brains and brawn do not always beget brains and brawn, and bad traits can be inherited too.

Do you know someone who inherited most of the bad traits from each parent and little of the good? I do. I also know outstanding athletes that produced offspring who have no physical talents, nor any interest in sports.

Likewise, if you're counting on your son or daughter to acquire your brains or your spouse's ambitions, forget it. How many famous inventors have given birth to inventors? Artists to artists? Success and/or talent seems to skip a generation, and wealthy entrepreneurs tend to beget heirs-in-waiting more than they do self-made businessmen.

Of course, there are exceptions to the rule, and sure we're curious what a child of ours would have become, but it's risky, and certainly not a sound reason to bring a human into this world, as these two point out:

> One could easily argue wanting to have a mini-me to carry on my genes is far more selfish in an already overpopulated world, than simply acknowledging that the world probably would not significantly benefit from my offspring. —E.T., 36, Ann Arbor, MI

> The best parents I know had kids because they genuinely believed their children can make the world better for future generations. These kids are now 22 and 20, and they're awesome, amazing people. The worst parents I know are the "mini-me" ones. —"I'm Not Kidding," 46, Portland, OR

## Pressure from Family and Culture

Most of my friends had kids because of huge pressure from family and
religion. I've been yelled at, called dirty names just for saying I'm not
interested in kids. It's hard to choose something that's
not popular, so most give in to the pressure.
—Kimberly Jean, 34, San Diego, CA

Are you a product of your nationality or the region in which you were raised? Many people have children simply because the pressure to do so from family and culture is too ominous to elude. Vincent Ciaccio—the former Spokesperson and Director of Strategic Planning for No Kidding! International—says that as most of his friends and family are children of Italian immigrants, many have children due to "cultural expectations."

Children are also the center of Hispanic culture. When asked for reasons her friends and family had children, one woman answered:

Cultural. I'm Mexican-American and I live in Texas on the U.S.-Mexican
border. In Mexican-American culture, there is pressure on people to have
kids, more so than in mainstream American society. Everywhere I go, I
see many people with kids. I have no kids and I'm happy that way, but it
frustrates me to see too many people with babies and kids.
—Veronica, 37, McAllen, TX

In spite of her culture, Veronica has chosen not to parent, and—although she's happy being kidfree—she admits it's not easy:

I feel left out, because in my part of the country many people have kids
and I'm one of the few who don't. In general, however, I'm not going to
have kids just because it's the "thing" to do or because "everyone else is
doing it." I just have to do what is right for me, no matter what anyone else
thinks. —Veronica, 37, McAllen, TX

Statistics show that Veronica's courage to belie her cultural pressure in order to follow her own path is still a rarity in the U.S., in that childless numbers are low for Latinos compared to non-Hispanic whites and African Americans. Of course, Italians and Hispanics aren't the only ones who ingrain the importance of childbearing. Non-parents from India say theirs is a very child-centric culture that shuns the choice not to parent; and in Eastern cultures, one's offspring are often a measure of status:

Status. Having children is a way to compare yourselves to others. Part of
my family is Chinese, so measuring oneself through a child's accomplishments is part of the culture. —Pollo Vermont, 35, Brattleboro, VT

According to author Elizabeth Gilbert's (*Eat Pray, Love*) experience, the first thing Indonesians ask is, "How many children do you have?" And if the answer is none, the next question is either "why not?" or "when will you be having them?" They honestly assume everyone wants children, and fear there must be something physically wrong with you if you don't.

Different regions put more cultural pressure on women to procreate than others. For instance, the Midwest and South in the U.S. are much less tolerant of rewriting the life script than say California or New York, as I suspect this Michigander is referring to:

It's expected where I grew up. You can be a career woman, sure, but you also have to give that up, eventually, and have children.
—Amber S. McGrath, 30, Lansing, MI

Pressure from family is not always due to culture and region. A sibling may want cousins for their kids and a parent may long for grandchildren. In fact, almost 40% of survey respondents checked "their parents wanted grand-kids" as a reason some friends and relatives had kids.

## Religious Reasons

They thought they should have kids because "God" wanted them to. They couldn't and still can't afford it (the kid), but since the invisible sky bully told them it was OK then they were happy.
—Male, 26, Elwood (USA)

Not far behind family and culture comes the influence of god and religion. More than one in five survey respondents say they have friends and/or family members who procreated for "religious reasons," often because they believe "it's God's plan for them."

Catholics and evangelical Christians proclaim that God commands us to "Go forth and multiply" and wills that young women marry, bear children and guide the house. Mormons—who have the highest birthrate in the U.S.—place family at the center of their religion, with women expected to serve as child-bearers and caregivers throughout their adult life.

Two of my high school classmates had large families because their religions (Catholic, Mormon) set them up with those expectations.
—Laurel Acheson, 39, Colorado

The religions of Islam, Judaism and Mennonitism also promote child-bearing, and the Amish are among the fastest growing populations in the world, with an average of 6.8 children per family.

Natalism is a belief that promotes human reproduction and parenting. One recent trend among conservative Protestant natalists is the Quiverfull movement, which advocates large families and eschews all forms of birth control. Chapter 16 explores further how the church pressures people to procreate, and points out a countertrend developing among Christians.

## Built-In Caretakers for Old Age

I suspect there are a lot of people out there who want someone
to take care of them when they're old, but thankfully I don't
know anyone who stated that reason.
—Susanne, 44, Cincinnati, OH

One fear tactic people use on those who announce they don't want children is to ask, "but who will take care of you when you're older?" More than 36% of my survey respondents cited this expectation as a reason their friends and family had kids.

Some find solace in the symbiotic notion that "I will take care of you when you're young and you will take care of me when I'm old." Others see it as a deal only agreed to by one party, as the offspring doesn't always hold up their end of the bargain.

Governments often play on our fears of "what might be" in order to prod us into procreating, but many in the younger generation are not assuaged by such campaigns:

People from the older generation tend to have the "take care of us in old age" thinking but for my contemporaries it doesn't seem to be a major consideration. It would be nice but it's not the main reason. The Singapore government is actively promoting this way of thinking (have children to care for you). Personally I think they're just trying to pass the burden of healthcare to the next generation instead of taking it up.
—Eveline How, 32, Singapore

We'll discuss this notion that our kids will be there to care for us when we're older, in a later chapter.

## To Appease A Partner

Reluctant but nagged into it by a spouse who had baby rabies.
—"Free and Loving It," Female, 40, Elizabethton, TN

Goodness knows how many parents out there did not actively want to procreate, but did so because their partner wanted to. Dozens of non-parents wrote in that they knew people who procreated due to "pressure from spouse" (Bren, 36, Massachusetts), or simply "to please their partner" (Kate, 38, New York).

Several non-parents tell of brothers who have been tossed into parenthood by a persuasive wife:

My brother mainly had kids because his wife wanted kids and our parents wanted grandkids. I don't remember him ever saying he wanted or didn't want any. I think he just assumed he had to. —Male, 25, USA

Brother: didn't want kids, married somebody who later decided SHE wanted a kid. ("We can have one, but it's YOURS. YOU wanted it, YOU raise it!") Poor kid. Why they didn't discuss this before marriage, I don't know. Smart me: I married someone I knew didn't want kids either.
—Female, 43, California

The #1 reason, of course—because their wife convinced them to do it—happened to my twin brother. —Female, 35, Tucson, AZ

Although it seems men acquiesce more than women (giving credence to the myth that childbearing is largely a "woman's issue") there were several respondents who knew women that had children simply because their husbands wanted them.

My father adores children and was wonderful with us. My mother claims that she didn't really want kids and wouldn't have had them if my father had not wanted them; she claims it was the best decision of her life.
—Rebecca, 32, Alexandria, VA

Although it can work out as with Rebecca's mom, becoming a parent solely to please your partner is a risky move with lifelong consequences for you, your spouse and your child, which we will discuss in Chapter 22.

### Carelessness
Although most of the "noble" reasons are checked,
most of my friends came under the "it was an accident" category.
—Michael Lawrence Alford Jr., 44, Santa Rosa, CA

Of course, there are mindless reasons people have children, which don't even involve intent, ego, love or desire. When asked to list why their friends and family had kids, almost half said, "It was an accident."

Are there that many people opposed to birth control? Or is it that they don't know how to use it properly? It's both, according to the director of the Office of Population Research at Princeton University, James Trussell. In analyzing government reports, he found that about half unwanted pregnancies are from improper use of birth control or method failure, while the other half from is from no use of birth control.[2]

Surprisingly, a study by the National Center for Health Statistics shows that the use of birth control for sexually active adults is *decreasing*, which experts fear could lead to an increase in unintentional pregnancies.[3] Some surmise this is due to birth controls' rising costs and undesirable side effects. Either way, it equates to more unwelcome babies; and raising a child is a heck of a lot more costly than birth control!

## They Never Questioned It

I don't think most people think of having children as an OPTION.
They think of it as a GIVEN. This has always perplexed me.
—Patty, 40, Philadelphia, PA

The other "unthinking" reason people procreate is because—like blinking—for some it is an automatic behavior that is not prone to questioning. It is simply a standard element of human existence that to many is a given, as this Californian states:

I don't think they ever questioned the paradigm of growing up and making a family. I don't think all of them really even WANTED kids...
—"smartypants," (female with PhD), 36, California

## Less Than Altruistic Reasons
### *The Selfish and The Sinister*

I was amazed at the number of self-serving and downright sinister reasons respondents gave for their friends' and family's procreation plans. But upon pondering the list, I'm not surprised, because I do know of—or have heard of—at least one parent that fits into each of these categories.

Following is a partial list—as gleaned from the survey—of self-serving, sleazy, sinister and sometimes stupid reasons some choose to reproduce. I've picked just one or two survey quotes for each category.

### To Entrap a Man

To trap a man. (I know MANY women who have done that). I also know of someone who got her husband drunk and conceived her fourth child within weeks of finding out her pregnant sister-in-law was getting her tubes tied after her delivery. She wanted to steal the baby thunder and be the mother of the youngest grandchild. —Vespertine, 31, Lafayette, LA

### To Receive Financial Support / Inheritance

Because they wanted financial and emotional support from others (family money, tax breaks, etc.), and having children is a bargaining chip.
—Jillian Finn, 34, Pittsburgh, PA

My sister's husband insisted on children. His parents are wealthy and he knew grandchildren would ensure his inheritance.
—Vicky Thomas, Orlando, FL

### To Get Government Perks / Avoid Government Punishment

Baby bonus in Australia is $5,000 a child, which you get when you give birth to the child. Now our government is giving all parents $1,000 for each child in a family to get the economy moving again. I think people are having children for the wrong reasons. —Cats16, 36, Picton, Australia

In Soviet Russia where I grew up, the communist government used to tax people for childlessness after they turned 25.
—"Irish girl," 30, Dublin, Ireland

### Status Symbols

They see having kids as a "status symbol." —Melanie, Tacoma Park, MD
Because kids are a sort of "status symbol" amongst certain groups.
—Female, 38, Colorado Springs, CO

### Sibling Competition

I feel like it's a competition in my own family. If you have kids, you are a winner and if you don't you're a loser. Always a negative connotation.
—Penny, 41, Phoenix, AZ

### Fashion Accessories

These days, people seem to treat children as accessories. Now, in addition to the little black dress, you need a little Kaeighley or little Myckaul to go along with it. Kids are the new black. You heard it here first.
—"The Space Cowgirl," 31, Arkansas

I know many people who had kids just so they could have the trendy "accessory baby" that seems so in style today.
—Roxanne Brennan, 38, Estell Manor, NJ

### Women: To Opt Out of the Working World

A couple of my friends had kids so they wouldn't have to work anymore. (It was the only way their husbands would allow them to stay at home.)
—Teresa V., 37, West Des Moines, IA

One friend never found the job she wanted in the working world. She told me once she decided to have a baby because the job of mom sounded better than a lot of other jobs. —Heidi Morgan, 31, Apex, NC

### Men: To Prove their Virility or Manhood

Prove their virility. My friend's husband likes to say how he's "filled a pram twice." (Plus he shouts and swears at his kids.)
—Jo Jager, 42, Kent, England

I know one man who I think had children because he wanted to be able to boss them around and have power over them. He has seven kids, by the way (shudder!). —Cheryl, 39, St. Charles, MO

### The Desire to Abuse Them

With the number of adults who were abused as kids who I know, and the way parents talk about their kids, i.e. when a parent says something bad their kid did, get a response of "If MY kid ever did that I'd…(describe horrific abuse)"—I think the desire to abuse kids is behind it! Or, at least use them as servants, sometimes. —Beth, 45, Oklahoma

### To Use Them as Servants

They like having someone help them with chores, etc.
—Tom & Judy, 28, Denver, CO

This final reason—"helping with chores"—held more weight in pre-industrial America when kids helped tend crops and animals on the family farm. But in today's Walmart world—with few families homesteading—kids actually *add* to the chores of modern life rather than subtract.

## The Laundry List

As gathered directly from Kidfree Survey responses, following is a laundry list of reasons people might procreate.

**Reasons People Procreate** *(From the Saintly to the Sinister):*

1. They Love Kids
2. They Like Kids
3. They Love Babies
4. They Really Wanted Children
5. They Want To Be Parents
6. They Want To Live The Family Lifestyle
7. They Think They'd Be Good Parents
8. To Pass Their Values On
9. To Achieve Purpose or Fulfillment
10. To Experience The Milestones In A Child's Life
11. To Have A Friendship With Their Kids
12. It's The Norm
13. It's "Part Of The Script"
14. Instinctive Drive
15. Biological Urge
16. To Appease a Partner or Spouse
17. To Give Their Parents Grandchildren
18. They Never Questioned It
19. Didn't Know They Had A Choice
20. It Was An Accident
21. They Were Forced Into It / "Oopsed" by a Partner
22. Pressure From Family
23. Pressure From Friends
24. Pressure From Culture
25. To Follow Tradition
26. Religious Reasons
27. To Fit In With Friends
28. Someone To Care For Them In Old Age
29. To Carry On Their Genes
30. To Carry On Their Family Name
31. Someone To Leave Their Legacy To
32. Someone To Continue The Family Business
33. They Wanted A "Mini-Me"
34. To Prove They Are Responsible Adults
35. To Replace Themselves On The Planet
36. To Perform A "Great Civic Duty"
37. Worried They'll Regret Not Having Them
38. It's "Human Evolution" / The "Purpose of Our Existence"

39. To Fill A Void
40. To Give Them Meaning
41. To Prevent Boredom
42. To Prevent Loneliness
43. To Relive Their Childhood
44. They Thought It Would Be "Fun"
45. They Need Structure
46. They Need To Be Needed
47. They Can Afford To, So Why Not?
48. To Create A "Symbol Of Love"
49. To Strengthen Their Relationship
50. To Save Their Marriage
51. To Improve A Spouse's Behavior
52. To Gain "Unconditional Love"
53. To "Fix" What Was Wrong In Their Childhood
54. To Show Their Parents They Can Do A Better Job
55. To Live Vicariously Through Their Kids
56. So Their Kids Will "Make The World A Better Place"
57. Sibling Competition / "Evening The Score"
58. To Validate Their Worth
59. To Feel Important / "Badge Of Legitimacy"
60. It's Fashionable / Kids Are "Accessories"
61. For Status
62. For Power
63. For Attention
64. "Consumerism"
65. To Keep Up With The Joneses
66. To "Have It All" (Career & Parenthood)
67. Men: To Prove Their Virility/Manhood
68. Men: To Have A Son To Coach
69. Women: To Opt Out Of The Work World
70. Women: Worried They'll Run Out Of Time
71. Women: To Prove They Are A Real Woman
72. Women: To Experience Pregnancy
73. To Entrap A Partner
74. To Receive Financial Support
75. To Receive Government Benefits/Rewards
76. To Avoid Government Punishments/Taxes
77. To Receive Employment Benefits & Perks
78. To Ensure An Inheritance
79. To Use Them As Servants
80. To Abuse Them
81. _____ (Your own addition)

The following quote from a non-parent in Santa Barbara is the most thoughtful I could find on the subject of reproducing:

> It is difficult to understand why exactly people choose to have kids. I feel that unless one decides to devote their lives to creating a secure, loved child, they should not have them. Children deserve all possible advantages in life that will enable them to be healthy minded happy adults. —Tina Takaya, 45, Santa Barbara, CA

*   *   *

The reasons for having children seem to range from the insightful to the inane and from the caring to the cruel.

But what would a kidfree non-parent know about the desire to reproduce anyway? My knowledge is more acute—and my expertise more aligned—with our following topic: Why We Don't Want Kids…

# CHAPTER 3

## Why We Don't Want Kids
### *101 Reasons Not to Parent*

I'm just really not interested in the job requirements.
—Female, 32, California

When I Google searched "reasons not to have children" in 2012, I got more than 400 million results. This is ten times the amount I got the year before. Either there are more reasons than ever not to have kids or more people are discussing the option of non-parenting—or both.

Either way, there are some entertaining lists—authored by parents and non-parents alike—espousing good reasons not to have kids: "The Top 100 Reasons Not to Have Kids (and Remain Childfree)," "24 Reasons Not to Have Children," "50 Reasons Not to Have Kids," etc. Each list has a unique angle, and I encourage you to check them out—whether you are undecided or just up for a little entertainment.

I purchased Corinne Maier's *40 Good Reasons Not to Have Children* to get the inside scoop from a mother of two. With statements like "breast-feeding is slavery," "child-rearing is war" and "child-parent dialogue is insanity without relief," she confirms our beliefs that we have dodged a bullet—and she does so in an acerbic tone only a parent can get away with!

Following are 101 reasons why one might not relish being a parent. These reasons were garnered from my two surveys of more than 4,400 adults without children, and many of their quotes are sprinkled throughout. This is not an exhaustive list. There are dozens of reasons not listed here that people give for not procreating—from as trivial as "pregnant women are not attractive" or "my dog would be mortally jealous" to as serious as "they might mistreat my cats" or "I'm afraid I might do harm to them." Feel free to add your own reasons to the list as they come to you…

## 101 Reasons *Not* To Parent:

**Childbirth is…**

   **hard on your body**

   **medically dangerous**

   **painful**

I have an incredible fear of dying in childbirth. It's like a nightmare. Just another reason I'm anti-kid. —Mandi B, 31, Austin, TX

**Daycare is…**

   **costly**

   **not ideal for children**

**Kids…**

   **act up in public**

   **break things**

   **cost an average of over $300,000 each to raise[1]**

   **cry a lot**

   **demand attention**

   **embarrass you in public**

   **fight with each other**

   **get in accidents**

   **get sick a lot**

   **have allergies (i.e. to your favorite foods or pets!)**

   **nag for the latest fad or gadget**

   **play parents off on each other**

   **spread colds & infections**

   **want instant gratification**

   **may not take care of you when you're older**

In my opinion, kids are just too disruptive and loud (running all over the place). What makes it worse are parents who don't make any effort to discipline them. —Veronica, 37, McAllen, TX

**Kids are…**

   **difficult to travel with**

   **messy**

   **needy**

   **noisy**

Why should I sacrifice myself for kids when I want to be a slave to no one? Not to mention the mess a kid creates.
—Shaheen Banu, 23, Mauritius

**Kids *can* be...**

> a disappointment, no matter how well you raise them
>
> born with birth defects
>
> manipulative
>
> mean to other kids
>
> ungrateful
>
> spoiled brats

Kids are not only a financial drain, but also a psychological drain!
—Sylvia Losier, 44, Halifax, Nova Scotia, Canada

**A Parent can't...**

> be flexible with his/her job or vocation
>
> be spontaneous
>
> come home to a quiet house and read
>
> dine at quiet adult restaurants (even though some do!)
>
> leave a child home alone
>
> leave a child in a car alone
>
> return a child, if he doesn't like them
>
> sleep in whenever he/she wants

I see so many women who are completely stressed out, overworked and exhausted because they have families. It seems to create undue stress on their marriages also. It seems like they are always caretaking others and don't get a break. —"AB," 35, Valley Village, CA

**Parenting can...**

> age you prematurely
>
> be an unrewarding job
>
> cause anxiety & stress
>
> cause arguments
>
> cause lost friendships
>
> damage your career
>
> damage your sex life
>
> drain your energy
>
> ruin a good relationship
>
> lead to divorce

Children of Divorce, need I say more? —Elizabeth, 37, Northern California

**Pregnancy...**

> can change your body permanently
>
> is difficult and dangerous

I REFUSE to put myself through nine months of discomfort and the agony of labor and delivery when I can't stand kids in the first place...
—Faith, 47, North Carolina

**There are no guarantees what you'll end up with**

Scared to have an unhealthy child (Down syndrome, autism, etc.).
—Female, 39, Brooklyn, NY

**You might...**

> **be a bad parent**
>
> **disagree with your spouse on how to raise them**
>
> **get stuck single parenting**
>
> **have to give up your pet(s)**

I would rather be a THINKER (two healthy incomes, no kids, early retirement) than a SITCOM (single income, two children, oppressive mortgage). —Female, 38, Colorado Springs, CO

**You will be...**

> **adding to the overpopulation of the earth**
>
> **bringing them into a corrupt world**
>
> **less happy, according to statistics**
>
> **passing on your (or your spouse's) bad genes**

My family has a history of cancer on both sides, heart disease on both sides, diabetes on both sides—why would I want to pass on those genes? —Laura Bennett-Kellay, 35, Battle Creek, MI

**You will have less...**

> **freedom**
>
> **money**
>
> **privacy**
>
> **time for exercise**
>
> **time for hobbies & sports**
>
> **time for sex**
>
> **time for travel**

It's too time and money consuming. You tend to lose your freedom—that is no travel, personal or business—which is damaging to the career itself. Moreover, I can't see my life being run according to the school timings and school holidays. —"crystalcarbon6," 32, Bangalore, India

**You'll probably have to...**

> **be around other people's kids you don't like**
>
> **buy a family car**
>
> **buy or rent a larger home**
>
> **buy car seats**
>
> **change diapers**
>
> **childproof your home**
>
> **clean up after them**
>
> **deal with other parents**
>
> **do more laundry**
>
> **constantly find babysitters**

You'll probably have to (cont.)...

>constantly buy new clothes
>
>cook for more people
>
>eat at "kid-friendly" restaurants
>
>find childcare you can trust
>
>help them with their homework
>
>move to a good school district
>
>taxi them around to school & events
>
>vacation during crowded school holidays
>
>watch children's movies & videos
>
>watch what you say in front of them

My main reasons for not wanting kids are financial, emotional, and environmental. Other reasons...I don't want to live in a certain neighborhood so the kids can go to a certain school, I don't want to drive a SUV/minivan, I don't want a messy house/car, I don't want to take orders from a two year old, I don't want to do homework...again, I don't want to watch what I say or do, and I don't want MY life to stop.
—Bob M., 39, Milwaukee, WI

You will worry about...

>drug & alcohol abuse
>
>keeping them safe
>
>kidnapping/child abduction
>
>online social groups
>
>online predators
>
>other kids' bad influence
>
>pedophiles everywhere
>
>"sexting" (texting sexual pictures of themselves)
>
>teen sex & pregnancy
>
>their predeceasing you
>
>violence in schools

Too many horrible things can go wrong: diseases, kidnapping, sexual predators, mental illness, developmental disabilities.
—Lynn O., 28, Rhode Island

Your spouse...

>may not be a good parent
>
>may resent the attention you give them

We feel that this could put a lot of strain on our marriage with the corresponding disagreements. —Male, 32, Ontario, Canada

Your child...

>could become a criminal
>
>may commit suicide
>
>may not like you

Somehow that last one stings the most. What if, after all is said and done, decades of love, sweat and expense, your child does not like you? Don't say it's rare, preventable, or only happens in troubled families, because there are too many cases to the contrary. I can count on both hands cases where an offspring loathes a parent for no justifiable reason. How heartbreaking must that be? Of course, I also know cases where a parent doesn't like his own child, which could be equally miserable I suppose.

You might be thinking, "Well, my kid(s) wouldn't have all the bad behaviors listed here, because I would be a good parent." I used to hold this belief myself, until over the years I saw honest, caring, loving and/or strict parents end up with spoiled, rude, troubled and/or addicted children.

While the preceding was a laundry list of the negatives of parenting, most don't need that many reasons. All it takes is one good reason, and the following graph reveals the top 12 reasons—according to the Kidfree Survey—that adults choose not to have children:

| If you DON'T want children, what are the reasons you don't? And if you are NOT SURE you want children, what are some reasons you might not. (Please check ALL that apply): | |
| --- | --- |
| I don't have the urge or drive to be a parent | 84% |
| I would have to give up my lifestyle | 79% |
| It is financially restricting | 72% |
| I would have to restrict my sports, hobbies and/or travel | 69% |
| Overpopulation / I don't think the world needs more people | 62% |
| I don't particularly like kids | 55% |
| I don't like the way kids are being raised today | 53% |
| I don't want the physical wear & tear on my body to bear children | 53% |
| I don't want to bring them into this corrupt and/or dangerous world | 44% |
| I don't think I would make a good parent | 44% |
| My spouse or significant other doesn't want them | 31% |
| I would have to give up my career | 30% |
| Other (please specify) | 19% |

Under "Other," respondents were able to write in their own reasons that weren't listed. One in five did so, and I've included many of their quotes herein. One reason I kept coming across was the concern they *might genetically pass on harmful mental or physical conditions or diseases to their offspring*. This is a thoughtful, unselfish reason not to procreate.

Mental illness runs in both of our families, and I fear passing that on, which seems unfair. —Rachael, 36, Boston, MA

Another theme in respondents' comments (which we'll discuss later) had nothing to do with bad genes or the horrors of kids and parenting. Rather, they focused on the world as it is today and where it's headed in the future as a reason for not wanting to subject any new offspring to it.

Most of all, the future looks bleak for future generations—environmentally, economically, socially, politically—not sustainable.
—Leslie Chow, 37, Ontario, Canada

### Top 10 Reasons to Stay Kidfree

Instead of seeing the downside of parenting, many non-parents focus on the upside of non-parenting in their comments. Following is a list of the ten most positive aspects of non-parenting (not necessarily in this order):

1. More Freedom
2. More Money
3. More Time
4. Less Worry
5. Less Stress
6. Less Noise
7. Better Relationship with Spouse
8. More Energy to Help the World
9. More Privacy
10. More Happiness

Some parents might take exception to #10 above. But studies show—as we'll see in Chapter 24—that childless couples are happier than childed.

\*     \*     \*

One respondent sees all the goodies she gets from not succumbing to a life of motherhood. When asked why she doesn't want kids, she wrote:

More $, more sex, more free time, more time to rescue animals, more laughter. —BattleCat, 33, Houston, TX

The next eleven chapters take an in-depth look at each major reason non-parents choose not to procreate, whether they are *confirmed childfree*, *kidfree by circumstance*, or *still on the fence*.

# CHAPTER 4

## "I Have No Urge or Drive to Parent"
### *...And Dabbling Doesn't Do It!*

"I don't feel the *need* to *breed*."
—Tammy T., 41, Los Angeles, CA

Do you feel the "need to breed?" The most common reason people choose not to have children is they simply don't have the urge or drive to do so. When asked the reasons why they "don't want children" or "might not want children," 84% of the Kidfree Survey respondents answered, "I don't have the urge or drive to be a parent."

If you are in the camp that believes—like I do—that parenting is such a huge responsibility you had better want to take on the job with all of your being, then why would you have kids if you simply don't have enough interest? I suppose some do it to please their spouses or parents, and perhaps others do it because "it is the norm" and everyone else is doing it.

However, most childfree who have carefully considered the responsibilities of parenthood do not think these are good enough reasons to have a child. Rather, we are of the belief that parenting is such a serious, all encompassing, and important responsibility, that one better have a significant urge or drive to do it in order to do it well.

*Urge* is defined as "a strong desire or impulse," and *drive* as "an innate, biologically determined urge to attain a goal or satisfy a need." So, if one does not have the drive to be a parent, they do not have a strong desire toward that goal. Most people probably *do* have the urge and/or drive to parent, but—because of societal pressures—it's hard to determine what percentage.

## Instinct vs. Reasoning

Humans are the only animals that have children on purpose
with the exception of guppies, who like to eat theirs.
~P.J. O'Rourke, political satirist, journalist, writer

Although meant in jest, there is truth to satirist P.J. O'Rourke's above quote. Guppies do like to eat their fry (as do swordfish, mollies and other common livebearers), and humans do have the ability to choose whether or not to have children. (O'Rourke does have children, by the way.)

As discussed earlier regarding "why our friends and family had kids," many of us believe they had an instinctive drive to be a parent. This is a key ingredient to being a successful parent, especially when coupled with the means to do so. Conversely, the lack of such inner motivation is an excellent reason not to bring a child into this world.

"Instincts" are defined as innate behavioral patterns, while "drive" includes the motivation and desire to carry them through. Humans are born with certain instincts, but, unlike most animals, we have the ability to guide these instincts with higher reasoning—i.e. the ability to consider the future and make choices.

Humans possess the instinct to reproduce in order to propagate our species, which is manifested through our physical desire to have sex. But, unlike animals, humans have the ability to choose sex without bearing offspring.

It is said that the only animals that have sex for other than reproductive reasons are humans and dolphins (both of which, interestingly enough, engage in homosexual activity). But the advent of birth control—such as "the Pill" introduced to the public in the 1960s—allows humans to engage in heterosexual sex while preventing pregnancy.

So, even if all humans possess the instinct to breed (a fact that in itself is debatable), the childfree do not confuse this with a strong desire to have children. When we deduce that we don't have the drive it takes to parent, we take precautions to prevent pregnancy—i.e. we engage in what could arguably called "responsible sex."

Many non-parents believe it is irresponsible to follow one's basic instinct to procreate without having both the means and the motivation to be a good parent. The term (as you'll see in the Appendix) the childfree use to describe those who proceed to procreate irresponsibly is "breeders."

## "Biological Clocks"
### *And Other Baseless Brouhaha*

"My biological clock is ticking!" says Lisa to Vinny as she stomps her feet with each word for emphasis, in the film *My Cousin Vinny*. Here the cliché is used by a woman—albeit comically—to threaten her man to speedily marry her before it's too late to bear children. Isn't it funny that it's also used by society to convince a woman to change her mind about not having children? Several friends of mine (mostly males) used the cliché—"but your clock is ticking!"—on me in my thirties when discussing marriage and children (or my lack thereof), and I tried to laugh it off.

While they may have meant no malice, did they honestly think that factor alone would make me change my mind? That somehow my future inability to create something would predispose me to want to create it now? Does that mean that since my hands will be shaky when I get older, I should want to become a sharpshooter *now*? Simply because I *can*?

Many a female has been talked into racing to motherhood on just this argument. The premise is: "You may not want to be a mother *now*, but if you do later, it might just be too late." This is taking action based on fear, rather than one's inner calling. Childfree women just say "No." In fact, they've developed a series of jocose comebacks for the ticking biological clock, most of which you'll find in Chapter 17, but here's a good one:

If I *do* have a biological clock, someone stole the batteries.
—Suzanne, 37, Sydney, Australia

Well, Suzanne does have a biological clock, just as all humans do. And the reproductive portion of it starts ticking away in a woman's mid-twenties, making her less fertile and—after 35—less capable of carrying a healthy baby to term. There are, however, women who actually *do*—by tubal ligation or hysterectomy—remove their reproductive abilities. These women literally did take the batteries out of their clocks!

By the way, it's not only women whose biological clocks are ticking away. Men's are too. As men age, the decline in their testosterone causes the volume, speed and quality of their sperm to decline. In a review of male fertility, the journal *Fertility and Sterility* (2001) found that "between ages 30 and 50, the average man's sperm declines by up to 30 percent in volume, swims up to 37 percent slower, and is five times more likely to be misshapen."[1] Since a higher number of misshapen sperm equals a greater potential for genetic abnormalities, older men are not only less likely to impregnate a woman, but are more likely to pass on genetic disorders like Down syndrome and schizophrenia. The difference is: While a woman eventually reaches menopause, a man can usually produce sperm through-out his lifetime, which is why we see senior men fathering children.

## Dabbling Doesn't Do It
### Having the Means Without the Motivation

Don't have them if you don't want them. It would be better for you to respect your desire to *not* have children than to have a child out of "obligation." Bring children into a world when they will be loved, cared for and wanted by the parents.
—Dewey Fairbanks, 33, Minnesota

Some choose to reproduce solely because they can afford to do so. One need only turn on the TV or open up *People* magazine to see how fashionable it is for the mega-rich (and super busy) to have children.

Besides celebrities, we all know examples of the detached parent who has the means to breed many children, but does not have the motivation to give them the time and energy they need. No amount of money can substitute for a parent's love and attention. And, if one does not have a strong desire to have kids, nor the energy to devote to them, it is selfish to go ahead and have them just because one can *afford* to do so.

While the percentage of prisoners who were raised in lower income, broken families is staggering, I wonder about the statistics for unhappy, dysfunctional, well-to-do progeny of parents who didn't want to parent?

Dr. Loren G. Yamamoto, author of *Tidbits on Raising Children*, stresses the importance of parents spending time with their kids, citing that "in the eyes of a youngster, providing time with them is at least as important as material wealth," and that:

In the pursuit of our careers, jobs and material wealth, all our time spent working is time taken away from our children. Highly successful, busy, working parents have often chosen to pay others to take care of their children. If given a choice of low, medium or high income, we would pick a high income. But if this choice requires that we must sacrifice time spent with our children, would we pick the same choice? Do we really want someone else raising our children so that we can work to gain career advancement and material wealth? Perhaps we should prefer a medium income with more of our time spent with our children so that we can raise them and instill them with our values.[2]

Many of us don't have children, because we simply don't have the time or energy to devote to them.

## No Burning Desire

I think you should only have kids if you have the BURNING DESIRE to have them. I never had that feeling, and I fully accept that most women/men do have that feeling and they should definitely do it!
—Annette, 39, St. Paul, MN

Nannies aside, there are a lot of people out there who just don't have a strong desire to do the things that parenting entails. Some men and women just crave the family life and the entire parenting package, which may include—but is not limited to—changing diapers, cleaning up messes, taxiing kids around, attending PTA meetings, helping with homework, and countless cartoons, videos, pizza parlors, play dates and time-outs. Did I mention noise and toys? But seriously, along with the rare "miracle moments," much of this list defines being a parent.

The list of parenting responsibilities usually won't deter a person who has a deep longing to have children. There are logical reasons not to procreate, and sometimes logic doesn't apply. It's a case of inner calling.

When asked why she doesn't want kids, the following woman—who is working on her master's degree—checked eleven reasons she didn't want them, and then wrote in:

But the big one is, I just don't want kids. I don't know why—it's just the way I am. I wonder if it isn't just something we're born with—not necessarily something we choose? Lots of people recognize the logical implications/restrictions inherent in having kids, but if they WANT to do it, feel the urge to do it, they do. All the reasons I checked above are simply logic, but the feeling I have, the urge I have is to focus on other things—growth, education, working in the community as a counselor with people who are already here. I just have a different urge than most people (or else, I'm more willing to follow the urge than others are). I *want* to do other things and I just can't accept the judgment from others that this is because I'm a bad, selfish, stunted, immature person. I really don't think any of those things are true—in fact, I'm a very compassionate and self-aware person. —"Childfree in Charlotte," 31, North Carolina

And why should she be judged any less compassionate for wanting to help the community rather than her own (unborn) offspring? Another good question she poses is: Why do the childfree have less of an urge to reproduce than most people? Are we born with a deficit of the gene that gives us the "instinct to procreate?" Or, is it our knowledge of parenting that prevents us from blindly jumping onto the carousel with everyone else? Perhaps it's a combination of both.

"Maternal urge" was never really there for me like I sensed in almost everyone else! —Female, 57, St. Louis, MO

"Maternal instinct" is defined by Elyse Rubenstein—a Philadelphia psychiatrist who counsels new mothers—as "an inborn tendency to want to protect and nurture one's offspring."[3] Many childfree women say they just don't have that tendency.

> I have never been interested in spending time with babies or children, so I naturally have chosen not to have them. I do not have the "ticking biological clock" that some other women talk about. "Uninterested" is the best way to describe my feelings about children. —Grace, 34, Seattle, WA

Sometimes our maternal/paternal instinct may lean more toward animals than humans, like Christine Walls who says she has an "avian maternal instinct," and dozens of other respondents who spoke of their desire to nurture pets more than little people. But does this mean we are "wired wrong," like this woman from Wisconsin professes?

> I am wired wrong. I hear or see a baby, and feel repulsed and disgusted. A baby *animal*, and I go weak and get all bubbly for it. That's where my maternal instinct went. —"MayhemKB," 29, Green Bay, WI

Others, like "Childfree in Charlotte," have no instincts to nurture small things, but have an "urge" to focus on personal growth, education, and helping the world instead. And as this Iowan put it:

> The only people who should have children are the people that *want* to have children. —Female, 30, Iowa

### Knowing Young
*Or Not*

It takes some women forty years to realize they never had a strong desire for kids to begin with, while others, like Tracy, knew from a young age:

> Absolutely nothing that revolves around being a parent appeals to me. Just as women know from a young age that they've always wanted to be a mom and have however many children, there are women like me who know from a young age that they never want them. All the things I envision for myself and my future don't involve kids. —Tracy, 32, Iowa

Although I am not one of the non-parents who knew from a young age they didn't want children, I imagine it would make the path in life simpler—not *easier*, but more straightforward. In my case, I didn't give parenthood much thought in my youth, and—although I wasn't crazy about babies—just assumed I would have them someday.

One of the problems with this "not knowing, yet assuming" is that you spend a lifetime deluding yourself and others about your goals and desires. Hence, your subconscious desires are at odds with your daily actions.

For me, it started in my twenties when I would run from guys who wanted to settle down and get married. Then, in my thirties, when I was ready to get married, I would find myself breaking up with boyfriends who started talking children (even though I *thought* I wanted them!).

When I finally figured out, in my late thirties, that I didn't have a strong urge to have children, I could look back and see the pattern. If I had known in *advance*—like many of my childfree cohorts did—I may have made some different dating choices, and could have saved others time and grief by being frank with them.

From observing non-parents, it appears that those who knew from a young age they didn't want kids—the *confirmed childfree*—tend to be more upfront with the people they date. But those who aren't sure or just really haven't pondered the issue may find themselves in a more nebulous situation—i.e. either by telling others what they want to hear, or by falling victim to their desires.

There are ways to avoid this. Books that explore the "non-parenting option" were not available when I was in my twenties, and are a good way for young adults to find the answers in themselves, and to plan life accordingly. Then, as Jan Flemmons of Jacksonville, Florida, puts it so succinctly: "If you don't want them, don't have them!"

\*    \*    \*

Of all the reasons not to have children—and we will explore dozens herein—"no urge or drive" seems the most basic and least cerebral of the lot. It is also the most important. Parenting is such an all-consuming task and life-changing force that one had better embrace it with all his or her being in order to rise to the challenge.

Here's a poignant quote from a survey respondent about entering parenting "half-baked" so to speak:

> If you don't want kids with all your heart, and you don't have the gift for raising them, and you can't afford them, you will produce a monstrous human being that will be a curse and a burden to society all of its life. Having kids is like brain surgery—you aren't doing anybody any good by DABBLING. —Female, 43, California

# CHAPTER 5

## "I Like My Lifestyle"
### *Why Change It?*

I am thrilled that I don't have children.
I have the thing that I love, which is freedom.
~Helen Mirren, 2007

What did you do last weekend? What are you doing tonight? Where do you like to dine? Where do you like to travel? Could you do any of these things if you had a young child in tow? Maybe. But probably not as easily or as often.

In fact, instead of doing what you're doing right now (reading this book in peace), you might be watching a kiddie video or helping a child do homework. According to the Kidfree Survey, the second most common reason the childfree don't want kids is because they would have to *give up their lifestyle*. About 80% checked this response, and over two-thirds also checked: "I would have to restrict my sports, hobbies and/or travel."

There is no doubt that having even *one* child will change your life dramatically—perhaps in ways you never even imagined—and definitely in ways that will restrict your freedom of movement and opportunity.

In this chapter we'll explore more than a dozen ways in which becoming a parent will change your lifestyle.

## Forgoing Our Favorites
### *(Sports, Hobbies and Travel)*

We have traveled all over the world. I have been able to
continue my sport, and have never looked back.
—Shelby Richardson, 49, Wisconsin

About once a year, the childfree network group starts an online thread about "What We Are Thankful For," and dozens reply with our list of blessings, many of which include our health, loved ones, pets, favorite sports, activities and travels. Kristel replied with a list, which included her childfree husband, her pets, and the following:

We are lucky to have good jobs and enjoy what we do for a living. We are lucky to get to travel whenever we want, and do last minute things on a whim, without the irritation of dealing with a child or sitter.
—Kristel, 33, Phoenix, AZ

When the childed say we are shallow or selfish, they are often referring to the fact that we prefer to have a carefree lifestyle—and all the travel, sports, hobbies, fine dining, sleeping in, peace and quiet, and clean homes—that comes with being childfree.

There is some truth to this, although "self-aware" would better describe our choice, since we know ourselves and what we want. We know what we would have to give up to have children, and—to many of us—it is not worth the "rewards" of parenthood.

While homebodies are well suited for nesting, world travelers would have a tough time with child in tow. And even if they wanted to schlep their kids all over the planet, for most it would be financially restricting. Romantic vacations to exotic places are one of the first luxuries most child-laden give up (which is commendable, considering the alternative).

Is it not selfish to go ahead and have children, and then leave them at home with a sitter because we do not want to sacrifice our travel or hobbies? These are the parents who try to "have it all," but don't excel at any one part.

But what about the parents who do give up their favorite sports and hobbies to have kids? Do they feel better in their martyrdom? We all know someone who—like my friend Jack—has cut back severely on golf since having children. He used to love golf. He enjoyed the weekly bonding with his buddies (plus he was getting quite good at it!).

Jack now finds himself with less time, because he is working harder to "keep the family engine going." And when he does have any spare time—

like weekends—he feels he should spend it with his kids (and rightly so). The only reason he goes to his golf club at all these days is to take his kids to the pool. His friends try to coax him to play hooky from the family, but then they feel guilty that he is a "better father" than they are to their kids. It seems like a lose-lose situation to me: It's either guilt or martyrdom.

Contrast this with Brian (my soulmate) and I who play it by ear as to when we will hop on our bikes or go play tennis. On the weekend, it may be after we've digested our brunch, read the paper or futzed in the garden. We just drive to our club for two hours of uninterrupted sports. And afterwards? We might walk on the beach, drive to the local nursery, or go eat somewhere. Literally none of this could be taken for granted if we had a baby. Sure we could try to arrange for a sitter, but—if my siblings are correct—it's not easy to find one at the last minute. The fact is: Freedom and spontaneity go out the window when you have even *one* child.

### Loving Our Lifestyle
Why *have* a kid, when I *am* the kid?
—Brian, 50, Santa Barbara, CA

"Lifestyle" encompasses more than just "sports, hobbies and travel," which is why 17% more survey respondents checked the former than the latter as a reason for not having kids. *Lifestyle* includes everything from sleeping in to being responsible for another human being's life.

When asked at parties and functions, "Why don't you have kids?" Brian's favorite response is "I am the kid!" This may sound trite, shallow or even selfish, but it is an honest answer, and a smart reason not to have children. There is a world of meaning in this statement. On the surface it means: "I want to play and do all my favorite sports and hobbies, instead of watching my kids do them." But deeper down it means: "I do not want the burden and responsibility that comes with being a good parent."

Some take this a step further by not even welcoming the responsibility of a pet. It's safe to say most of you don't go this far, since my research has found that the vast majority of non-parents are both pet owners and pet lovers (which we will explore later).

Let's face it, more than bringing home a playful and poohful puppy, there is a huge burden of responsibility the day your child is born, and for at least 18 years thereafter. You are no longer the kid, you are the *parent*.

The days of spontaneously going to an art opening or wine tasting, jumping in the car to get a bite to eat at that quiet little café, taking off on a weekend jaunt, or just sleeping in and hanging around the house reading a book all day are—gone.

They are replaced by: waking up early for the kids, feeding the kids, dressing the kids, then shuffling them around all day to school, doctor's appointments, play-dates, games and practices, followed by helping them with their homework, feeding them, watching kiddie shows, bathing them, and trying to get them to bed again. Alone at last, you say? Not if they decide to come and jump into bed with you!

Being a parent truly is a 24/7/365 responsibility. And if it's not, you're probably not being a responsible parent. Think about it: The two of you can't even leave the house to walk the dog together. That would be child endangerment!

### Trading Sports for Strollers

The magnitude of the responsibility really hit home with me a few years ago when Brian and I were at the club playing tennis. Onto the court next to us strolled an odd group: a mother and father pushing a stroller with an infant, and what appeared to be grandpa close behind. They started off by all three trying to hit the ball together, but the infant started crying when left alone. So, the husband acquiesced to take the child for a stroll while his wife played with her father.

Not ten minutes later the husband was back with the crying baby, so mom had to take the baby for a stroll. Back again, and now it was grandpa's turn.

Good tennis players, but not one of them got a chance to warm up and play before being interrupted (not to mention their embarrassment about the disturbance the baby was causing at our normally quiet tennis club). When grandpa came back and said, "I think she needs a new diaper," they all decided it was time to head back to the car for the diaper and leave.

We never saw that couple and their baby again. Did they decide to quit the club—or quit tennis altogether—because it was too much of a hassle? It got me thinking: Would I want to give up my favorite sport for a child?

Here are some lifestyle changes a new parent might need to make:

- **Buy a larger home, or add on**
- **Move to a good school district**
- **Childproof the house and furniture**
- **Pay for daycare (if both work)**
- **Buy a larger family car (picture "minivan")**
- **Eat at family restaurants**
- **Cook kid-friendly meals**
- **Watch kid-friendly shows and videos**
- **Fence in yard/make it safer**
- **Be surrounded by toys and noise**
- **Taxi kids to school and events**
- **Constantly buy new clothes as kids grow**
- **Miss work when they're sick**
- **Help them with their homework**
- **Buy them school supplies**
- **Attend parent-teacher meetings**
- **Plan vacations around school breaks**
- **Plan ahead for hiring babysitters**
- **Host play-dates & kiddie parties**
- **Cut back on your social life**
- **Curtail your sports and hobbies**
- **Carpool to kids' practices**
- **Clean up after the kids**
- **Do more laundry**
- **Go to bed earlier**
- **Wake up earlier/no sleeping in**
- **Schedule a proper time and place for sex**
- **Discipline and police your kids**
- **Save money for college**
- **Worry more**

### Blindsided by Burdens

We all know people who actually embrace these lifestyle changes wholeheartedly when they have kids, and we know others who were aware, but had no intention of making these changes—shuffling them off instead to a spouse or nanny. But what about the poor soul who had no idea what he/she was in for? After all, they don't teach parenting in school. These folks are literally caught blindsided by the burdens of parenting.

In his article for *The Sydney Morning Herald*, "The Hidden Truth About Parenthood," Sam De Brito says the reason so many are in the dark about the negative aspects of parenthood is because parents are less likely to admit them to others. [1] He says most parents say "it changes your life" and "you don't know what love is until you have a child," while only a few admit "if I'd known what it was going to be like, I probably wouldn't have done it" or "I'm really struggling. I want my old life back."

Why don't they admit the downsides? De Brito believes, "these disclosures are usually accompanied by a sense of guilt or fear that they will be judged a lesser person, or at least parent, because of their 'failings.'" Not having taken the parenthood plunge himself, De Brito sardonically cites some of the changes he has seen in his friends who have become parents:

> First they all get rather fat, their social life evaporates and they look 10 years older from lack of sleep; a little further down the track and the suggestion of international travel is still met with an amused snort, their sex lives have curled up to die under the doona and, as their sprogs sprout further, they become obsessed with backyards and moving to moonscape suburbs. Is it any wonder some people generate a touch of resentment towards the screaming turd-machine that has lumped them in this parallel universe? Where they watch their child-free friends stroll off to the beach or brunch while they load up the Bugaboo like it is a Humvee about to enter Baghdad?
> ~Sam De Brito, from "The Hidden Truth About Parenthood."[2]

This is probably why the older we kidfree get, the more convinced we are we took the right path. Every year we see more and more examples of the negative aspects of parenting. We see young people race into parenthood expecting it to be a "bundle of joy," only to find their youth snatched from them, and their lives changed drastically forever.

### Treasuring Time and Space
I Need a Lot of Alone-Time…
and that would disappear with children around.
—Julia, 43, Ohio

Do you ever long for more alone time? I do, and I don't even have kids. Are you around people all day, and need a reprieve when you get home at night? Or, are you a private person—like 43-year-old Elizabeth from Chicago—who doesn't like being around people in general? She says, "I am very private and need a lot of personal space. Children are inherently demanding and needy." Amen!

> I love having time to myself, and the mothers I know have damn little if any at all. —Juju, 41, Maryland

It would be difficult to be a private person and have kids at the same time, as "privacy" and "parenthood" are antonyms. Although my friends wouldn't call me a "private person," I do cherish my alone time and seek it whenever possible. It centers me and clears my mind of daily clutter. I can't imagine going straight from working with clients all day to picking up children from school and driving them home to parent all night. (Or worse yet, just being at home all day with crying infants or toddlers!)

Parenthood leaves little or no time to be alone in peace, and to many this would be an unwelcome adjustment.

> Limited time to do the things I want *now*. With kids, this would be compounded. —Bob Dietz, 33, Loveland, CO

Forget about "alone time," how about time in general? Even as a kidfree, I find myself always trying to catch up on my To-Do List and wondering how mothers fit it all in. From mundane errands like grocery shopping, banking, car repairs and laundry, to the chosen activities like beaching, biking, gardening or reading, it seems like there's never enough time in the week to do it all. With a kid or two in tow, I might as well chop the "chosen" hobbies right off the list!

### Craving Clean, Calm & Quiet

> Can't stand noise, dirt, clutter.
> —Female, 39, Lehigh Valley, PA

Are there plastic toys on your living room floor? Yapping cartoons in the background, or children yelling down the hall? Not if you are kidfree. The cacophony of noise and clutter may seem like a menial reason not to have children, but it is all part of the parenting lifestyle.

In the Kidfree Survey, dozens of childfree wrote in—under "Other reasons not to have kids"—everything from simply "I like white couches" (Female, 21, Miami, FL) to "I am hypersensitive to noise, particularly high-pitched noise" (Kate, 37, London, England). Some people really are hypersensitive to noise, but most of us just don't welcome it.

> I don't care for the excessive noise that seems to go hand in hand with children. —Tara Aiken, 35, Salem, OR

> I like CALM—hate noise and screaming from anybody but especially from kids, they are SO loud! —Suzie, 34, Quebec City, Canada

> I love silence! Plus, I'm a nervous personality type and I think I would be prone to a nervous breakdown! —Ms. Green, 27, Fayetteville, AR

Kids are by nature messy, and are not good candidates for white couches. There's a reason Howard Hughes never had kids (or none that he claimed). Neat freaks might experience acute stress around a cute toddler with chocolate melting in his hands.

### From Bach to Barney

"I'm pretty sensitive aesthetically, and it does something for me when I look at a pretty room," says new mom Deborah Cherney, who resigned to changing her interior after having twins. "Looking at what the room used to be was the visual equivalent of listening to Bach or Mozart. Now it's the visual equivalent of listening to Barney." [3]

According to the *New York Times* article "Parent Shock: Children Are Not Décor," Cherney felt the full impact when she put their 18th-century mahogany dining table and chair set in storage.

"When I bought the table I was envisioning these beautiful, lovely dinners with fine china," she said. "Once you have kids and once you give up those things, it was like, 'Who was I kidding?'"[4]

Saying good-bye to your formal dining room and your cherished antiques for a playroom and childproof furnishings is yet another by-product of becoming a parent and embracing the family lifestyle.

### Sleep, Sweet Sleep

I care too much about sleep,
and raising a child would affect my sleeping habits.
—Tamlar, 39, Athens, OH

Another lifestyle element we childfree cherish is our ability to have a complete, uninterrupted full night of sleep—at the hours we choose. This is the first thing to go—with the white couches—when the bundle of joy arrives home from the hospital. Infants are not on *your* schedule; you are on *theirs*. They may require you to wake up several times a night for feeding, or they may just cry for seemingly no reason.

Although not everyone requires a full night's sleep, I agree with 38-year-old Lynn W. from Virginia who says, "I need at least 7-9 hours of undisturbed sleep at bedtime...really!" And rightly so, considering the Better Sleep Council says most adults need seven to nine hours of sleep each night, and that "sleep deprivation destroys not only physical health, but mental health as well. It can cause everything from minor irritation to outbursts of temper to full-scale mental illness."[5]

The irony is that the very entity that causes your lack of sleep is the very entity that needs you to be fully rested. According to sleep expert Dr. Amy Wolson, "it is most important to pay attention to getting a sufficient night of sleep when one is responsible for driving, operating machinery and/or responsible for taking care of children."[6]

Terrific! Just when we need more sleep, we'd be getting less sleep than ever before. And forget about sleeping in. Although babies outgrow the nightly feeding stage, they grow into children who wake up early, have to be fed and dressed and taken to school.

Although "lack of sleep" sounds like a petty reason not to have a child, for those who require a good night's sleep to function well it can be a serious consideration. If nothing else, it is just one more in a list of dozens of unwelcome changes one must make to be a parent.

Some of us are not afraid to admit that we just want it *all*:

> I want lots of sleep and sex, adult conversation and free/flexible options
> with how to spend my time each and every day.
> —"Grateful Female," 37, Mukilteo, WA

### Ahh...FREEDOM!
I have thought long and hard about this subject.
Life without kids means one important thing to me: FREEDOM.
—Robert, 49, New York, NY

Besides our favorite sports, hobbies, travel, sleep and dozens of other interests we'd have to curtail—if not give up—to raise children, there is also that essential thing called "freedom."

To many childfree, freedom is the main benefit to not having kids. And, if you've had your freedom for 37 years, like the following female from Pennsylvania has, it's pretty darn hard to give it up:

> I'm so used to my personal freedom, it now feels almost impossible to give
> up, and I don't believe I could make such a huge commitment.
> —Biscuit, 37, McMurray, PA

When asked, "Are You Happy Being Kidfree?" Biscuit answers:

> Yes. How much time do you have? I love my freedom, physically and
> financially. I love staying up late or sleeping in late. I love having no forced
> schedule or accountability besides myself, my husband and my dog. I live
> a very relaxed lifestyle, and I don't want that to change. I love taking a trip
> at the drop off a hat, or eating dinner at 11 pm if we feel like it.
> —Biscuit, 37, McMurray, PA

What are we "free" of when we are "kidfree?" Many things, but most significantly we are free of the stress, worry, commitment and responsibility that parenting brings. The phrases "huge sacrifice" and "serious commitment" came from dozens of survey responses.

It begs the question: Are the childfree more aware of the burden parenting brings, or do we just take the commitment more seriously? Or both? Non-parents put it so well in their survey responses that I picked a few quotes from each category to illustrate our concerns about parenting.

### Responsibility

I believe children are an awesome responsibility and don't feel up to the challenge. When I am around other people's kids I feel so responsible for them, because the parent isn't paying attention and it wears me out.
—Marcia Lemaster, 36, Spokane Valley, WA

The idea of being responsible for them and them ALWAYS being there scares me. There are no take backs once you have birthed them. You can't change your mind and return them. —Female, 33, Phoenix, AZ

It's all about them, all the time, until YOU die. Also, and more importantly, flat out fear of the responsibility. —Liz, 48, Miami, FL

### Commitment

I think I would have made a good father, but only because I take my commitments very seriously. Being a "good" parent requires a substantial time commitment that I wasn't willing to make. —Male, 36, Denver, CO

You are committing yourself to an "unknown" and must give that unknown your full commitment from the day the child is born, regardless of what that will entail. —Cara, 40, New York, NY

### Hard Work & Sacrifice

It's a huge sacrifice and responsibility and I am uncertain I could handle it well. —G. Nancy Cafiero, 48, Chandler, AZ

I have heard good parents who love their children be honest about the huge sacrifices and hard work involved. I am just not convinced the rewards are there. —Sandra Howell, 32, Hobart, Australia

You have to sacrifice so much, and I don't see what makes it all worth it. —Cindy L'Esperance, 43, Charlotte, NC

### Stress & Worry

Stress involved in both raising them and worrying about them and grandkids in the future. —Scott Johnson, 40, Fayetteville, AR

I have always been a "worrier" and would be extremely anxious until the kids were at least stable adults. And no, I am not depressed or clinical in any way. —Barron, 32, Denver, CO

I think the mental and emotional strain would be too much to handle. —Meg, 38, Chicago, IL

Keith does a good job of wrapping the whole "freedom/stress/worry/lifestyle" issue into one diaper (sorry) in his following comment:

> Both my wife and I enjoy the freedom that not having kids gives us. The ability to go wherever, whenever we want, and not have to worry about the hassle of finding a babysitter. My wife has never had the drive to be a mom, and having kids, while I wouldn't mind having one, has never been a top priority of mine. While most of our friends are worried about not getting pregnant, going though the stress of fertility treatments and such, we are enjoying ourselves and the freedom we have.
>
> We also know a few people who have said if they had to do it over again they would not have had kids. They love their kids, but they just don't think they are the parents they should be because they never really wanted kids but gave in to pressure from family and friends. My way of thinking is, it is easier to regret not having kids than it is to regret having them because you can't give them back once you have them.
> —Keith Zimmerman, 36, La Salle, IL

### Revelling in the "Parent Package"

Some might say, "But having a child is worth all this," and to them I tip my hat. It is worth it to them. Is it worth it to you? You have to ask yourself that question. Would you revel in being a soccer mom or dad and taxiing kids around town in a minivan to pizza and ice cream parlors?

Would you enjoy watching kiddie videos in place of your favorite adult shows? Do you like the idea of a bustling family vacation as opposed to a peaceful, romantic getaway? How about dining at kid-friendly franchises rather than eclectic bistros? Are you ready to switch over from doing your own sports and activities to watching your kids do them? These are a few questions to consider before procreating.

There are parents that are so into the above-mentioned lifestyle—and so good at it—that I wonder if they were happy before having children. Many of them live vicariously through their offspring, and enjoy making them the center of their lives. These are the people who should be having kids. But many non-parents have observed the "parenting package," and just don't see themselves fitting into that role.

> I don't want to get together with other women to set up "playdates," don't want to administer "time-outs" and use all the other buzzwords that are so annoying. Don't want to fight others so my kid is "the smartest, most athletic, etc." Don't want to be part of the consumer attitude. Don't want to trade babysitting. Don't want to be saddled with all the housework, babywork. I can't stand those high-pitched screeching voices. Everyone's kid is "Number One." (How can everyone be Number One?) Basically, I can't think of a good reason to do it. —Female, 46, Michigan

Unfortunately, there are adults who don't want the lifestyle changes, but have kids anyway, and find themselves merely tolerating it, resenting it, and/or checking out altogether. Here's the scenario: The father that can't wait for his "boys trip" to escape the madness at home and be a kid again; the wife that resents the husband for not doing his part to raise the children; and the kids that act out because they're not getting enough attention. (Often followed—I might add—by divorce and single parenting!)

### "Life Is Good"
I like my life the way it is, and kids would change it.
—Christine, 39, Greenville, SC

Searching through the written-in responses to "Why don't you want kids?" I was pleased to find so many content childfree people. From simply "Why ruin a great thing?" ("Fly," 37, Milwaukee, WI) to "I have a very happy and fulfilled life right now. Why would I want to change it?" (Patty, 40, Philadelphia, PA), there were dozens of responses from childfree who were simply too content with life to mess with it.

> I like my life the way it is without kids, why would I want to risk having to change that? Also, it takes all my effort to take care of myself sometimes, let alone having to worry about someone else as well.
> —Karla, 30, British Columbia, Canada

\*　　\*　　\*

At first glance, "lifestyle" may sound like a superficial reason not to have children. But when you consider it, lifestyle is…well…life itself! It is what we do, and how we do it, on a daily basis.

Whether it's watching your kid play sports or playing sports yourself, eating escargot or Spaghetti-Os, driving to Gymboree or flying to Jamaica, living in a Bach world or a Barney world, lifestyle is all-encompassing, and you better be comfortable with the choices you make, since there are…no returns on children!

# CHAPTER 6

## It is Financially Restricting
### *(To Put It Mildly)*

Mother Nature, in her infinite wisdom, has instilled within each of us a
powerful biological instinct to reproduce; this is her way of assuring that
the human race, come what may, will never have any disposable income.
~Dave Barry, Humor Columnist

Although the above quote by Dave Barry was meant in humor, there is much truth to it. Biological instinct aside, kids are expensive. Raising even *one* child for 18 years can take a huge chunk from a couple's disposable income and can entirely deplete their discretionary income.

Did you know that if you lived in a city in the Western U.S. with a total household income between $57,000 to $99,000, it would cost you over $240,000 to raise one child? And that does not include college. Add about $79,000 to put them through public college or $109,000 for private college—for a potential expense of over $350,000 per child! [1]

If you live in the Northeast you can expect to spend at least 5% more than this, and if you have a six-digit household income over 30% more.[2] These figures were found on the "Cost of Raising a Child Calculator" at BabyCenter's website, and are based on annual reports from the U.S. Department of Agriculture and The College Board.

To find out how much it would cost you to raise a child in your region of the U.S., with your income, with or without college expenses (or to find out how much you are saving by not!), check out their website:

www.babycenter.com/cost-of-raising-child-calculator

## Forget Financial Freedom

We'd never get close to financial independence if we had kids.
—Female, 30, Alexandria, VA

With the average cost per child at about a quarter million bucks in the U.S., it's no wonder a whopping 72% of survey respondents checked "It is Financially Restricting" as a reason they don't want kids. Of the 13 reasons listed, it came in third place behind "I would have to give up my lifestyle."

This makes sense, because lifestyle and finances are not mutually exclusive. Rather, they are joined at the hip. Take for instance your current *discretionary* income (you know, that extra moola left over after life's necessary expenses). How much do you have to spend on travel, events, your favorite hobby, your pet(s), your home, or just dining out? Is it more than $30,000 per year? Because that's about what you'll need per year for 22 years if you want to raise two children and put them through a good four-year college in the U.S.

Even if we can afford to raise kids, it will directly affect our lifestyle. A friend of ours has three kids ranging from teens to twenties, and he told us it cost him about $250,000 per child, not including college. That's three quarters of a million dollars he could have invested in his dream company, bought a vacation home with, or just socked away for retirement! Some non-parents would rather use the money to help their community:

> According to a study by the USDA, one child will cost his or her parents almost $300,000 from birth to age 18, a few hundred thousand more for college alone. Call me selfish, but I could use that money to beautify my city, improve an orphanage, or found a library instead.
> —Tripp, 21, Arizona

Becoming a parent also affects our job choices. Perhaps you're like Viki from outside Chicago who says, "Money is not a big factor in my life, and I don't want to have to get a job I hate because it pays more in order to make children financially feasible."

If money is not a big thing in your life *now*, it will be when you have kids! There will be worries like: If my spouse and I both have to work to pay the bills, can we afford daycare? What if I lose my current job? What if there are unexpected health costs? What if the child is born with a defect? Can we afford the medical bills? What if the economy gets worse?

Some people never consider these risks before becoming parents. For those who can afford it, it works out. For those who can't—what a quagmire they find themselves in.

## Kids Demand More These Days

I constantly have to listen to my children complain that
so-and-so has the latest, greatest name-brand whatever.
~Michelle Singletary[3]

Is it that kids today are more demanding, or is it that there's more for them to demand these days? Either way, they have a lot more gizmos than we had when we were young, as we'll explore in a later chapter.

Suffice it to say, 30 years ago parents didn't have to buy us cell phones, computers, the latest video games and equipment, or even iPods and MP3s. Of course, parents don't *have* to buy these things for their kids, but it's hard not to succumb to their demands when other parents are.

In her *Washington Post* article "Spare the IPOD, Unspoil the Child," Michelle Singletary laments the pressure from her kids to buy things they don't need. Here are some excerpts from her article:

As a parent, I know there are certain things I have had to get used to. I know that children will always want what you know isn't good for them. They will relentlessly beg for things until your head nearly explodes.

However, what I didn't anticipate—and what I can't get used to—is dealing with the overindulgent decisions made by many of the parents of my children's friends and classmates.

My 10-year-old daughter can't understand why I won't buy her an iPod. My 8-year-old son points out that all his friends have video-game systems or the handheld versions—most of the time both.

And it's not just about the money. Okay, it is a lot about the money.

First, it's the initial outlay for the game system. But then there's the endless badgering to supply them with new games to feed their habit. Sorry, I'd rather put that money into my son's college fund.
~Michelle Singletary, "Spare the IPod, Unspoil the Child"[4]

According to research, cell phone ownership begins as young as age six, and over half of all tweens (aged 8 to 12) now have cell phones![5] This recent phenomenon of parents giving in to the technological whims of their offspring will be discussed further later. But suffice it to say that cell phones bills for 18 years are a huge expense that our parents never had.

Singletary (whom I like to quote because she's a parent) also reminds us of the financial outlay for children's events these days. "Don't even get me started," she says, "on the pressure to compete with the birthday parties that are equivalent to coronations." Have you been to one of these lately? It's not just kids getting together for ice cream and cake. It's more akin to hiring a full-blown carnival with rides, live music, catered food, clowns and entertainment. As one childfree network member posted:

> I just can't imagine spending $50,000 on a birthday party. I saw one on TV recently that was a kid's FIRST BIRTHDAY!!!!! There were all these rides—it literally cost $50,000. That's just freakin' insane.
> —Michele Drake, Childfree Network member

One could also argue that the demand for pricey celebrity name-brand apparel (à la "Hannah Montana") did not exist when we were kids. And, the prime consumers of high-end clothing—once reserved for well-to-do housewives—are now high school girls packing mom's credit card.

### Good Schooling is Expensive

> If you think education is expensive, try ignorance.
> ~Derek Bok, lawyer, former president of Harvard University

If you agree with the above quote and all the bumper stickers stating that "ignorance is expensive," then you probably know the importance of good schooling. The problem is it's getting harder to find, as the public school system in the U.S. (and arguably England and Australia) is in bad shape. Some say the system has collapsed, and that to ensure your kids get a good education you have to send them to private schools.

Here's an excerpt from *SFGate* columnist Mark Morford's article "American Kids, Dumber than Dirt," in which he discusses the education system with a longtime Oakland high school teacher and friend:

> We are, as far as urban public education is concerned, essentially at rock bottom. We are now at a point where we are essentially churning out ignorant teens who are becoming ignorant adults and society as a whole will pay dearly, very soon [...] It gets worse. My friend cites the fact that, of the 6,000 high school students he estimates he's taught over the span of his career, only a small fraction now make it to his grade with a functioning understanding of written English.[6]

When Morford offers counterevidence of some very talented young people to his schoolteacher friend, he concedes that there are exceptions, but these are usually the "lucky, wealthy, foreign-born, private-schooled."

This teacher is confirming what many fear to be true: The public school system is failing students so terribly that it's worth spending the extra money—if you have it—to send your kids to private schools. Morford concludes that:

> Most affluent parents in America—and many more who aren't—now put their kids in private schools from day one, and the smart ones give their kids no TV and minimal junk food and no video games. (Of course, this in no way guarantees a smart, attuned kid, but compared to the odds of success in the public school system, it sure seems to help.)
> ~Mark Moreford, from "American Kids, Dumber than Dirt"

If you think this teacher's being an alarmist, check the statistics. Report cards don't lie, and the NAEP Report Cards show that students in private school score well above the national average, with more than twice the percentage of 8th and 12th graders scoring at the advanced level in math, reading and writing. [8]

Studies also show that private schools are safer and have less violence than public schools—an important factor since the emergence of school shootings. In 2006, the Indicators of School Crime and Safety report found that public school students were *five times more likely* to be "threatened with harm at, or on the way to/from, school," and *six times more likely* to have "street gangs present at, or on the way to/from, school."[9]

In another study, public school teachers reported far more cases of drug abuse, student apathy, tardiness, absenteeism and disrespect for teachers than did private school teachers.[10]

The stickler is, the average annual nonsectarian private high school tuition is more than $27,000.[11] So, to put two kids through a four-year high school, it would cost us almost $220,000 in tuition alone. We'd be hard pressed to afford sending them to college after this.

## What About Retirement?
The question isn't at *what age* I want to retire, it's at *what income*.
~George Foreman, boxing champion with ten children

Let's say you can afford to have kids, send them to good schools, and still live the lifestyle you desire. Bravo! But what about retirement? How much more money could you put aside each year if you didn't have kids and their expenses? Some parents don't start saving for retirement until after their kids are out of college, giving them few years for their money to grow, and pushing their retirement out to an older age.

Unlike George Foreman's quote above, it is important to Brian and I at what age we retire. We are not living to work, we are working to *live*. We plan to enjoy our retirement long before we are too cranky and crotchety to travel or too stiff and sore to ski or snorkel.

Not having kids may allow us to retire in our late fifties, instead of late sixties—ten years that make a world of difference. Although I love work and will always dabble in it, I look forward to knowing that one day I no longer have to earn money to survive. I simply don't want to be too old and weary to enjoy life to it's fullest when that day comes.

## "Unaffordability"

The major reason that I do not have children is because I cannot *afford* them. I would adopt if I could but even that's not possible. The expense is just ridiculous.
—Penny, 41, Phoenix, AZ

Affordability is a very real issue for some, and a good reason not to have kids. The childfree do consider the costs of having kids, and many—like Penny above—realize they couldn't afford them even if they *wanted* them. How much less pain, suffering, starvation, disease and violence—not to mention overpopulation—would there be in the world, if those who could not afford to raise children would accept this fact and either have fewer children, or refrain from procreating altogether? To put it bluntly:

Can't Feed 'Em? Don't Breed 'Em! —Roddy D., 38, Dallas, GA

The above advice by Roddy—"if you can't feed them, don't breed them"—was echoed by *dozens* of non-parents throughout my survey. It seems like a no-brainer, but apparently not to all. There are billions of impoverished people around the world who—whether out of ignorance or for religious reasons—do not use birth control or abstinence, and find themselves with several hungry mouths to feed. And many in developed countries—who do not have the ignorance or religion excuse—have kids simply because they know someone else will pick up the tab.

To the people who know they simply cannot afford a child and thus refrain from having one in spite of their biological urge or government perks, I'm sure I speak for most of us when I say, "We laud you!" It may be a difficult decision, but a smart one. Too many statistics show that children born into poverty are at an extreme disadvantage from the beginning. Most importantly, they are more likely to commit violence.

According to Mike Males, author of the article "Wild in Deceit: Why 'Teen Violence' is Poverty Violence in Disguise," the major factor, buried in teen-violence stories and rarely generating any remedies, is poverty.[12] He cites a study that found the U.S. raises three to eight times more children in poverty than other Western nations, which accounts for our higher rates of youth violence. Other effects of poverty include increased likelihood of being born with a disease or birth defect, and later becoming depressed, addicted, suicidal or incarcerated.

In our current economy, I don't feel we have the financial means to raise a child and provide the way I would want to. —Female, 44, Denver, CO

Even if you're not impoverished (which you probably aren't), do you feel you have the income to raise a child in the manner you would like, come what may? I knew a woman whose grandchild was born with a brain defect and required shunt surgery and extensive medical work. Even with medical insurance, the parents did not have the money to cover the costs.

So what did they do? They threw fund-raising parties and sent out fliers and emails soliciting financial contributions from everyone they knew—and even people they didn't—from coast to coast, to help cover the costs of "little Johnny's medical bills."

I was one of the strangers who threw in a little cash, but I wondered how far these donations would get them. Perhaps his first year, at best?

And what about the rest of the child's life? He would need ongoing medical assistance. Did they consider the risk of medical complications with their small bank account when they set out to have this second child? Probably not, although in their defense I don't think most parents do.

More parents should consider the risk. According to a report published in January 2007 by the Center for Disease Control (CDC), birth defects affect as many as one in 33 babies born in the U.S.[13]

The CDC found that the initial cost of having a baby born with a birth defect ranges from $75,000 to $503,000 per case.[14] To most couples, this can be financially crippling. Of course, for those who can't pay at all, taxpayers end up footing the bill through state and federal programs.

Finances aside, caring for a child with a defect for the rest of its life is an enormous burden.

The tragic ending to the story about Johnny is that—after all the stress and medical expenses—little Johnny died just a week after he was born, much to everybody's sorrow.

If you find yourself on the fence about having kids, take a look at your current situation. Besides the vital question of, "Am I physically and mentally prepared?" ask yourself whether you are *financially* prepared to raise a child. What is your current situation? Are you struggling to pay the bills now? Do you live in a safe neighborhood with good schools, or would you need to move? Are you in debt? Can you afford even your current lifestyle? Because—even if you enlist the aid from your parents, friends and taxpayers—your expenses will increase with a child to care for.

We can't afford to support the lifestyle we currently have, so it's impossible to add the expense of children. —Heidi, 34, Ohio

> Not only is having kids financially restricting, having enough money in the first place is very difficult. —Female (university student), 19, England

Whether you can afford kids or not, you may not find the "rewards" worth the costs. In the *BusinessWeek* Debate Room, the pros and cons of the issue "Kids Are Worth the Cost" were debated. Vincent Ciaccio gave us the con—"Thanks, But No Thanks"—side of the argument:

> The idea of something being "worth the money" can be a strange one... Society still operates on the idea of kids being "worth the money" for everyone. With the advent of reliable birth control, I think it's time we changed that mindset.
>
> The Agriculture Dept. estimates that for most people, raising a kid from birth to age 17 will run about $290,000. This doesn't take into account things like private schools or higher education, which can raise the total significantly. Nor does it factor in things like lost wages or fewer promotions due to child-care needs.
>
> My wife and I came to the decision years ago that we wanted to remain child-free, but financial concerns weren't the only motivator. All the same, the lack of that strain on our budget is significant, and that means less overall stress for our relationship. The emotional costs of raising kids get glossed over just as much as the financial ones.
>
> Also, while most big-ticket investments, such as real estate, have expected returns when one sells, having kids doesn't necessarily pay for itself. People may argue that kids will take care of parents as they get older, but that's not always the case. Our nursing homes are proof of this.
>
> I'm not saying children are categorically not worth the cost. It's hard to put a price tag on a kid's first words or seeing your child off to the high school prom. Having a child is supremely rewarding for many people, and worth any price. But not for everyone. [15]
> ~Vincent Ciaccio, former spokesperson for No Kidding! International

Notice how Ciaccio mentions the "emotional costs" as well as the financial? Both can be equally daunting.

\*   \*   \*

Many people do consider the expense of raising kids before having them, and still find their desire to have them far outweighs the financial negatives. To those who can afford to raise kids in a good, clean, healthy environment (with lots of love I hope), I say "right on!"

But parenting is not for everyone. And while, for some, lack of finances may be the main reason for not having kids, for others the cost of raising them is just one in a list of many reasons for not having children.

# CHAPTER 7

## Earth Doesn't Need More Humans

Instead of controlling the environment for the benefit of
the population, perhaps it's time we control the population
to allow the survival of the environment.
~David Attenborough, *The Life of Mammals*

Global warming, deforestation, desertification, air pollution, contaminated water, animal extinction, greenhouse gas emissions, thinning ozone layer—these are just a few ways humans are hurting the earth, and hurting ourselves. In return, we may be leading ourselves to gradual extinction.

One of the more altruistic reasons people choose not to have children is their concern for the health of our over-burdened planet. About 62% of respondents to my survey checked "Overpopulation/I don't think the world needs more people" as a reason they are not procreating.

It doesn't surprise me that it was the fifth highest reason on the list of thirteen, in light of the fact that the childfree tend to be a conscientious group of people. For most childfree, like this schoolteacher, overpopulation is one of several reasons they choose not to procreate:

> My biggest social concern is overpopulation. However, my husband and I sincerely lack the desire to be parents most of the time. I am an elementary schoolteacher and also involved in community youth theatre. I believe I contribute to our next generation in this manner rather than in simply adding another body. —Lisa F., 35, Cedar Park, TX

But for others, it was the *main* reason not to have children:

> Overpopulation was by far the strongest reason that I chose to "get fixed." That was 15 years ago, and my reasons haven't changed.
> —Kathleen, 41, Fort St. John, Canada

## The Population Problem
### *Poisoning the Petri Dish*

There are too many people in the world today.
The breeders need to get a clue and either slow down or stop!
—Debby McMichael-Delo, 46, Big Lake, AK

Every second on Earth, more than four people are born and less than two people die. That's an increase of 2.3 human beings on Earth per second![1] With the current world population at over seven billion, sources say we are headed to more than 9.3 billion by mid-century.[2]

The growing numbers of non-parents in developed countries have certainly helped slow the population increase, but humans are still multiplying by an annual rate of 1.1% worldwide.[3]

Overpopulation is an extremely important reason to me, as humans are breeding to an extent that disgusts me. —Marion, 35, Montreal, Canada

Like bacteria in a petri dish, organisms can only survive as long as the resources that sustain them are replaced faster than they are depleted. If organisms reproduce too quickly, they deplete their own sustenance, poison their environment and—ultimately—die. If the planet is our petri dish, humans cannot continue to populate without killing ourselves.

In fact, signs are everywhere that we are approaching full capacity of the planet, and many say it is a good reason to obtain from procreating:

Clearly, overpopulation. To even visualize how, in negative ways, that this is the root of ALL other problems with THE WORLD, would be a start in the right direction for humanity. I don't see any issue (i.e. global warming, crime, starvation, you get the idea), that wouldn't be made even a little bit better if everyone in the world stopped procreating for just a day, let alone controlling themselves to 1 child per couple.
—Michael Lawrence Alford Jr., 44, Santa Rosa, CA

According to EnviroHealth expert Olivia Rose-Innes, nearly one in three people in rural areas lack safe drinking water, and over half the people in the world live below the poverty line?[4] The Optimum Population Trust has found, "Human consumption of renewable resources is already overshooting Earth's capacity to provide. Resources are becoming scarcer and the number of hungry people increasing year by year."[5] Two of their solutions include the following:

1) Politically, governments can give attention and resources, such as education and contraception, to the 200 million women and millions of men who need it worldwide.

2) Individually, couples can choose to have smaller families or stop at two.

## Disposable Diaper Danger
### *and Tons of Trash*

Environmental impact of even *one* child is amazing! I've always believed
it's important to adopt a "lost" child rather than create new ones.
—Cheryl S. Levinson, 62, San Jose, CA

Huggies and Pampers and Luvs…Oh My! Babies generate eight to twelve dirty disposable diapers daily. And—thanks to housewife Marion Donovan who invented them in her home in 1950—these plastic puppies are not biodegradable.

Of course, rather than environmental health, Mrs. Donovan was concerned with the *mental health* of the mothers who had to continually wash out the poop-filled traditional cotton versions that had to be reused. (Can we blame her?) Henceforth, disposable diapers came to dominate the developed world.

Since the typical child runs through 8,000 to 10,000 diapers before becoming potty trained, the soggy stinky bundles are a major trash item. And where do they go? To landfills. In fact, diapers account for almost 5% of all developed countries' landfills, and more than 18 million a year are buried in U.S. landfills alone!

In his piece "The Disposable Diaper Myth," Carl Lehrburger sheds the ugly truth about diaper-disposing danger:

> The truth is, most of the plastic-lined "disposables" end up in landfills. There they sit, tightly wrapped bundles of urine and feces that partially and slowly decompose only over many decades. What started out as a marketer's dream of drier, happier, more comfortable babies has become a solid-waste nightmare of squandered material resources, skyrocketing economics, and a growing health hazard, set against the backdrop of dwindling landfill capacity in a country driven by consumption. [6]

Trash production in the U.S. has nearly tripled since 1960. Americans generate trash at an astonishing rate of 4.6 pounds (2.1 kilograms) per day per person, which translates to 251 million tons per year. This is almost twice as much trash per person as most other major countries. What happens to this trash? Some gets recycled or recovered and some is burned, but the majority is buried in landfills. The amount of trash buried in landfills has doubled since 1960.[7]

A non-environmentalist would be hard pressed to argue the fact that reducing the amount of babies born would help decrease the amount of trash buried in landfills. But he may counter, "Who cares, if trash is buried in landfills where we can't see it?"

The problem is twofold, according to Greenpeace co-founder Dr. Patrick Moore. The first is space. "There's less current landfill capacity and fewer potential sites—which also means that disposal costs are higher."[8] But more than dwindling space, Moore says the second problem with landfills is where they're located and how to control pollution. There are often trapped landfill gases comprised mostly of methane and carbon dioxide—both of which are major culprits of smog and global warming.

Human garbage is not just a problem on land. Our oceans are increasingly littered with plastic bottles, bags and bottle caps that choke and kill birds and fish. In just one year, 15 billion pounds of trash is dumped into the sea worldwide.[9] Just one massive cruise ship alone will dump millions of tons of solid waste and sewage into our oceans.

## Detrimental Depletion
### of Earth's Resources

The raging monster upon the land is population growth.
In its presence, sustainability is but a fragile theoretical construct.
To say, as many do, that the difficulties of nations are not due to
people but to poor ideology or land-use management is sophistic.
~E.O. Wilson, January 1995

Deforestation, desertification, over-hunting, over-fishing—these are a few ways our growing population is depleting the earth's resources. We are simply taking more than we are giving back.

The world's forests are key to a healthy ecosystem, not only because they provide habitat for millions of species of plants and animals, but because they regulate our climate, prevent droughts, provide the oxygen we breathe, and absorb the earth's toxic amounts of carbon dioxide. We depend on trees to cleanse our atmosphere.

Due to humans, the world's rainforests are in danger of becoming extinct. According to the Time Multimedia Almanac, "if present deforestation rates continue, all tropical rainforests will be completely cleared in 177 years."[10] These rainforests are located mostly in the developing countries of South America, Africa and Asia, where the population is growing fast and the poor are seeking ways to survive.

Every year satellite images pick up tens of thousands of fires burning across the Amazon and Brazil, which hold about a third of our remaining rainforests. Deforestation and slash-and-burn farming have wiped out roughly 90% of West Africa's rainforests, and now Central Africa's Congo

Basin has come under the axe too. While earth-watchers decry such destruction of endangered plants and animals, these countries call us hypocrites, because we—the developed countries—certainly had our era of land clearing for economic expansion.

Desertification—the transformation of habitable land to desert—is another by-product of human's overuse of Earth. According to E. O. Wilson's *The Future of Life*, desertification is induced by factors that are mostly man-induced including: over-cultivation, overgrazing, increased fires, overdrafting of groundwater, and deforestation, to name but a few.[11]

## The Faltering Food & Water Supply

Water tables all over the world are falling, as world water demand has tripled over the last 50 years. When these aquifers are depleted, food production worldwide will fall.
~Earth Policy Institute, March 2003

Are we running out of food? Not quite yet in the developed countries. But according to the UN Food and Agriculture Organization, in 64 of 105 developing countries, the population is growing faster than food supplies.[12] In the recent economic downturn, the UN warned that the world food supply is dwindling rapidly and food prices are soaring to historic levels, causing a "very serious risk that fewer people will be able to get food."[13]

Since 70% of the world's fresh water is used for irrigation, food production is highly dependant on the availability of water. Demand for water soars as populations grow, and by 2025, 48 countries comprised of three billion people will face shortages.

For the first time in history, urban demand for water is outpacing farm demand, as city users outbid irrigators, and by 2050 cities will consume half the world's fresh water—reducing that available for food production by a third. —UTA Foundation[14]

Our thirst for bottled water and long showers is directly affecting our farmland food supplies. Since humans know how to farm and raise our own food, we may not run out of things to eat soon. However, there is already a shortage of quality wild food available on the planet.

A number of fisheries are in trouble in North America, and the Department of Commerce declared a disaster in 2012 for cod and other groundfish in New England, as well as oyster and blue crab fisheries in Mississippi, and wild Chinook salmon in Alaska. California too has seen a marked decrease in the numbers of wild salmon spawning in our rivers.

Unfortunately, farmed salmon is a poor substitute, as it attracts parasites, damages the marine environment and poses a danger to human health.

The depletion of sea life started years ago in other parts of the world where humans have fished for centuries longer. Now we are increasingly forced to buy frozen fish shipped from halfway around the world or to farm them ourselves—both of which are substandard in taste and nutrition.

## Global Warming and Carbon Footprints

I wouldn't myself choose to be born today (global warming). I can see no reason that is not ultimately selfish for having children.
—Allie, 30, Ontario, Canada

Global warming—which is connected to many environmental problems discussed herein—is a major issue today, and too huge to delve into here. Since the earth's climate fluctuates over time, there is controversy over whether global warming is a man-made or natural event. But there is no doubt that human activity—by adding carbon dioxide to the atmosphere at rates faster than it can be absorbed—is adding to greenhouse gas emissions, which are warming the planet.

In his report "Population, Consumption Key to Climate Solutions," environmental expert Bob Doppelt explains global climate change succinctly through his "IPAT" formula:

Climate Impacts = Population x Affluence x Technology.[15]

Basically he's saying: The impact on the climate is equal to the size of the population, times its affluence, times its technology. This is why countries like the U.S. have a far larger carbon output than the lesser developed. But Doppelt says too much emphasis has been put on changing technology, and not enough on the core problems of population and consumption. Environmental writer Dr. John Feeny agrees with this:

It's the great taboo of environmentalism: the size and growth of the human population. It has a profound impact on all life on Earth, yet for decades it has been conspicuously absent from public debate.[16]

Why is stabilizing the population a taboo subject? Some say it's because it sounds anti-immigration or anti-life. It may be also due to the shortsighted desire of governments to grow their populations for economic gain. Either way, many non-parents know that the best way to reduce one's carbon footprint on the earth is to simply not have a child.

I get carbon offsets for not having kids! —George, 51, Fresno, CA

## Circular Logic
*Politicians Pushing Population Growth*

Governments measure their economic success—however short-term—on their GDP (Gross Domestic Product). If a country's GDP rises during a president's four-year term, he may use this statistic to get reelected. One way to increase the GDP is to increase the nation's number of working citizens. So, leaders of the developed nations devise ways to persuade their citizens to have more children.

One argument governments give in justifying their "baby bonuses" is that the elderly need young workers to support them after retirement (i.e. by taxing them for Social Security, Medicare and other programs). This is not only fear mongering, it is circular logic. By producing more offspring to support the poor, sick and aging, we are continually adding to the populace of poor, sick and aging that will need support!

## "Quality of Life Inversion"
*Quality vs. Quantity*

Democracy cannot survive overpopulation. Human dignity cannot survive
it. Convenience and decency cannot survive it. As you put more and more
people into the world, the value of life not only declines, it disappears.
It doesn't matter if someone dies. The more people there are,
the less one individual matters.
~Isaac Asimov (1920-1992), biochemist, humanist

Overpopulation is not just an environmental issue; it's a human decency issue. I agree with Isaac Asimov (above) that the value of human life declines as the quantity increases. It's becoming increasingly apparent that *quality of life* is inversely proportional to *quantity of life*.

In fact, many—like RT Wolf below—believe that a decrease in population would help solve many of the world's problems:

If the population of the world would decrease instead of increasing, it
would solve poverty, famine, food and water shortages, land shortages,
the energy crisis, global warming, and many other things.
~RT Wolf, Mind-Manual blog[17]

Obviously there are others—like the Duggars with their 20 and Nadya Suleman with her 14 children in one home—who carry the opposing philosophy of "the more the merrier." But I doubt these kids are getting the quality attention and upbringing they would in a family of four.

Is it a coincidence that the quality of food, housing, and medical care is much lower in overpopulated areas of the world? Or, that there exists a lower lifespan and higher incident of HIV/AIDS and other endemic diseases in countries with high birth rates? The population experts think not.

Not only does adding to the overpopulated world turn many people off; so does the idea of subjecting a child to the blight of our future planet.

One reason I'm quite happy not to have children is that I don't have very much faith in the future, with the combination of potentially catastrophic climate change, peaking of world oil supplies, general over-population and environmental degradation. It's as though my choice not to have children is a vote of no confidence in the future. —Kylie, 36, Perth, Australia

Pessimism about the future of humanity and the planet. Not just overpopulation but that the population will be decimated in the next 50 years or so and people will suffer greatly. I don't want to subject anyone to that deliberately. —"Hellboundforjoy," 40, Orange, CA

### The Adoption Option

There are plenty of kids already in the world that could use help
and be taken care of. So I feel it is inappropriate to bring
more children in to the world.
—Seana-Marie Weaver, 41, Ventura, CA

Another elephant in the room is the fact that there are already plenty of children in the world that need a home and/or parent and don't have one. Why not help one of these kids instead of producing another? Many survey respondents commented that—if they were to have children—they'd adopt. This obviously removes the ego factor of reproducing a "mini-me," and helps the world at the same time.

I think it is absolutely one of the most selfish things a person can do. There are lots of kids out there who need good homes. Why add to the overpopulation just to feed your ego, or to "fit in," or because of peer pressure or parental pressure? —Linda Kay Marshall, 43, Slater, IA

\*     \*     \*

While there are self-serving reasons the kidfree choose not to procreate, the fact that many are refraining because they are concerned about our earth and do not wish to poison it for future generations is quite unselfish.

Perhaps if more people around the world take our lead, the progeny of those parents will be praising us for not poisoning their petri dish!

# CHAPTER 8

## "I Don't Particularly Like Kids"
Learning to dislike children at an early age
saves a lot of expense and aggravation later in life.
~Robert Byrne, author, billiards expert

"Noisy, messy, needy, demanding, little stinky things." Am I describing a new puppy, or perhaps a pet weasel? No, this is one childfree woman's (who shall remain anonymous) description of kids. These were the adjectives she used to describe why she doesn't particularly like kids or want kids.

Why bear children if you cannot *bear* children? If you do not like weasels, would you have them live in your home 24/7 for 18 plus years? What if your spouse liked them and you didn't? Would you acquiesce? How about if they cost over 300 grand to raise and a lot of time, sacrifice and emotional heartache? Just as liking kids is a good reason to have them, not liking kids is a great reason not to have them.

Although most childfree are not child-haters, 54% of survey respondents answered, "I Don't Particularly Like Kids" as a reason they are not having them. This distaste for children can range from a mild aversion to absolute abhorrence and is caused by a host of factors—not to mention an abundance of annoyances.

While not all respondents elaborated on their disdain for children other than to say "I really don't like children" (Debbie, 35, Hastings, England), some revealed in detail *when* they developed their repulsion and others *why*. Following are some findings from the Kidfree Survey…

## "I Never Liked Kids, Even When I *Was* One"

As a child, I thought I hated everybody,
but when I grew up I realized it was just children I didn't like.
~Philip Larkin (1922-1985), poet, novelist

Think back on family gatherings when you were a child. Were you the one who'd rather be hanging out with the adults than out playing ditch 'em or dodgeball with the kids? You're not alone. Many of us—like Michelle below—preferred spending time with adults over time with tykes:

I've never had the urge to have children and have never particularly enjoyed children. When I was a child, I preferred the company of adults. I didn't like to play house like the other girls my age. I remember being told that I was <insert appropriate age here> going on 40, and was darn proud of that! —Michelle, Saskatchewan, Canada

If playing with kids seemed mundane to you *then*, it probably still does now. In fact, I checked to see if Michelle—who never particularly liked kids even when she was one—ever wanted to have kids. Her answer was "absolutely not." Disliking kids from a young age helps make that decision easier.

Even when I was a kid, I was not keen on other kids; I wanted to be an adult. When I was 4 my mother took me to playcentre to try and get me to interact with other kids. She would set me up doing an activity with other kids and inevitably chat to the other kids and stop focusing on me for a moment. I would always disappear, she would usually find me in the kitchen drinking tea with the adults or chatting to a parent. I was always more comfortable at dinner parties than playing on jungle gyms! —Female, 32, Victoria, Australia

Although the Australian above did consider having kids at one point, she too has never been interested in child's play, and tends to drift away from friends who become parents. She finds the conversation centered on kids to be boring. Perhaps—once it's cultivated—the desire for adult conversation and culture is not always curtailed by a biological clock.

## "I'm Not Crazy About Kids in General"

I admit I am not a fan of kids in general, but I have met children that I like
and don't mind being around. I prefer older children because you
don't have to do everything for them and they usually
know how to behave and speak clearly.
—Psylocke, 35, Houston, TX

On a scale of one to ten, how do you feel about kids in general? Perhaps, like Psylocke above (who rates kids a "5" on the Kidfree Survey scale) you don't love them or hate them, you just feel neutral about them. Perhaps you like more mature kids and try to avoid screaming babies and toddlers. Or, like many of us, you enjoy children, but only in small doses and as long as they're well behaved.

This category of feelings toward kids—the "yes sometimes, but only if"—can be classified as conditional like, and may be where most of us fit. When I asked survey respondents, "On a scale of 1 to 10 (1 being "Hate Them," 5 "Neutral," 10 "Love Them"), how do you feel about kids in general?" the most common rating was a "5/Neutral."

The chart of the survey results below shows that—although most non-parents don't hate children—about 45% rate them below "neutral." While about 7% of us give "kids in general" a generous "9" or "10," more than three quarters of us fall somewhere between "3" and "8"—revealing our mixed feelings toward young human beings. Here are the results:

**On a Scale of 1 to 10 (1="Hate them" 5="Neutral" 10="Love them"), how do you feel about KIDS in general?**

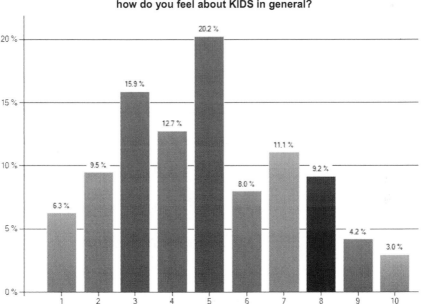

This indifference toward kids does not give one the impetus to embark on a lifelong journey to raise them. We can only hope that parents score somewhere between an "8" and a "10" or we'd have a lot of unhappy moms and dads to contend with!

## "I Don't Like Kids *Today*"
### *Nor the Way They're Being Raised*

My kids would be brought up properly, as I was,
and who would they have as friends to play with?
I wouldn't have any one else's misbehaved kids in my home!
—Paul Patch, Buffalo Grove, IL

For other non-parents, it's not so much an aversion to the attributes and antics of young developing human beings, as it is a disdain for the *modern* child. In other words, it's not kids we don't like; it's *kids these days*.

When I told my friend Bob (a grandparent in his 70s) I was writing this chapter and how the issue for many of us is not so much that we dislike kids as much as we don't like what they've become today, he completely agreed.

"I have always liked kids. But I honestly don't enjoy being around my grandkids anymore, because of what their parents have made them into." Bob said it was a joy to be around them when they were young, but it's sad to see the signs of how their parents and society have tainted them.

"They have no respect for their elders, feel the world revolves around them, manipulate their parents into getting what they want, need constant stimulation, and are more entertained by video games than playing their own games outside," he said. And that's just the short list.

While the childfree community often laments the laundry list of bad behaviors in kids these days, we are well aware that—as with unruly dogs—the trainers are usually to blame. This is why when I asked for reasons you might not want kids, 53% checked "I don't like the way kids are being raised today." Because, as many of us are aware:

Even if your kids are perfectly behaved, you will still need to be around other children. —Lynn P., Silver Spring, MD

Whether it's their imperious attitudes, lack of respect, or the fact that they think the world revolves around them, kids these days don't appeal to many childfree no matter who is to blame. Even those who work with them daily prefer to pass on procreating:

My wife is a school teacher, and after years of it—and seeing how bad kids today are—we decided not to have children.
—M, 29, Leicester, England

We examine how parenting has changed in the next chapter, but suffice it to say, it's not as easy to like kids these days when they have been shaped into little irreverent monsters. And even if we can do better,

I'm with Kelly who says:

I don't want to have to hang around with other people's children.
—Kelly, 40, Lexington, KY

I would be remiss, however, not to mention how all generations of adults seem to think that the new crop of kids are more misbehaved than they were growing up. It seemed my dad's favorite three words when we grew up were "kids these days…" (murmured while shaking head in disgust). Now I find myself echoing these same words.

Perhaps it could be argued that each generation of humans is, in fact, declining and degenerating to a lower quality than the one before.

Shakespeare poked at youth in some of his plays, and we can even look back to 400 BC to see complaints about the children of "today":

Children today are tyrants. They contradict their parents, gobble their food, and tyrannize their teachers.
~Socrates (469 BC-399 BC), Classical Greek Philosopher

A timeless statement, as true today as it was over 2,000 years ago. The difference is, parents didn't have to buy them cell phones, computers and iPods back then…

### Techno Tykes Are Trouble

I think society spoils kids too much. In my day we had to amuse ourselves by playing with friends, playing outside, etc. Now kids are too "plugged-in." Society tells kids they need expensive gaming systems, personal computers and even cell phones. They don't.
—Char, 33, Indiana

Society gets some of the blame for the changes in parenting and kids. How could we become addicted to violent video games when we were kids if they didn't yet exist? How could we demand iPods and iPhones if they weren't yet invented? And how could we tarnish our reputations through texting and sexting when we had not the tools? Sitting around becoming obese was much harder to do back when we had to build forts, ride bikes and run around the block for entertainment.

America is cultivating a generation of "vidiots"—video idiots. Now, when families go on road trips, they have the car equipped with videos, so kids don't have to look out the window and learn about the country they live in. Even stores, waiting rooms and gas stations are adding TV and video for the stimulation-starved.

Parents take videos with them to friends' and family's homes, so they can slap one in and shut their kids up when they start having meltdowns. Videos have become the modern day pacifier to whiny kids. Mothers plop the kids in front of them in the other room when they need peace and quiet.

But video entertainment is just the tip of the tech-berg. Think of the stuff kids crave these days that weren't even around before the early 80s:

- **Personal Computers (first IBM PC in 1981)**
- **Mobile Phones (first commercially available 1983)**
- **Cellular Networks (early 1980s)**
- **Video Games (early 1980s)**
- **MP3 (1991)**
- **BlackBerry (1999)**
- **Smartphone (first one launched by Palm, Inc. 2001)**
- **iPod (2001)**
- **Mobile Instant Messaging (2002)**
- **MySpace (2003)**
- **Facebook (2004)**
- **Twitter (2006)**
- **iPhone (2007)**

…And the list goes on. The problem is, parents are satisfying their children's cravings at increasingly younger ages. This teching and texting complicates an otherwise simple childhood—say, of playing outside throwing a ball—by exposing kids to stimulus they might not be ready for. In two words, they are: overexposed and overstimulated.

The technology boom that has bombarded kids in the past 30 years has not only corrupted what it means to be a child, it has created in youth an insatiable demand for more, which can be quite costly for parents financially and emotionally.

Technology has made kids into a different kind of mindset. They seem like leeches who will use every single resource and drain you of your time and finances, only to take off at age 18 and just call you on holidays.
—KS, 43, Virginia Beach, VA

## Yes, Some Truly *Do* Hate Kids!

I hate kids and especially the weird sounds they make.
—Isabel, 32, New York, NY

OK, let's cut the P.C. B.S. and come out and say it: Some non-parents truly do *hate* children. Twice as many respondents—16%—rated kids a one or two than did a nine or ten on the Love/Hate scale. In fact, more than 6% rated their feelings about kids a "1" on a scale of 1 to 10.

Jared of Houston, Texas, rates them a "2" and simply says, "They are annoying." Others find harsher adjectives to describe children, like this Canadian who rates kids a "1" on the scale of 1 to 10:

I have never liked babies or children—puking, crapping, whining creatures. I find them truly revolting. —Lederfrau, 37, Ontario, Canada

How do you feel about baby pictures? Do you wonder why some folks go googoo gaga over them, while you just gag over them? One woman in our childfree network described Anne Geddes's photos (the babies dressed as pastel flowers, butterflies or bunnies, etc.) as "creepy and gross."

What's your physical reaction to the sound of a crying infant or a screaming child? Does it make your breathing stop, heart pound, muscles tense up and/or hair stand on end? It's a fight or flight response. I thought all humans felt this way, but I've seen too many parents carry on in total disregard while their child screams bloody murder a toy's throw away from them to conclude there is a universal aversion to such outbursts. And then there's the stickiness and the ickiness:

To me, children are little noisy hurricanes with perpetual sticky fingers, running noses and dirty diapers. —Emily, 44, Audubon, NJ

Kids are disease housing, stinky, slimy and in general icky, useless wastes of time, money and energy.
—The Crazy Cat Lady, 25, Phoenix, AZ

Let's face it, modern day techno woes aside, kids are by default needy, noisy, messy little creatures whose primary goal is to get what they want—and now. Many childfree fail to see the charm in them that their parents do, and, in any case, do not wish to house one of their own.

Perhaps it's not the nurturing knack you lack, but yours is channeled to animals rather than small humans, like the following two women:

Really don't like babies. Don't like modern kids, and don't want what I see of other peoples' kids. Don't need a pet substitute!
—Gaynor, 53, Canberra, Australia

I have absolutely no patience for kids and their loudness and hyper-ness. I cannot stand anything about them. I do not have a maternal instinct, but I do have an Avian Maternal Instinct. —Christine Walls, 29, Glendale, CA

Whatever your reasoning, if it's wry child-bashing you enjoy, pick up a copy of *I Hate Other People's Kids* by Adrianne Frost. It's a funny poke at the nasty little beasts that includes ingenious quips like the following:

And they say Jesus loved the little children, all the children of the world, but he never dined with one. He chose the lepers.[1]

One non-parent said, "this book lists every single reason I've chosen to remain childless…and it's done with sass and humor." If nothing else, reading Frost's book will help release your pent up, politically incorrect anger toward ill-behaved kids with some therapeutic belly laughs.

\* \* \*

Although there are exceptions, and good kids still do exist, it is our observation of the majority that pushes us away from the group as a whole:

The older I get, the more I realize I seriously just hate children. I see nothing redeeming in well over 90 percent of them.
—KarenMR, 45, Denver, CO

Whether it's babies or teens, modern day kids or kids in general, whether they're too techno for your taste or just too dull and tiresome, too noisy, smelly or messy—do yourself a favor by acknowledging your disdain for kids *now* and opting not to have your own.

After all, unlike a weasel, you will not be able to lock them up in a cage when they annoy you!

# CHAPTER 9

## Parenting:
### *The Good, The Bad and The Inept*

The pressures of being a parent are equal to any pressure on earth.
To be a conscious parent, and really look to that little being's mental
and physical health, is a responsibility which most of us, including me,
avoid most of the time because it's too hard.[1]
~John Lennon (1940-1980), The Beatles

A childed friend of mine told me, "I don't think you should have a chapter about parenting in your book when you're not a parent and your readers aren't parents." Well, I beg to differ.

*Parenting* is a major reason so many childfree choose *not* to parent. Some don't like the direction parenting has gone today and don't wish to fight it, succumb to it, or even be around it. Others know what the job entails, and are aware that they are not physically, mentally and/or emotionally cut out for it.

Since having kids is all about parenting, not wanting to parent and/or not being equipped to parent are two very good reasons not to have children. Let's explore each…

## Parenting Has Changed
### *...and Not for the Better*

Being a GOOD parent is A LOT harder than it appears
(or how society portrays parenting should be).
—Molly Ray, 35, Seattle, WA

Let's face it: Parenting has changed. Neither the childed nor the childfree would dispute this statement. I would further it by saying "not for the better." Mostly due to societal changes, parenting has become more difficult and complex than it was when we were kids.

"There was a time when parenting was a simple job," says Tom McGrath in his article about parenting in *Philadelphia Magazine.* "Not easy, but fairly straightforward: You had kids, you provided them with food, clothes, shelter, an education, and a decent sense of right and wrong, then you pushed them out into the world, hoping that at the very least they wouldn't be a burden on society."

"Today, in contrast," says McGrath, "parenting has become not only vastly more complicated, but seemingly more important than ever before."[2]

With thousands of books and articles written on the subject, the pundits have analyzed parenting to death, frustrating moms and dads with conflicting messages on how to do it right.

Everyone is a purported expert on how to be the perfect parent. The complexities of parenting are so overwhelming that, frankly, many of us are turned off by the daunting task.

There are dozens of new laws regarding parenting that didn't exist when we were young. My mother would have been a criminal today for not using child car seats, for letting us ride bikes without helmets, and for leaving us in the car while running in to get milk at the store.

Spanking (also called "smacking") is now illegal in over two dozen countries,[3] and several groups in the U.S. are trying to initiate bills to make it illegal here.[4] As of the mid-90s, parents became liable for their minor children's crimes in the U.S., yet it is also more common for kids to sue their parents. So parents have fewer rights and more liabilities than ever.

Consider the dangers parents have to worry about that our parents didn't: Online predators, Internet pornography, toxic toys, trans fats, mercury poisoning, ozone alerts, global warming and navigating the national car seat regulations—to name but a few.

"We no longer live in those carefree days of unlocked doors and children romping through neighborhoods unwatched for hours on end," Howie Rumberg points out in his article "The Pitfalls of Parenting: If it's not toys, it's something else to fear." He cites Alicia Barlow of Connecticut remembering a childhood of playing in her friend's tree fort full of rotting wood and rusty nails. "Now a mother of two," Rumberg says, "she half-jokingly talks about inspecting her children's pristine swing set before play dates to ensure that she won't get sued."[5]

Remember the list of electronics in the last chapter that kids want that weren't even around before the 1980s? The manufacturers have done their best to create a demand in kids to have it all at younger and younger ages. And, despite their high cost and ill effects on kids' physical and mental well-being, parents dole them out to offspring at an ever-increasing rate.

Addiction to these techie toys—along with parents' fears of outdoor danger—has caused today's youth to spend far too much time indoors. Research links a lack of outdoor activity to depression, obesity and stress in children. The problem is so bad it prompted Liz Baird, director of school programs for North Carolina Museum of Natural Sciences, to launch the "Take a Child Outside Week." In an article pondering this problem, Jackie Donaldson asks:

> Don't you remember roaming free when you were a kid? Today's children may not have such fond memories unless we shove them out the door because unstructured outdoor activity is down by half from the previous generation.[6]

Times have changed. If you had told my parents back then that one day there would be a national holiday to get your kids out of the house, they would have laughed. (They couldn't get us to come in for dinner!)

Many of us aren't prepared—emotionally or financially—for the onslaught of material demands society has created in the children of today. In any case, we wouldn't relish the frustrating, thankless, always saying "No" and being the bad guy side of parenting.

But what would a non-parent know about raising kids when she doesn't have her own, right? Most parents are quick to point this out. You can be assured that we can have a well-educated opinion and a more keenly objective eye than even parents themselves.

## Bad Parenting

*Choosing to have children is like choosing to play the bagpipes:*
*you must do it well or not at all. Anything in between*
*and you'll really annoy your neighbors.*
~Nina Paley, cartoonist and animator

Not only is parenting more complex these days, but many of us believe that *bad parenting* is more prevalent. It's ironic that we have to get a license to drive, but not to do one of the most difficult jobs on earth: Parent. Nobody teaches us how to raise children, and just because one can *conceive* a child does not mean that he or she is qualified to parent.

One of the most oft-discussed topics in the childfree community is *bad parenting* and the effect it has on the offspring it produces and on society in general. As noted earlier, well over half my survey respondents (53%) said they "don't like the way kids are being raised today."

Being a bad parent does not equate being a *bad person*. To the contrary, many parents are loving individuals—who often care *too* much. It's the parent's *tactics* at childrearing that are often misguided and counterproductive. From *underparenting* to *overparenting*, we see how the childed are making bad decisions.

The childfree have coined terms to distinguish the different types of parents (see the Kidfree Glossary). "Breeders" are defined as those who bear children without the knowledge or means to raise them properly. They have too many kids in spite of the fact they can't afford them and/or they don't discipline them properly. Likewise, a "MOO" is a Mother Operating Offensively (read: mom pushing her way to front of line with Hummer-sized baby carriage, mindless of her screaming toddlers in tow).

On the other hand, because we acknowledge there are *good parents* out there who are bucking the trend, saying "no" when they should, and using tough love to teach their kids manners, we have the acronym "PNBs" (Parents, Not Breeders), and to them we take a bow! Believe it or not, although there is a fair amount of parent-bashing in these childfree forums, there is a surprising amount of parent-praising, when praising is due.

We often hear that "kids have changed these days" and they have, but not on their own. Children have not just genetically mutated to be more spoiled, materialistic, lazy, obese, violent, suicidal, rude in public places and generally less respectful to adults. The parents have *allowed* this to happen, both by the way they raise them and the way they don't raise them.

## Counterproductive Control

Don't handicap your children by making their lives easy.
~Robert A. Heinlein (1907-1988), novelist

Have you noticed that parents have a propensity to micromanage their children these days? While guiding is a parent's responsibility, the definition of micromanage is "to manage or control closely, often so closely as to be counterproductive."

Parents are increasingly *doing* for their kids, instead of teaching them to do for themselves. Just Google search "micromanaging your kids" or "helicopter parenting" to find thousands of books, articles and essays on this recent phenomenon. Parents who micromanage may mean well, but they get too involved in controlling every aspect of their child's life, from choosing their play dates to bargaining with their teachers and coaches. In their defense, some experts are telling them to do so.

Case in point, at a friend's house I came across Rick Wolff's book *The Sports Parenting Edge*, claiming to teach parents how to do everything for their little "athlete" from "Deciding if your child should specialize" to "Handling their sub-par coaches"—all so one can "Ensure a great sports experience, from T-Ball through college." [7]

On the inside flap of the book, the author asks parents:

Did your son get cheated out of playing time in yesterday's soccer game? Do you not see eye-to-eye with your daughter's basketball coach? Are you concerned that your child's athletic gifts are going unnoticed by colleges? [...] For kids today, playing organized sports has become a kind of uncharted territory, and it's important for moms and dads to map out the guidelines for their youngsters as soon as possible. [8]

Why? So our kids don't have to think for themselves? Or is it to ensure that our kids don't embarrass us by failing? How in the world did we ever survive without these books 30 years ago? I guess kids just had to mature and learn how to interact with adults on their own.

"Helicopter Parents" are those pushy moms and dads known to complain to colleges that didn't accept—or employers who didn't hire—their beloved Brendan. They may even be found accompanying said child to job interviews!

In his report "The Future of Helicopter Parenting: The trend is gathering speed in the U.S." Kevin Osborn says, "they are micromanaging their offspring not just in kindergarten and elementary school, but all the way through college and into adulthood." [9]

Osborne says that as a result of this *helicopter parenting*, "some educators have called the 80 million children of baby boomers the most protected and programmed children ever."

I must confess that—given my personality and today's pressure to be the perfect parent—I might fall into this trap of over-controlling if I were a parent, and I wouldn't like myself for it.

## A Dearth of Discipline

*The thing that impresses me the most about America
is the way parents obey their children.
~Edward VIII (1894-1972), Duke of Windsor (non-parent)*

I don't think this British Duke was complimenting the Yanks with his above observance on parenting in America. But I've heard non-parents from other countries complain about the same thing: The lack of discipline parents give children these days.

It seems only logical that it is more effective to parent one's children than it is to befriend them, doesn't it? Yet, when I googled "being friends with your kids," at the top of the list of 249 million choices was the article "Ten Ways To Become Best Friends With Your Teenagers." Hello! Your 16-year-old daughter does not want to be your best friend. Nor should she be when she's learning to grow up and become an independent person.

Why do parents feel a need to be buddies instead of parents today? Is it out of guilt, or the need to be liked? Or is it a product—as Diana West, author of *Death of the Grown-Up* surmises—of the generation raised in the 50s and 60s, whom themselves never grew into adults?

While seemingly harmless, the negative by-product of trying to be friends is that the first thing to go out the window is discipline. It's this lack of boundaries from a young age that causes kids to scream like banshees and run around in restaurants like apes, when decades ago we had to mind our manners lest we incur the wrath of dad.

*There was a time when we expected nothing of our children but obedience, as opposed to the present, when we expect everything of them but obedience. ~Anatole Broyard (1920-1990), literary critic*

This lack of authority causes kids to disrespect adults and show no manners around strangers. Then what happens when they get that first job and have to play by the rules? The negative consequences of parents who can't say "No" can be seen in the sense of entitlement in today's youth.

## Hard to Buck the Trend

How does all this bad parenting affect us non-parents? One way is that we are grooming a generation of self-righteous incompetents that will one day run the country. But on a more personal level, "bad parenting" makes those of us without kids hesitant to join the group. Even if we know we'd do it differently ourselves, it's hard to buck the trend. And, as this Texan puts it:

> It doesn't matter how well you raise them or treat them, they still have to be around the other kids, and in today's world the other kids are more damaging than anything else. —John C., 38, Texas

Sadly, it is the parent who replies "No" to their nine-year-old asking to buy a violent video game that becomes the "bad guy," not the neighbor's dad for allowing them to sneak over and play *Grand Theft Auto V* or *Bulletstorm* for hours unsupervised.

You can't shelter kids from all outside influences, and to try to do so would be controlling and counterproductive. Thus, parenting can be a lose-lose situation, or—at the least—a heartbreaking and thankless job.


## Inept Parenting

Having children makes you no more a parent
than having a piano makes you a pianist.
~Michael Levine, author

The word "inept" finds its root in mid-16th-century Latin "ineptus" meaning "not apt" or "unsuitable." How many parents do you see in this world who are unsuitable for raising kids? Unsuitable parents would include those who cannot financially afford to have children (but have them anyway, knowing the government or someone will pick up the tab), and those who are mentally or physically incapable due to drug use, physical problems, genetic disorders or mental illness.

It's hard to imagine why a drug addict would want to have children, but many intentionally do just that, in order to collect per-child welfare checks that governments hand out to the impoverished. Although in the late '90s the United States' SSI (Supplemental Security Income) tried to crack down on issuing welfare checks to drug addicts and alcoholics,[10] many of these people have turned to faith-based welfare handouts.

In most developed countries, no matter how poor, drugged up or unqualified one is to parent, there will be a government program or group that will enable them to bear children by picking up the tab.

Millions of starving women around the globe give birth to children who will grow up hungry, malnourished, and with no hope of a healthy childhood. And yet, for reasons unknown to most (but pondered for decades by sociologists and scientists), these people choose not to use abstinence or birth control, and continue to breed.

This situation was discussed earlier in Chapter 7, but suffice it to say it is a tragedy that the people of the world who are the least qualified to rear children, are the ones who are least likely to refrain from having them.

The good news is: There are many out there who do know in advance that they would not make a suitable parent, and choose not to. In fact, when asked why they don't want kids, 44% of respondents to my survey checked "I don't think I would make a good parent." Their reasons range from personality problems to serious disorders:

I have an anxiety disorder that could get worse if I had kids because (a) the antidepressant I'm on has been proven to cause birth defects, so I would have to go off it and (b) what's more anxiety-producing than parenting? —Female, 29, Minneapolis, MN

Knowing you would be an unsuitable parent—for any reason—is the best reason I can think of not to procreate.

### Lone Parenting
*Just Say No!*

I have never had a desire to be a parent and honestly think I wouldn't have the patience. I also believe parenting is a two person job and have not been in a secure relationship where it has been an option since 2002. —Justine, 40, Perth, Australia

If you agree with Justine (above) that parenting is a two-person job, you won't be pleased with the statistics. Currently one in three children in the U.S. are being raised by only one parent, and the numbers are increasing.[11]

The situation is similar in both the UK[12] and Australia,[13] where "lone parent families" (children with one unwed parent), make up about one in four families, and those numbers are increasing. Arguably, the odds are stacked against these kids before they are even born.

Studies show that children born to single parents are more likely to suffer from depression, anxiety, alcohol and drug abuse and thoughts of suicide, than even those from divorced families. Plus they are three times more likely to drop out of high school than children from "intact families headed by a married mother and father."[14]

Another study found that boys reared in single parent families were twice as likely to end up in prison than boys reared in an intact family.[15]

If you are single and not having kids only because you know they should be raised by two parents—good choice! And, if you are single and contemplating having a child on your own, please consider the downsides.

Clearly, many single parents are not inept, and many are single for reasons beyond their control (i.e. divorce or the death of a spouse). But to *intentionally* set out to raise a child with only one parent is—arguably—to do a disservice to yourself and your child. As Kiki from Hawaii puts it:

I think the only people who should be parents are committed couples (it really is hard on just one person alone), who both really want children more than anything and are willing to make the sacrifices involved...The consequences to the child of the wrong decision are just too great to be made selfishly. —Kiki, 40, Hawaii

Besides the challenges of lack of finances and time, studies show that single parenting also hinders the child's development. A critical factor in healthy emotional development is the amount of contact that children have with both parents. According to the Department of Health and Human Services (HHS) "Children need emotional and financial support from both parents in order to become productive, successful adults."[16]

The number of single mothers in the U.S. more than doubled from 11.5% to 26% between 1970 and 2004, and 33% of all births are now to unwed mothers.[17] You probably know at least one woman who decided to *go it alone*—raising children without the help of a father, either by "oopsing" an unsuspecting suitor, or by using a sperm donor. I know of two women who have done just this. Are they happy? Are their kids well adjusted? I wish I could say yes.

In one case, the mother is forever trying to collect child support from the wealthy deadbeat dad who has chosen to have no part in his son's life. In the other case, the mother has developed a physical condition that keeps her home-ridden, causing her son to forgo his favorite sport to stay at home and assist her.

This is not uncommon, as statistics show that more than 25% of lone parents have a "long-standing health problem or disability" as do many of their kids.[18] So not only are these parents (mostly women) trying to raise kids without the help of a spouse, but in many cases they or their children have serious health problems or disabilities.

A good friend of mine "Charles" (who, by the way, warned me away from parenting years ago) tried to convince his daughter not to make this very mistake. At 43 years old, "Kathryn" (who has no partner) had decided she wanted to get pregnant and raise a child on her own. Upon hearing this news from his daughter, a worried Charles sat down and wrote her a letter outlining his concerns about how it will affect everyone involved. The letter is so pertinent here that I've reprinted it with his permission:

Dear Kathryn,

It was quite a surprise last week when you mentioned that you were thinking of having a baby, since I had the impression that you didn't particularly like children! Having a family has the potential of providing personal fulfillment and a joy to both parents and grandparents. Your having a family of your own certainly has my blessing, especially if: there are no illusions, you fully assume the burden of raising the child, and there is a reasonable chance of success for you and your child.

Since I entered marriage and parenthood without any experience or advice from anyone, and I didn't do such a hot job, I thought I would exercise my parental rights and relate some of my experience and cautions. You might give the following four thoughts some consideration. I do this with the intent of having you *not* repeat my mistakes and maximizing your happiness.

First, raising a baby through infancy, childhood, teen years, young adulthood and adulthood is, I think, the most difficult job on earth. It is often a nasty job that commands your full effort 24 hours a day, seven days a week, 52 weeks a year, for nearly two decades. There is no more difficult or demanding or important work in industry! It absolutely requires the total commitment of your time, energy, mental focus, patience, self-denial, tolerance or disappointment, hard work, and all of your finances.

Raising a family with a loving husband who shares the burdens and earns a good living is the ideal. The problem is that he may not be up to it all, may get distracted, and may leave for some reason. It's very difficult to judge personality, character and other aspects, even after several years, until a special situation arises. Your mother misjudged me. I even misjudged myself, as I didn't expect our relationship to work out as it did. I turned out to be immature, self-centered and selfish. I wasn't as committed to the family as I should have been.

Not having a spouse to support the family emotionally, with energy, work, etc. more than doubles the task of the mother and substantially reduces the probability of success of everything. It seems to me the single mother has a nearly impossible task, but the job goes on... Remember, you will be about our age, 65, when your child, hopefully, will be through college.

My second thought has to do with a good friend, Karen. When she was almost 40 she thought she wanted to have a child. She had a good boyfriend, an active life and all that. I must say though, I had difficulty imagining her with a baby with her personality and lifestyle, as I knew her.

So, one time when she raised the subject, I asked her "Have you ever volunteered to take care of your brother's child for a week, so he and his wife could have a vacation together? Have you volunteered to babysit so they could go to a movie?" Her reply was "No, not really," to which I asked "If you really don't enjoy interacting with children, why do you think spending a lifetime raising them would be your thing?"

Well, I don't know if our conversation had any impact, but she and her boyfriend have been living together happily for eight years without kids. She told me she is very happy and thought her "maternal instinct" had kicked in for a while, and she got over it.

My third suggestion is that I would recommend you investigate what are the possibilities your child might have a birth defect, as some are sensitive to the mother's age. You could do so by talking to your doctor, or checking the Internet or the library. My friends Tim and Pam have a Down's Syndrome girl and fortunately they are saints. For me, it would be an impossible nightmare.

My fourth thought is that I believe it would be an immoral act to create a family assuming the grandparents would be providing major support, for several reasons. First, you should know your mom and dad could be dead within a year or so. After all, my good friend Jean died when she was about my age now. Secondly, no one has the right to deliberately create a major obligation of work, commitment, time, money, etc. and pass it on to their parents.

Your mom and I have worked very hard all of our lives. In this, our declining years, we have an absolute right to spend our few good years the way *we want*—and not the way someone else wants. While your mom and I would enjoy a grandchild, and would probably provide some occasional support, you should *not* expect any significant time, work, increased financial commitment, etc. than you now receive. The care, raising, and support of a child would be your responsibility.

I'm sure you know that raising a child is *not* like getting a toy, a car, or a pet—it is a lifetime of many commitments. It may not have occurred to you, but having a child requires many hundreds of thousands of dollars. Your mom and I have supported you all of your life. We are simply too old to assume the burden of a new family. I know that is not your intent.

In closing, I say again—you certainly have my blessing and best wishes to start a family, especially if you have no illusions about the incredible chore of following through, and if you have created the conditions to allow you to fully assume all the burdens of raising a child.

Love, Dad

Good letter! If only all fathers (or mothers) could impart this kind of wisdom and experience to their daughters.

\*     \*     \*

If you are torn between becoming a parent or a non-parent, there are some well-balanced books you can read (*The Parenthood Decision*[19]), as well as online articles you can browse ("Should I have a baby?"[20]) to help guide you in your decision.

But if you feel parenting is too complex and convoluted, or that you would not be a suitable parent for whatever reason, you are astute to realize this now before jumping in.

If only more people would ponder parenting *before* they procreate, the world would be a much better place.

# CHAPTER 10

## "I Fear Childbirth"
### *(And What it Might Do to My Body)*

If nature had arranged that husbands and wives should have children
alternatively, there would never be more than three in a family.
~Lawrence Housman (1865-1959), English playwright

Something tells me Lawrence (above) witnessed his wife giving birth.
Either that, or he is a very shrewd man. Men can be babies when it
comes to pain, so if *they* were the ones experiencing nine months of
pregnancy and childbirth, there might be fewer children in the world.
However, there are women too who feel the *physical trauma of pregnancy*
and the ensuing *painful childbirth* are reason enough not to procreate.

About two-third of all female survey respondents—when asked for
reasons they don't want children—checked "I don't want the physical wear
& tear on my body to bear children."

Interestingly, more than 9% of males checked this too, implying they
were looking out for their mates. Some men said they don't want their wife
or partner to go through the physical trauma, while others admitted they
didn't relish what it would do to her body.

For most, this is just one of *several* reasons they didn't procreate, but
for some the prospect of pregnancy and/or childbirth brings a tremendous
amount of fear and anxiety. Many women took it a step further by adding
comments in their survey like "I fear childbirth." *Tokophobia* is the
psychiatric term for this fear that can even cause panic attacks.

The following survey respondent reveals her serious phobia of the entire reproduction process, from pregnancy to preschool:

> Besides all the other tons of reasons out there to not have kids, I have a horrible, horrible phobia of pregnancy, childbirth, and small children. How could a woman do that to her body? It's so gory and creepy!
> —Xantres, 22, Indianapolis, IN

## Avoiding Pregnancy Like the Plague

> The thought of being pregnant scares the living hell out of me!
> —Gabs, 34, Fort Collins, CO

While Tinseltown and tabloids make big bucks on revealing the bellies of über-pregnant celebrities, many non-parents wince at the sight. For many, a belly full of baby simply bombards us with bad thoughts of what would be if we embarked on the pregnancy pilgrimage. Thoughts of nausea, pain and stretch marks will not be selling us your magazines. No, they'd more likely have us protesting your publicity stunt!

Evelina from Helsinki, Finland, says, "I'm really scared of giving birth, and the idea that something would grow inside of me is not tempting either," while Sara from Auckland, New Zealand, quite simply says, "Pregnancy disgusts me." Others use words like distress, anxiety and torture to describe their view of pregnancy:

> I think pregnancy and childbirth is horrible torture and I can't imagine willingly submitting myself to it. I have very low pain tolerance. Also, I think it's very easy for men (and family and friends) to want kids, as they are not the ones sacrificing their bodies or the ones that end up stuck with a child for years... —Emma Miller, 22, Ontario, Canada

There is sound reasoning for wanting to avoid the physical effects of pregnancy. Besides the proverbial "morning sickness," weight gain and fickle food cravings, many women embark on pregnancy unaware of the numerous medical problems that can come with it.

Here is a list I found on BabyCenter.com of maladies that can occur within a pregnancy term.[1] (Warning: You may want to skip this part!)

> **Ectopic Pregnancy**—Occurs when a fertilized egg implants outside the uterus, typically in one of the fallopian tubes. If left untreated, it can rupture (causing severe pain, bleeding and shock) and be life threatening.
>
> **Miscarriage**—The loss of a pregnancy within the first 20 weeks. Vaginal spotting or bleeding is generally the first symptom, followed by abdominal pain a few hours to a few days later. It's possible that as many as 50% of pregnancies miscarry before implantation in the womb occurs.

**Preterm (Premature) Labor**—Starting to have contractions that efface or dilate your cervix before 37 weeks of pregnancy. Symptoms include: excess vaginal discharge, vaginal spotting or bleeding, menstrual-like cramps and low back pain.

**Placental Abruption**—A serious condition in which your placenta separates from your uterus, partially or completely, before the baby is born. A variety of symptoms include: sudden and obvious bleeding or bloody fluid if your water breaks, uterine tenderness, back pain, or frequent contractions, and possible decrease in the baby's activity.

**Preeclampsia**—A complex disorder of pregnancy that causes changes in your blood vessels and can affect your liver, kidneys, brain and the placenta. Symptoms may include swelling in face and hands or puffiness around the eyes, and excessive or sudden swelling of the feet or ankles. In serious cases, you may have intense pain in the upper abdomen, a severe headache, blurred vision, or nausea and vomiting.

**Urinary Tract Infection**—Pregnancy makes you susceptible to urinary tract infections of all kinds. Symptoms include pain when urinating, pelvic or lower abdominal pain, frequent urge to urinate, and cloudy, foul-smelling or bloody urine. An untreated bladder infection can lead to a kidney infection and premature labor.

**Kidney Infection**—A serious infection that requires immediate medical attention. Can cause high fever, shaking, chills or sweats; pain in your lower back or in your side just under your ribs (and possibly in your abdomen); nausea and vomiting; and possibly pus or blood in your urine.

Have you broken out in a sweat yet? If you're lucky enough not to experience any of the above complications during pregnancy, chances are your nine months will not be devoid of the less harmful discomforts of gas, bloating, constipation, abdominal pain, nausea, sleepiness, back pain and cramps. But seriously, pregnancy is not without health risks, and some women feel unsure they could physically handle it:

I'm not sure that I'm physically capable of having a baby and do not want the agony of miscarriage to be the way that I find out that the doctors were right. —Danielle, 32, Salem, IN

For others, it's not the medical problems that have them petrified, but rather the pain of the pointy prickly tools that are all too often used by obstetricians during pregnancy, as this Canadian shares:

I have a severe needle phobia. When I have had to have blood drawn in the past I've been too terrified to eat for days at a time. If I were ever forced to go through 9 months of pregnancy—and all of the needles that go along with that—I'd fear for my physical and mental health. —Female, 23, Toronto, Canada

This "blenophobia"—or fear of needles—is shared by millions worldwide, including 20 million in America alone. It is serious enough to cause many women to ixnay the idea of pregnancy and childbirth.

## The Trauma of Childbirth

Giving birth is like taking your lower lip and forcing it over your head.
~Carol Burnett

Although coming from one of my favorite comediennes, the above quote makes me cringe more than chuckle. This is probably because it contains more fact than folly. If you've seen pictures of live birth, you know what I mean. I'll never forget seeing a video of live birth in college, and wanting to run to phone my mom and apologize. Oh the pain, the horror, the ripping and tearing, as this poor woman tried to push this large head past the threshold of her body. A good video for population control!

No wonder so many women in my survey echoed these sentiments:

The thought of giving birth alone scares me to death.
—Female, 30, Hamburg, Germany

And it's not just the pain that scares us. When I was a young girl, I told my friends that "god made it fair between men and women," because men had to fight and risk their lives in wars, and women had to endure the pain of delivering babies. Had I known the facts, I would have added "risk their lives" to the latter as well. Indeed, there is mortal risk in birthing a child.

In fact, women are now dying in childbirth at the highest rate since 1977. According to the National Center for Health Statistics, in 2003 the maternal death rate jumped from 10 to 12 women per 100,000 live births. The following year—2004—it increased again to 13 deaths per 100,000. And in my state of California, the maternal death rate increased to 16.9 per 100,000 in 2006—triple what it was a decade before![2]

Experts think this may be due to three risk factors: the rising obesity in women, an increase in Caesarean section deliveries, and the older age at which women are now giving birth.

But I'd be remiss not to point out that the current odds of maternal death during childbirth (1 in 7,692) are still lower than your odds of getting killed in an auto accident. Ninety years ago—before antibiotics, ultrasound and epidurals—the odds were something to give pause to, as one in 100 women died while giving birth!

These days, death to the *infant* is much more common—671 per 100,000 live births—than death to the mother.[3] I'm sure the fact that your child is over 50 times more likely to die in childbirth than you are, is not a consoling fact, however.

## The Pain of Labor

The pain, the pain!
—Peggy G., 42, Warwick, NY

You can rest assured that death is much less common than extreme pain and physical complications during childbirth these days. But you won't rest assured if you are petrified of the potential pain! Many childfree women—like Peggy above—when asked why they don't want to procreate, simply responded about the pain. Some don't want to endure childbirth, and others are afraid of it:

I'm deathly afraid of going through the pain of labor! I'm selfish. And there's nothing wrong with that! —Female, 30, Loves Park, IL

Pregnancy and childbirth frighten me. —Female, 25, Georgia

My mom once told me that humans do not have a memory for pain, otherwise they would not give birth to more than one child. I figured either she was speaking from experience (she had three) or she had read it in one of her psychology books, so I believed it.

But years after I broke my leg in a ski race, I could vividly remember the pain I was in as I was carried down the mountain in a ski sled. Granted, I can't relive the exact pain of my fractured tibia and fibula, but I certainly don't want to go there again, and the memory always slows me down on a steep icy slope! Thus, I find it hard to fully believe my mom's pregnancy pain parable, and—at any rate—don't wish to test it.

If I were to create my own allegory from the ski incident, it would be that: In spite of the pain and trauma—and due to my love for the sport—I did return to skiing, just as a mother returns to pregnancy. The risks are worth the perceived rewards to each of us.

## Complications of Childbirth

Fear of suffering during pregnancy and childbirth.
Fear of miscarriages and stillbirth.
—Anneke, 43, Brattleboro, VT

Being squeamish or fearing pain may sound weak or selfish to some, but giving birth does carry with it a host of risks and complications worth giving pause to, even in our modern era of medicine. When a 40-year-old female from Manchester, England, told me she didn't have children because of her "terrible fear of childbirth," she was not just referring to pain, but to the dozens of things that can go wrong in the process.

Following is a list of problems that can occur before, during and after childbirth. (Please don't throw this book at the wall!)

**Prelabor/Braxton Hicks Contractions** – Irritating irregular contractions which produce a "false labor" that can cause preterm rupture of the membranes.

**Preterm Rupture of the Membranes** – Water breaks prior to 37 weeks, and may trigger premature labor and delivery. Can cause stillbirth.

**Rupture of Membranes and Infection** – Amniotic fluid can get infected and be dangerous to the baby if inhaled during pregnancy.

**Premature Birth** – A birth that occurs before the 37th week. "Preemie babies" do not yet have fully developed lungs, heart function or central nervous system, thus are not able to breathe or eat on their own and are susceptible to many health problems.

**Stillbirth** – The birth of an infant that has died in the womb, after surviving the first 28 weeks of pregnancy. Odds are one stillbirth in 115 live births in the U.S.

**Abnormal Presentation** – Improper positioning of the fetus upon delivery, including Breech Birth and Shoulder Dystocia.

**Breech Birth** – When the baby doesn't enter the birth canal head first, causing difficult labor and delivery, head entrapment and/or brain injury.

**Shoulder Dystocia** – After the delivery of the head, the shoulders cannot pass below the pubic area. May cause damage to the nerves in the baby's shoulder, arm and hands, and possibly even fetal death.

**Forceps or Vacuum Delivery** – When normal delivery can't take place due to breeching or other problems, forceps or a vacuum may be resorted to. Nerve or brain damage may result if done improperly.

**Umbilical Cord Prolapse** – When the umbilical cord, before or during labor, slips through the cervix, preceding the baby into the birth canal and possibly through the vagina, it can get blocked and stop the flow of blood to the baby through the cord.

**Umbilical Cord Compression** – When the umbilical cord gets wrapped around the baby from movement during pregnancy. The cord may harm the baby, but mostly it gets stretched and compressed causing sudden drops in the fetal heart rate.

**Episiotomy During Labor** – A painful incision between the vagina and anus to aid in delivery. May cause infection, increased bleeding, prolonged healing and discomfort during intercourse.

**Prolonged Labor** – "Dystocia" is an abnormally slow, painful and difficult labor due to many causes. Not healthy for mother or baby.

**Caesarian Section** – "C-Section" is surgically removing the baby through an incision made in the lower abdomen, when natural delivery is not possible or advised. Risks of infection and blood clotting are higher, and maternal death rate is 5 times greater.

**Postpartum Depression** – Beyond just the "baby blues," 10% of new mothers experience PPD—a more severe form of emotional distress lasting up to six months after childbirth.

After reading the previous list of possible complications in childbirth, it's hard not to agree with the following non-parent who believes the medical procedures should be more safe and advanced by now:

I have a fear of childbirth. I don't have a problem with C-sections, but the thought of giving birth is very disturbing and to me seems somewhat like torture...I don't think medical practices are good enough. If it were a man giving birth, they would have come up with a better way by now.
—Genova Boyd, 27, Bavaria, Germany

## The After Effects
*Both Mental and Physical*

I do not want the emotional distress and possible psychological side effects a pregnancy could have on me, as I have seen how women became completely different persons after their pregnancies.
—Barbayat, 29, Bremen, Germany

It doesn't always end there. After nine months of carrying around a melon in your stomach, feeling sick, tired and achy—then going through a painful labor and ripping your body open in childbirth—you'd think there would be months of joy and endless rewards thereafter. Well, not likely.

Most women experience the "baby blues" in the first ten days to two weeks after childbirth. This includes a roller coaster of emotions ranging from feeling happy one minute to crying the next. They may lose their appetite, have a hard time sleeping (even when the baby's asleep), lose their concentration and feel a bit depressed. If this doesn't end or worsens after two weeks, the woman may have postpartum depression (PPD), which lasts up to six months. According to FamilyDoctor.org, the symptoms of postpartum depression include:[4]

- **Feeling sad or down often**
- **Frequent crying or tearfulness**
- **Feeling restless, irritable or anxious**
- **Loss of interest or pleasure in life**
- **Loss of appetite**
- **Less energy and motivation to do things**
- **Sleep difficulties**
- **Feeling worthless, hopeless or guilty**
- **Unexplained weight loss or gain**
- **Feeling like life isn't worth living**
- **Showing little interest in your baby**

Basically, you could become a basket case after giving birth.

Many childfree are aware of the emotional dangers inherent in the changing hormonal levels that occur during and after pregnancy, and they fear the toll it may take on their mind and body.

> The first 9 months and the next 18 years. Not just the physical, but the hormonal and emotional wear and tear on my body.
> —Sheri, 36, West Palm Beach, FL

Even if you're lucky enough to miss all the hormonal and emotional side effects of having a baby, you still may not escape the physical damage it inflicts. A friend of mine told me she was never the same after having even her first child. Without going into detail, there are changes to the female body that may occur much to the chagrin of both the husband and wife, as this candid-yet-anonymous male puts it:

> Child birthing ruins a woman's body. Even if she were to enter a rigorous rehabilitation program (and most women I know would not even enter into a mild exercise program), the damage is not even surgically repairable.
> —Married male, 44, Center Line, MI

While this may not always be the case, I understand his concern, and I'm certainly relieved I don't have to test it!

\*　　\*　　\*

Whether you are squeamish (or scared stiff) about the idea of pregnancy, petrified of pain or needles, traumatized by the thought of birthing a child, or worried about the physical and emotional impact the event will have on you and/or your spouse, you are not alone.

While most of us have several reasons not to bear children, for some this one is all they need. On the bright side, perhaps this is nature's way of keeping the population down.

# CHAPTER 11

## "I Don't Want To Bring Them Into This World"

I don't want to bring them into this messed-up, already overcrowded world where life just seems to be getting more and more difficult!
—Dahlia, 40, San Francisco, CA

```
"Three infants found dead in freezer"
"Couple accused of ditching baby"
"Sex offenders found at child care homes"
"Teacher convicted of sexually exploiting minors"
"Man gets life in deaths of wife & baby"
"One in 50 U.S. babies abused, neglected annually"
```

. . . $A$nd the headlines keep coming. The above newspaper headlines all appeared within one month of each other and were all concerning child victims in the United States and Europe.

Almost half of Kidfree Survey respondents answered, "I don't want to bring them into this corrupt and/or dangerous world," when asked for reasons they don't want children. Some of us feel this world has gotten worse since we were kids, and others think it's just always been bad and don't want to purposely expose another human to it.

For many—like Renee—the putrid condition of the world is the *primary* reason they choose not to procreate:

> Sure the freedom is a bonus to being CF, but my #1 reason is because I think the world is a sick place and do not wish to bring anyone here.
> —Renee, Childfree Network member

Admittedly, the degeneration of society wasn't one of my original reasons for not procreating, but it has become a major *hindsight* reason. Over the past decade, what I've seen happen to my state, my country and the world in general makes me relieved I'm not subjecting any new humans to it.

## The Best Has Been

I think it is totally irresponsible to have kids in such an uncertain world. We have had the best, and things are just going downhill from here environmentally and society-wise. I couldn't stand the stress of being a parent and putting a child out into this.
—Bagfish, 34, Cumbria, England

Although I consider myself an optimist, I have to agree with the above Brit—a female with her PhD. The world, in many ways, is going downhill. Would you want to be born today? Would you want to live it all over again in today's world? It may sound cynical, but I wouldn't. I love the childhood I had, and know it would not be the same in today's world.

We've already discussed the problems of Earth's dwindling space and resources, society's pressure on procreators to be the perfect parents, and technology's role in complicating childhoods and draining parents' pocketbooks. But what about the moral and intellectual decay of society? What about the über-greed and the über-speed of life? Materialism, sensationalism and "instant gratificationism" seem to have replaced the hard work, patience and fortitude of our Industrial Age forefathers. You need to embrace this change if you want to raise a family in it, don't you?

I'm very glad that I don't have to worry about bringing a child into this world, which seems to be getting more polluted, wars and terrorism see no end, and certainly America's first place in the world is waning, so this may not be a dream country in another 30 to 40 years.
—Jaana G, 52, Roswell, GA

All signs point to what Jaana asserts, that America is indeed waning. We are slowly losing our "number one superpower" status, and we certainly aren't thriving like we used to. We are in debt up to our foreheads and are finding it harder to borrow money from the countries we so condescendingly referred to for years as "developing." They are developing while we are drowning, and it looks like they are getting the last laugh. Who would wish this dire debt dilemma on their offspring?

It's one thing that the U.S. may no longer be top dog, as we've had our glory and it's someone else's turn. But leaving behind a national debt that is piling ever higher to the next generation is almost criminal. It seems our once thriving country is going the way of the Roman Empire, whose greed and decadence caused its own demise.

Economics aside, America is just flat running out of role models. In the past decade, crime and corruption have inundated our politicians, church leaders, corporate CEOs and major sports figures. (Either that, or the *uncovering* of the corruption has increased.) Regardless, it instills in the helpless citizen feelings of suspicion, stress and general malaise. So many leaders and "upstanding" citizens abuse their positions of power, who can we trust anymore? Ultimately, our powerlessness leads to apathy.

It is also documented that our educational standards are slipping. One in three kids drop out of high school in the U.S., and in big cities like Los Angeles, over half drop out.[1] A 2008 Associated Press poll found that half of Americans say U.S. schools are doing a "fair to poor job preparing kids for college and the work force." Statistics show that dropouts earn far less than college graduates, rely more on social services such as food stamps, are more likely to wind up in prison, and have children that are destined to repeat this pattern in a hopeless, endless cycle.

## The Onslaught of the Online World

To me people have children for very selfish reasons.
Wanting to carry on a line is selfish. The world today is
extremely dangerous. Why bring a child into that?
—Female, 30, Clarksburg, WV

Online predators, online pornography, online bullying, online suicides... None of these crimes and ills even existed three decades ago. And these horrors occur without your child even leaving home! How would you feel if your teen was bullied by peers on the Internet and killed herself? Or persuaded by a 40-year-old man to meet somewhere?

With the advent of the Internet, came the advent of *online predators*. Now, not only is it dangerous for your child to walk to school alone, but it's dangerous for her to sit in her bedroom alone—alone on the computer, that is. According to Clint Van Zandt, MSNBC analyst and former FBI profiler, "Federal authorities believe that at least 500,000 to 750,000 predators are online on a daily basis, constantly combing..."[2]

Crimes Against Children Research Center found that 1 in 7 youth received online sexual solicitations (about half of which are from other youth, not adults). Their online fact sheet reports that, conservatively, 4% of our youth are victims of online predators, as follows:[3]

- 1 in 25 youth got "aggressive" sexual solicitations that included attempts to contact the youth offline.
- 1 in 25 youth were solicited to take sexual pictures of themselves.
- 1 in 25 youth were upset or distressed as a result of an online solicitation.

Another ugly perpetrator on the family computer is *online pornography*. Children are not only *subjects* of Internet porn, but may become *addicts* of Internet porn. This latter problem was revealed on *Cyber Seduction: His Secret Life*, a TV movie on Lifetime (which by the way is a good network to watch to discover the hardships of parenting!).

The movie was based on the true story of a teen who found himself addicted to Internet porn. Affecting him physically and emotionally (i.e. grades, sports, sleep, social life), it nearly destroyed the previously healthy life the teen had enjoyed. It was a grueling journey for he and his parents to get the help he needed and finally overcome his obsession with sex and porn. And it all started innocently one day after school, on the computer.

According to My Kids Browser, the following stats on children's exposure to porn have been derived from reputable sources including Google, WordTracker, PBS, MSNBC, NRC and Alexa research:[4]

| | |
|---|---|
| Average age of first Internet exposure to pornography | 11 years |
| Largest consumer of Internet pornography | 12-17 years |
| 15-17 year olds having multiple hard-core exposures | 80% |
| 8-16 year olds having viewed porn online | 90% |
| 7-17 year olds who would freely give out home address | 29% |
| Children's characters linked to thousands of porn links | 26 |

Thirteen was the age that Megan Meier was victimized by *cyberbullying*—a powerful phenomenon of peer attacks in cyberspace. Megan's 2007 suicide was the result of a cruel hoax by kids and a mother getting thrills through the power of online social bullying.

Hers wasn't the first "bullycide" of its kind (recall 13-year-old Ryan Halligan who hung himself in 2003 after months of online bullying from kids), and it hasn't been the *last*. Now there even exists an Anti-Bullying Week, launched by the UK's Anti-Bullying Alliance (ABA). A survey conducted by the ABA found the following:[5]

- One in five (20.5%) of Year 6 primary school pupils surveyed (aged 10 or 11) had been cyberbullied in the past 12 months.
- 22% of Year 6 pupils did not know how to protect themselves against cyberbullying.

## Innocence Lost Young
*Sexting, Texting and Growing Up Fast*

The first time I held a mobile phone was in my mid-twenties. I was on a business trip and the rental car company included it as a promotion. The phone was about eight inches long, weighed at least four pounds and was strictly used for pricey business calls. Now, the cell phone—with its built in camera, access to the web, music and video games—has become a youth appendage. Texting is the center of teen (and pre-teen) life.

Whether you believe that this constant communication in the airwaves between kids is healthy or not, there is no doubt it has created some distasteful new phenomena. The latest of these is "sexting"—sending sexually suggestive nude or nearly nude images of oneself via text messaging. These images are used to sexually titillate others, and are often passed along to friends for their entertainment value.

A recent survey from Pew Research Center found that 4% of cell-owning teens ages 12-17 say they have sent sexual images via text messaging, while 15% say they have received such images.[6] It also found that teen girls often feel pressure to send these images and later regret it.

A friend of mine, upon finding her teenage son's missing cell phone, also found out about his "sexting" habits. Graphic images of his private parts had been sent out into the cyber world for all to see and enjoy. His mother did not enjoy it. And it's not just *photos* parents worry about these days, but actual *videos* of sex. What once was reserved for the eyes of adults in theaters and adult stores can now be viewed daily by kids on cell phones in a matter of minutes. No wonder they want to experiment sooner.

Timothy Jay, author of *What to Do When Your Kids Talk Dirty*, has also found that kids are swearing at younger ages and using more offensive words than ever before. The following survey respondent gave a long list of reasons she doesn't want kids, most of which had to do with worrying about the ill affects the world would have on them. Here are excerpts:

I don't want them to run with the wrong crowds and get into crime and/or drugs. I don't want them to be teased and/or bullied. I don't want them to be in a Columbine situation... I don't want them sexting or using My Space or Facebook inappropriately. I am a worrywart. I already suffer from insomnia. If I had a kid, I would constantly worry about their safety and well-being. Teenagers are confused, insecure, trying to fit in. You can't tell them anything because they think they know everything. They are having babies more than ever. [...] —Clara Michelle, 38, Milwaukee, WI

## Kids Are Commodities

I don't want the stress and worry that is involved with looking after a child.
I worry enough about my nephew (he's a great kid)...I worry about
something happening to him (knife/gun crime, car/road accident,
drink spiked with drugs, etc) where he is an innocent bystander.
So many terrible things happen to innocent kids/people everyday.
It breaks my heart just thinking about it.
—Ann G, 29, Greater Manchester, England

The Internet's not the only perpetrator of the young and innocent. When a child leaves the house, there is more crime that can befall him than ever before. Kidnapping is on the rise in the U.S., according to the FBI's National Crime Information Center.

From 1982 to 2000, the number of missing persons reported to law enforcement increased 468%—from 154,000 to over 876,000. Almost 90% of those missing are children under the age of 18.[7] That's over 2,000 children a day reported missing in the U.S. alone! The chances are now also higher that a child will be trafficked somewhere and sold into slavery. In his book on sex trafficking, Siddharth Kara writes that:

By my calculation, the total annual number of individuals trafficked for commercial sexual exploitation is between five hundred thousand and six hundred thousand, out of a total number of annual human trafficking victims of 1.5 to 1.8 million.[8]

Kara estimates that one woman or child in every sixty seconds somewhere across the globe is trafficked for sexual exploitation. With an estimated price tag of $5,250 per slave in the U.S. and $4,800 in Western Europe, a thief sees dollar signs on a child as he walks down the street.

Newborn children are coveted by baby brokers (who receive $60k to $120k per child on the street), as well as by emotionally obsessed infertile women. While writing this book, our small resort town saw a bold case of infant theft, when a woman just walked into a hospital maternity ward, scooped up a newborn baby, and walked out the door with it.

When hospitals everywhere upped their security in response to baby thieves, it prompted an entirely new—more gruesome—phenomenon to occur: fetus theft. Women will actually fake a 9-month pregnancy, then murder another woman to steal her unborn child from the womb! There have been 13 known cases of this crime since 1987, and 12 mothers and four babies have died from it. Just another crime against children and parents that didn't *exist* thirty years ago.

## Schools and Sanctuaries Aren't Safe
*Nor Are Their Leaders*

Schools have always had their tough kids. I remember fearing a surly girl in the 8th grade who threatened, "If you come to school tomorrow your ass is grass!" I was scared, but what did she mean? She meant she would bully me, taunt me, push me around and—at worst—beat me up.

Years later, knifings replaced bullying and fistfights. Now guns have replaced knives as the weapon of choice on campus—not to mention the occasional bomb! "Your ass is grass" now means you may get stabbed or shot if you show up to school.

School is also an easy place to procure and stash drugs these days. In 2000, more than 50% of all teens (including those in middle school) said that drugs were sold, used or kept at their school.[9]

Another trend—unless it's just reported more these days—is that of *teachers sexually exploiting students.* In addition to the cliché dirty old professor harassing a female student, many female teachers have been convicted of sexually molesting their male students in recent years. Even boys *coaches* may not be trusted these days. The Penn State child molestation scandal opened up a whole new worry for parents.

The Catholic sex abuse scandals of the late 20th century brought to light the fact that even *churches* are no sanctuary from predators. For years boys and girls worldwide have fallen prey to the very role models they look up to and trust—the priests and religious authorities in their churches.

## Bingeing, Barfing and Blackouts
*To Escape Life's Stress*

All signs point to kids drinking and drugging more today. After a decade of decline in teen alcohol and drug abuse, a study released in 2010 shows a marked reversal in the trend. The Partnership/MetLife Foundation Attitude Tracking Study (PATS) shows that, for teens in grades 9-12, the use of alcohol, Ecstasy and marijuana are all up dramatically, as is the attitude that it is acceptable and beneficial.[10]

Not only are more kids drinking today, but kids are drinking *more* today. Binge drinking (five or more drinks in a sitting) is now common, and is climbing fastest among 18-20-year-olds. According to a 2007 study by CASA (the National Center on Addiction and Substance Abuse at

Columbia University), both binge drinking and drug abuse increased in college students between 1993 and 2005. [11]

"Binge drinking frequently" is up 16%, "Drinking to get drunk" is up 21%, and "getting drunk three times a month or more" is up 26%. Over *half* of all binge drinkers report having had blackouts. The number of daily marijuana users doubled in the same period, and the use of illegal drugs, such as cocaine and heroin, went up 52%.

But the prescription drug phenomenon is a whole new bottle of opiates, so to speak. CASA found that, in the 12 years of their study, the use of opioids like Percocet, Vicodin and OxyContin increased 343%, and the use of tranquilizers like Xanax and Valium increased 450% for university students. Kids can now access them freely on the Internet. The main reason for usage cited by students? To "relieve stress."

America's not alone in its burgeoning of bingeing, barfing and pill-popping youth. According to an article published by the British Medical Association (BMA) entitled "Alcohol and Young People":

> There was a general rise in the proportion of 11 to 15 year-olds who drink alcohol regularly, but also there is an increase in the amount they are drinking on each occasion.[12]

Why should parents worry that their kids are drinking more and starting younger? Because alcohol is—by far—the number one cause of death in youth today. But death aside, what does it say about society that increasing numbers of young people depend on drugs and alcohol to escape life's stress? Probably that life's getting more stressful.

### "Life is Hard"
*And it seems to be getting harder*

Life can be very difficult for many people, and as the world evolves, it seems as though it becomes harder for kids to grow up in a balanced happy environment. I would feel the pain my child would feel and that is a difficult thought for me.
—Jen, 36, California

It used to be that adults envied children for their youth and innocence—a kind of happy-go-lucky freedom if you will. Not a care in the world. It's hard to envy kids today when we see the weight of a worsening world on their shoulders. I see an insecurity and self-consciousness inflicted by a society that directs them to "do well, look good and fit in." And I hear fear and anxiety in their louder and more frequent screams.

The number of college students counseled for depression doubled between 1988 and 2001, and the number reporting suicidal thoughts *tripled* in the same period.[13] Suicide is now the third leading cause of death among kids 15-24, and the second leading cause of death among college students. As with binge drinking, the top reason students cited for considering suicide was, "relief from emotional or physical pain."[14] Either there's too much pressure on kids these days, or kids can't handle the pressure.

> Life is hard. It's certainly been that way for me mentally and emotionally. I studied philosophy at university and investigated all of life's big questions. All I found were more questions. I have nothing reassuring to tell a kid when he/she asks. —"ryanpaddy7," 31, Tokyo, Japan

For some, like this man from Tokyo, it's not about the world going south as much as it's about life's difficulty from a psychological standpoint. Through his searching, he has found he would not have positive answers to give a child about life's big questions.

### "It's Cruel to Bring a Being into This World"

> Man is subject to innumerable pains and sorrows by the very condition of humanity, and yet, as if nature had not sown evils enough in life, we are continually adding grief to grief and aggravating the common calamity by our cruel treatment of one another.
> ~Joseph Addison (1672-1719), English essayist, poet, politician

The above quote from a thinker of the 17th century shows that life's difficulties have existed for centuries, and are nothing new to humanity. Technology and decadence aside, many non-parents—like the two below—feel that the world isn't necessarily worse than when they were young, but that it has always been crummy, cruel, and unfair.

> I distinctly remember thinking that it would be cruel to bring a child into this world when I was 17 and dating a guy I thought I would marry after high school. He wanted us to get pregnant right after graduation so we could be together, and I told him that was not a very good way to bring a child into this world. I guess even then part of me was unsure about becoming a parent. —"TheSpaceCowgirl," 31, Arkansas

> I could care less about decadence, but the less people forced to live in this crummy unfair world, the better. —Tasci da Synx, 27, Tracy, CA

For some, this cruel and crowded world is reason enough not to procreate:

> By far, my two primary reasons are: 1) feeling bad about bringing innocent people into this cruel existence, and, 2) overpopulation.
> —"smartypants," (female with PhD), 36, California

But, while some may see humans as the victims of a cruel world, others see us as the actual *perpetrators*—or the virus, if you will.

> There is the school of thought that Mankind is a virus, and a very good argument can be made to support it!
> —Trafferd Pryce, 52, Santa Barbara, CA

Likewise, kids are not only the victims of evil, but the doers of evil. Doesn't it seem there's an inordinate amount of kids killing their parents, shooting their siblings, attacking grandma and torturing each other lately?

Recently two British kids age 10 and 11 were convicted of robbing, beating, stabbing and torturing two other children almost to their deaths. The reason given by one of the boys: "There were [sic] nothing else to do."

So, if mankind is indeed a virus, who wants to bring a human into it? Especially without its permission, as Paul points out:

> Society and its ridiculous laws are getting harder and harder to live a happy life under, and imagine what it will be like 20 years from now. What RIGHT does anyone have to bring another life into the world without its consent and possibly against its will? Since you can't ask it, the right thing to do is to not make that decision for it.
> —Paul Patch, 41, Buffalo Grove, IL

Another theory among childfree—and many intellectuals in general—is that our species is due for a massive die-off. This may happen by way of natural disaster, human hand in nuclear war, or by the slow petri dish theory of overpopulation, disease and famine, as this Brit predicts:

> Regardless of whatever else they want their children to be once they grow up, ALL parents want their kids to be "happy." I think that, in the near future (one or two hundred years), our species is due to experience a MASSIVE die-off as part of the inevitable natural "correction" of our population surplus. As resources become scarce, people will fight wars for them. Many millions will die through starvation or communicable disease. Who wants THAT as the legacy they leave their kids to face?
> —Jim, 35, Staffordshire, England

Having never been a doomsayer, I have a hard time admitting that I am increasingly agreeing with this "massive die-off" camp. It doesn't depress me, because the earth needs to periodically wipe the slate clean and start over. But I would feel guilty if I were subjecting the next several generations to a slow, painful demise.

> I think their chances for living a reasonably suffering-free life would be remote due to the direction of the world. —Rich, 50, Santa Barbara, CA

## Perception Versus Reality

The world is NOT in fact getting more dangerous—it has never been
SAFER for kids or for adults. What has changed is the tolerance for
violence/corruption in the name of political "sensitivity."
—Wolfe, 33, New York, NY

There are those—like Wolfe above (a male with his Masters degree)—who actually believe that life has never been *safer*, and there are arguments that can be made to that point. Air pollution has improved in major cities since the 1960s; the percentage of smokers has decreased in the U.S.; child safety seat laws and airbags are saving more lives; laws against domestic violence are stricter; pedophiles must register and can't live near schools; toy safety inspections are stricter, and so on.

There are definitely some positive trends, if you look hard enough. But I wanted to verify Wolfe's point that violence has not increased, just our lack of tolerance. So, I looked at the FBI Crime Reports listing every year from 1960 to 2009, hoping for some good news.

The U.S. has indeed seen a decrease in violent crime four years in a row between 2007 and 2010. However, we still have more than quadruple the number of violent crimes (murders, rapes, etc.) than we did in 1960.[15]

Population increase is partly to blame for this increase, so I looked at the chart that adjusts for this. When indexing per 100,000 inhabitants, the *violent crime rate* has risen 250% since 1960 and the *total crime rate* has nearly doubled since then.[16]

It is true that our tolerance for violence and corruption has decreased over the centuries, as humans have attempted to become more "civilized." We've come a long way since the day it was acceptable to pull a human apart limb-by-limb in the town square, as folks looked on and cheered.

But even if all that has changed is our *tolerance*—does that make life any easier? If we tolerate these acts less and perceive them as worse, doesn't our level of stress rise? What percentage of reality is *perception*?

If I perceive it to be dangerous for my son to ride a bike to school, and thus take that healthy joy from him, isn't that still one less healthy joy for my son's childhood? Whether you believe the late politico Lee Atwater's assertion, "Perception is Reality," or its sister aphorism, "Life is 90% Perception, 10% Reality," it's hard to argue with the following viewpoint:

Reality doesn't bite, rather our perception of reality bites.
~Anthony J. D'Angelo, founder, Collegiate Empowerment

*　　*　　*

I confess: I hated writing this chapter. Not because I was short on material on why people don't want to bring another human into this world. Rather, I had so many negative topics to cover I couldn't do justice to each. Each issue—from Teen Suicide to Prescription Drug Addiction—could have filled a book in itself.

The fact that there are far too many problems facing our youth today to fit into one chapter—or even one book—saddens me. It's disheartening to discover that the world—like a pressure cooker—is under a lot of stress. How and when will the top blow?

> If we had kids, we would have to care about how messed up the world is getting. Now we know that once we die, everyone else can just live in the mess they created, we won't have anyone we have to worry about.
> —Kent Atwater, 35, Rockford, IL

I *do* care about the youth of today, and the plight of tomorrow—as I think most non-parents do. But—like Kent above—I do find comfort in knowing that I don't have any offspring of my own to worry about.

And, as I finally complete this chapter, I can honestly say: I have never before been as relieved to be...kidfree!

# CHAPTER 12

## "I Would Have To Give Up My Career"
### *(Or Alter it Greatly)*

To find a career to which you are adapted by nature,
and then to work hard at it, is about as near to a formula
for success and happiness as the world provides.
~Mark Sullivan (1874-1952), author, journalist

Some might take exception to the above quote. In fact, most mothers would bristle at the notion that "career" is more important than raising a child. But that's because they don't realize that *parenting* can be regarded as a career in itself.

The question is not which is *more important*, but which are you suited for: a career in the business world, or a career as a stay-at-home parent?

Some think they can have both, and others realize it is best to choose. Nearly one in three survey respondents cited *giving up their career* as a reason not to have children, while others say they may have to alter it greatly. Still others say they would not change their career at all if they had kids, but fear they may not do well juggling *both*.

In my twenties and early thirties—when flying about the country busily ensconced in my magazine career—I figured if I had kids one day I would find ways to make it all work. I'd hire a nanny or somebody to take care of them. All I knew was: *I wasn't going to quit my career to become a full-time housewife!* I thought I could "have it all."

The fact is, I was naïve and hadn't given the job of parenting much thought at all.

## Jill of All Trades / Master of None

There is little evidence that the role of housewife is any more frustrating
than the role of housewife and careerist rolled into one. (I have done both
roles and both are very difficult and not totally satisfying.) [1]
~Penelope Trunk, author of *Brazen Careerist*

While the above quote, along with her article "Your Family Would be Better Off with a Housewife, So Would Mine," may ruffle some feminist feathers, it is simply too rational to dispute. It is difficult to combine the roles of housewife and careerist into one, and arguably best to choose one or the other. Many of us believe parenting is too important to just dabble in, and kids deserve at least one full-time parent.

In my mid-thirties, I finally did give parenting the consideration it deserves, and—after years of witnessing both families with a full-time mom versus families with a working mom—I came to the conclusion it is not smart for two working parents to raise kids.

Of course, it *can* work, but it's not ideal for two full-time career people to raise kids "on the side." Studies show, it's not only unfair to the kids—who reach out in bad ways for the attention they crave—it's also hard on each parent and each of their jobs.

Many non-parents are well educated and hold demanding—yet rewarding—jobs they are dedicated to. And, although "house husbands" are on the increase, it is still usually the woman who must compromise—if not sacrifice—her career to raise the kids. In the U.S., she is still the one who handles two-thirds of the childcare duties.

The woman who foresees the sacrifices *before* popping out children, might conclude that the purported rewards of motherhood are not worth the relinquishment of a rewarding career.

I think that my husband and I would make good parents. However, there
are things that I want to do with my life (both career accomplishments and
personal things such as travel) more than I would want to raise children,
and I don't think it's possible to fit children in without sacrificing large parts
of my life. I say this particularly as a woman with a demanding career
(scientific research). —Nicola, 28, Atlanta, GA

Other childfree women with demanding careers admit they would not quit their jobs to have children, but know that it would be hard to succeed at both simultaneously:

I wouldn't give up my career, but it would be hard to do both well.
—SB (female with her PhD), 33, Durham, NC

In a seemingly sexist opinion piece on *Forbes.com*, Michael Noer gives the argument that men should not marry career women. He cites evidence that career women and families don't mix well:

> If a host of studies are to be believed, marrying these women is asking for trouble. If they quit their jobs and stay home with the kids, they will be unhappy (*Journal of Marriage and Family*, 2003). They will be unhappy if they make more money than you do (*Social Forces*, 2006). You will be unhappy if they make more money than you do (*Journal of Marriage and Family*, 2001). You will be more likely to fall ill (*American Journal of Sociology*). Even your house will be dirtier (*Institute for Social Research*).
> ~Michael Noer, "Don't Marry Career Women" [2]

While Noer may not be my cup of java (nor I his), his points are well taken. I've seen many a career woman get downright bored and frustrated after forgoing her life in the business world for a life in the kitchen and minivan. Some end up resenting their husbands who get to leave the house to interface with adults eight hours a day, while "mom" stays home and goes stir crazy with the babbling two year old. Many head back into the workforce, only to find that "having your kids and your career too" can be problematic. Take it from Penelope Trunk—who's been both a career woman and a mother—when she so frankly states:

> The point is that marriage and family work best when one person is taking care of them full time. Duh. Everything in the world is best off when it is cared for very carefully. I wish everyone would stop trying to deny this. It's barking up the wrong tree...The conclusion, that marriages and families work better with a full-time housewife, is hard to swallow but hard to deny. It's just that not every woman wants to take care of a family and marriage full time, and even fewer men do.
> Many people will say they'd rather face the challenges of a dual-career marriage than the challenge of a stay-at-home-spousedom. Fine. Just know the statistics are not in your favor. [3]
> ~Penelope Trunk, author of *Brazen Careerist*

Apparently career women are starting to realize that statistics are not in their favor, because although more than half the mothers of infants (53.3%) in the U.S. are in the workplace, that is down 6% from it's peak (59.2%) in 1997.[4]

Many of my female survey respondents agree that they would have to forgo their career if they became a mother. Since childrearing is still primarily the *female's* task, it's no surprise that over twice as many women as men checked "I would have to give up my career" as a reason not to have kids. While only 13% of men checked this, over 34% of women did.

## Down With Daycare

As a former teacher, I have seen the effects of daycare first-hand.
Of the children I taught, the ones with the most discipline
problems were those who were in daycare.
~John Espinosa[5]

Obviously, there are many people raised by dual-career parents who don't end up as axe murderers. The point is, kids who are shuffled between school and daycare or nannies lack the attention they need from their parents, and the results aren't positive.

Dozens of studies have uncovered the negative effects of non-maternal childcare on children's behavior. Two found evidence that the longer a child spends in childcare, the more stress they may experience, and that could lead the young to become aggressive and disobedient.[6]

This aggressive behavior might be explained by the finding in an Early Childhood Research Quarterly study that daycare children show increases in the stress hormone cortisol throughout the day, compared to children at home.

These studies reinforce earlier research by the National Institute of Child Health and Human Development, which found "children who spent most of their time in childcare were three times as likely to exhibit behavioral problems in kindergarten as those who were cared for primarily by their mothers." Some parents find out—after they have kids—that putting them into daycare is not a viable option, like this father:

I just pulled my 18-month-old little gal out of daycare after 4 days. She was so horrified by the experience that she screamed herself into losing her voice. Well, we got the message!
I regret ever having put her in daycare. My wife had just taken a new job so that she could go back to the "corporate working world." After we saw the affect that daycare (and a reputable one, too) was having on her, we both decided that we'd made an error. My wife quit her new job, and we pulled the baby out, back to the home where she belongs.
~Dan, "Daycares Don't Care, How Can a Daycare Love?"[7]

Where the baby belongs, but what about the wife? Would you be happy giving up your career to be an at-home mother? Whether you believe daycare is harmful or not, what's the point of having a child when you can only give him that little bit of time between dinner and bedtime when you're exhausted from a full day's work?

## Crowding Out Career

One of the MANY reasons that we are CF is that I don't feel
I could balance having a kid with a career. I wouldn't want to
give up my career and I would go mad staying at home
day after day with a child, even if it were mine.
—Darla, Childfree Network member

I remember going to a legal deposition, and one of the young female attorneys said—unabashedly, right in the middle of proceedings—"I have to go now. I'm late to pick up my two year old from daycare." You should have seen the glare darted at her by her clients, who, apparently, were expected to continue on their own without her. She scooped up her stack of papers, and darted out the door without even an apology.

Six months later, I saw her picture in the real estate section, pushing a low-end house as her first listing. I was not surprised that the law firm that hired her had finally said, "enough's enough." Or perhaps she demoted her *own* career, so that she could work out of her home and be a better parent.

Either way, it illustrates that career can—and often does—suffer from parenting. Despite new laws that don't allow employers to discriminate against mothers in the workplace (called "gender discrimination"), being a mom usually does cause one to miss more work in order to care for a child.

But this is not just a *female* issue. Men's careers can suffer too. In fact, not only are 15% of all single parents fathers, but increasing numbers of men are quitting their jobs or working out of the home, in order to become stay-at-home dads (SAHDs). Men now make up about 3% of the stay-at-home parents in the U.S. and 12% of the stay-at-home parents in Canada—these numbers have *tripled* in the past three decades.

Whether dads work at home or in the office, their wives are demanding more "task sharing" from them these days as well; expecting them to help out with parenting chores and taxiing kids. And the modern father feels compelled to choose time with his kids over time at the office. He is suddenly pulled in two different directions, as this father admits:

Career advancement is still possible, but climbing the ranks after the birth of a child often means spending less time with the child and not forming as deep of a bond. You end up feeling pulled in a lot of directions, and it feels quite stressful. ~Trent Hamm, "The Costs of Having Children" [8]

So, ironically, just as a new father's priorities change from climbing the corporate ladder to spending time with the kids—necessity calls him to work harder and earn more to make ends meet.

### "I'll Just Get a Nanny"

I'm training to be a surgeon and I worry about my obligations to patients.
Surgeons in my specialty commonly have 9-month wait lists for performing
life-altering procedures. Is it fair for me to make those patients wait even
longer (risking their health) so that I can cut down my hours and make
time to take my kid to soccer practice? But if I just hand him off to a
nanny all the time, what's the point in even having him?
(And would that make me a bad mother?)
—Heather, 24, Ontario, Canada

Heather (above) has thought the career conundrum through better than I had at her age. I was at least ten years older before I pondered the sense in pawning a child off to a nanny for most of the day.

A friend of mine travels over a third of her time on business, loves her career and is very good at it. When she said she was still considering having kids, I asked, "What about your job?" "Oh I would never quit my job," she said, "That's what nannies are for!"

My thoughts are: a) if you think you'll still prefer your job over your child even after it's born, why have a child? And, b) is it really fair to the child to be raised by hired help?

Research shows it's not just daycare centers that have a negative effect on children, but—more broadly—non-maternal childcare. In laymen terms: The kid needs its mother around.

To be fair, there are child development experts who oppose these findings and maintain there are no negative effects on the child from non-maternal childcare. Even so, would I want an adult living in my home and raising my child? It sounds both expensive and awkward.

Even if we are fine with hiring someone to care for our kids while we enjoy dual careers, there is the question of *will we feel guilty* or *will we be judged*? The below female attorney feels she would be judged harshly for continuing her career after having kids:

I wouldn't have to give up my career, but between work and kid, I would
have absolutely no time for myself or my husband, and I would be judged
harshly (including by my husband) for continuing to work as hard as I
want/need to do to continue to be a success at my career.
—Female, 39 (with her J.D.) Houston, TX

Brian and I both agree that when we embark on a challenge—whether it's having a pet or having a child—we like to give it our all. Leaving a child at home with a nanny while we work, play or travel (or leaving a dog alone in a yard all day to bark), is not our modus operandi.

**Despite Stereotype, "Career" Ranks Low**

While dropping me off at my office one day, a car mechanic asked me, "What do you do?" I showed him the magazine I publish and added, "I am also currently writing a book for the childfree." (Long pause.) "You know, people who choose not to have kids," I said.

After the initial look of bewilderment followed by a slow "Ah, yes" (a reaction I'm finding to be standard), this young mechanic with two small children (and already divorced) started launching into his sermon that *women these days are selfishly putting career and money in front of family*.

I found it odd that he assumed this was the only reason women don't want kids. He carried on a one-way heated conversation with himself, as I listened wondering if his anger was directed at a mom who'd left him too many years in daycare (or an ex-wife who didn't want to quit her job!). Nonetheless, I didn't bother informing him that *two-thirds* of my female survey respondents did not cite "career" at all as a reason not to have kids.

Admittedly, this was one of *my* major reasons for becoming childfree, initially because I did not want to be a "Master of None," and later because I concluded that nannies and daycare were not good alternatives.

I was surprised, however, that more female survey respondents did not check "I would have to give up my career" as a reason not to have kids, in light of the fact that most CF women are well educated. So, I tried to analyze why that could be. The reason 66% of women did not check this answer could be three-fold, and may reflect the wording of the question.

First of all, not every woman taking the survey *has* a career, and many are in college or grad school getting degrees. Perhaps they would more likely have checked "I would not be able to *start* my career," or "I would not be able to continue my schooling."

Secondly, of those who *do* have a career, many may have no qualms about hiring childcare if they were to have kids. (Coincidentally, the same percentage of mothers today—two-thirds—work outside the home.)

And thirdly, not everyone is happily wedded to her job, and many may have no problem dumping it for a good cause—that is, if *kids* were their good cause.

Whatever the reasons, the fact that only one in three women checked "career" as a reason not to procreate, negates the stereotype that *all childfree women find their jobs more important than having children*.

## Trading In Suits For Sweats
*Or "I'm No Domestic Diva"*

As illustrated in Pamela Stone's recent book, *Opting Out? Why Women Really Quit Careers and Head Home*, many working mothers—and even high-powered career women—do come to realize that balancing their career with being a mom is not working. And, although reluctant to do so—realizing it's not worth the hardship and time constraints, nor is it fair to their career or children—they quit their jobs.

The following telling excerpt is from an article, "Waving the Long Goodbye," by Sarah Achenbach, who decided, after six years of struggling to be a full-time worker and a full-time mom, to move home:

> At work, I generally drank my meals. Not the 1960s three-martini-lunch kind of meals, but the two-cups-of-coffee-followed-by-a-cup-of-soup-at-the-desk kind. My self-created rule was that, because I left each day at 5 p.m. on the dot to be able to make my son's daycare pickup, I should eat lunch at my desk. Leaving my desk meant less work done—and less work done meant more guilt.

> I finally admitted to myself that my version of Soupermom was a far cry from the heroic image of working mom I'd had in mind that day at the grocery checkout counter—not to mention throughout my childhood, college and early working years. Maybe a noodle is just a noodle, but I knew then that things had to change.

> It wasn't long before my prenatal theory of a happy co-existence between career and family had become more like a war zone with the different sides advancing or retreating, depending on work deadlines, ear infections and my daily struggle between need, want and expectation. The final breaking point came when I poured the powder into my coffee cup and drank the bitter soup down.

> A few months later, I made the hard decision to shed all my administrative duties and my title—not to mention a goodly portion of my much-needed salary—and said goodbye to daily face-to-face with colleagues I enjoyed and admired to work part time from home. Part time is often held up as the perfect solution to work/family conflicts—and don't get me wrong, it's the right solution for me right now—but that's not the point. The point is that I always wanted to be a full-time worker and a full-time mother, and after six years of struggle I discovered that it was impossible for me to do both the way I wanted to, or felt I should.
> ~Sarah Achenbach, "Waving the Long Goodbye"[9]

Achenbach is not alone in her desire to forsake the full-time career to be an at-home mom. She cites a poll by *Parents magazine* of 1,000 working mothers that reveals 46% said they'd rather be stay-at-home mothers, only 13% were happy with their work/family situation, and a whopping 99% admitted to feeling stressed nearly all the time!

The problem is, not all women are mentally equipped to be at-home moms. Many savvy working women miss the suits, the power lunches, the meetings, the deadlines, the challenges, and just the interfacing with adults. These are replaced by sweats and slippers, toddler toys, Gerber lunches, kiddie videos and challenges of a different sort (like treating colic).

Here's a letter from a new mom seeking advice from syndicated columnist Carolyn Hax:

> Dear Carolyn,
>
> I'm taking the year off to be at home with our new baby. My days are busy, but I'm pretty good about tidying up toward the end of the day so my husband comes home to a clean house. I'm not used to this level of domesticity, so sometimes things get pretty crazy around noon—clothes everywhere, kitchen dirty, etc.
>
> He came home unannounced at lunchtime the other day, and the house was a customary wreck. I tried to laugh it off, but he's now "very concerned" that I'm getting overwhelmed at home and that we should rethink our decision. I can't wait to go back to work, but that's not why.
>
> Would our relationship take a hit, do you think, if I "let" him talk me into returning to work and hiring a nanny without ever explaining that I'm not the slob he saw in action the other day?
> ~Stay-At-Home Mom (Carolyn Hax's "Tell Me About It" column)

This story is telling on so many levels. You've got a career woman who (probably begrudgingly) agrees to become a stay-at-home mom for a year. It seems she had no idea how overwhelming the task of mothering would be. She is not fond of "domesticity" and misses her work. She wants to use her husband's concern to hoodwink him into letting her go back to work. (Not a peep about what's good for the baby.)

Sadly, her dire situation is driving her to deceive her own husband, instead of communicating honestly with him—probably because she feels shame that she'd rather work than be at home with her child.

Carolyn's response was too lengthy to print here, but her first words of advice were to *quit playing games and be honest with her husband, before it ruins her marriage.* (Amen!) And, to let him take a turn at parenting all day one Saturday or Sunday to see things through her eyes.

On the "stay at home vs. go back to work" issue, Carolyn declined from advising, stating it "involves a topic on which biases run strong." But, as a mother herself, Carolyn did express the following creative insight on parenting in one of her final paragraphs:

> Somewhere between the cave and the gated community, being home with small children changed from a team sport to an individual one, with teammates replaced by gadgets, stuff and more stuff. I realize I'm projecting here but if being "at home with our new baby" means 8, 9, 10-hour stretches of just you, your baby and your stuff, then you'd really have to love babies or hate your job *not* to be dreaming of the office.
> ~Carolyn Hax, from her syndicated column "Tell Me About It"[10]

*　*　*

When it comes to dual-career marriages, both men and women have a tough time transitioning to parenting. Not only might they not agree on how to handle it, but if they do agree, one or both spouses may not relish the new role they've been thrown into.

The husband may feel pressure as the new sole provider; the wife may resent leaving the business world; or—if they choose to "do it all"—they may end up mastering none, and the child and career lose out.

After weighing the options, many non-parents conclude that neither Plan A (quitting a career to be a stay-at-home parent) nor Plan B (settling for daycare and becoming a part-time parent) sound like good options.

Many—like me—have considered these options and choose Plan C—Kidfree!

# CHAPTER 13

## "We Like Our Relationship"
### *(And Having Kids Could Ruin It)*

Having a first child is like throwing
a hand grenade into a marriage.
~Nora Ephron (1941-2012), screenwriter, producer, director

*" We never laugh anymore. She's so uptight," Mike laments to me over a Cobb salad one day. "I'm always doing something wrong with the baby. 'You're holding her wrong...That's not how you burp her...Where did you put her binky?' It never ends. And forget about sex. She acts like I'm some plague-ridden pariah, whose sole purpose is to be pocketbook papa."* I choke on my wine as I hold back a chuckle that would surely be seen as an insensitive jab.

You see, Mike knows I've chosen not to have kids, and I've given him many reasons, not the least of which is Brian and I are happy with our relationship the way it is. We fear throwing a needy third person into the mix might mess with the magical make-up of our union. And it would. It always does. Just as my friend Mike found out six months ago when the baby arrived home from the hospital.

Take a look at your childed friends and see if you don't agree. Is the pre-baby magic still in their marriage? This chapter explores the many ways becoming a parent can—and often does—change the dynamics of a relationship.

## Kids Can Mar a Marriage

I felt the happiness of my marriage was far more
important than having children.
—Joy, 44, Mammoth Lakes, CA

"I like my relationship the way it is, and having kids might ruin it." This answer did not appear on my survey under "Why don't you want kids?" But it should have. Under "Other," nearly one in ten non-single respondents wrote—in various ways—that their relationship was too important to mess with by having kids. Here are a few of their quotes:

> My husband and I are so comfortable, happy and content that we feel complete. There is no feeling that we're missing anything in life because we enjoy each other so much. We have a good thing going here—why mess with it?! —Linda Leschina, 36, Chicago, IL

> I respect and nurture my relationship with my husband. Too often I see couples who have become all about their kids, lose touch with each other, and ultimately end up in a loveless marriage or divorced because of their children. I could not sacrifice my relationship with my husband for a child. Therefore, I can't say it's a good idea for me. —Wendy, 28, Denver, CO

> My DH [darling husband] and I have been without children for so long that to have them now, I'm afraid would mess up the good thing we have going. I know what he likes, he knows what I like. I can spend every second catering to him and vice versa. We have a good life the way things are now. —Mrs. B, 31, from Smyrna, GA

The above non-parents are in truly happy relationships and are wise to know that kids might change all that. How did they know this? Did they find out through empirical observation? Did they see studies and statistics? Or did they hear it directly from the horse's—a parent's—mouth?

I searched online to see if there was evidence beyond what I'd acquired through observation—and boy was there! The proof that having children can make a relationship worse seems to be everywhere these days, not only through studies, but from parents themselves.

Where it used to be taboo to admit the loss of feeling toward one's spouse after baby's arrival, husbands and wives seem to be divulging these truths all over the worldwide web. As the following new mother wrote in her *Times Online* article, she had a marriage "made in heaven" filled with such "obvious happiness" that probably sickened her friends, until the night she gave birth to her child. "At that moment...

> He was no longer at my side. I heard a baby crying...and that was it. That was the night we lost each other. I have been in mourning for our marriage ever since. Having a baby is supposed to bring you closer together as a couple, isn't it? From night one, in the labour ward, we

began to unravel. I was given a private room in the NHS hospital, and then my husband and I went our separate ways. I gazed into the baby's unfathomable black eyes and felt the centre of my world shift.
~Anonymous mother, *Times Online UK*[1]

Perhaps it's survival of the species and a mother's instinct to protect her child, but just as my friend Mike's wife had done, this woman has shifted the center of her world from her husband to her baby, and will likely take 18 years, if ever, to shift back.

Having children changes the marital relationship, often eroding the level of emotional and physical intimacy between spouses. I like my marriage the way it is. —Mishka Rogers, 26, Oxford, NC

While most of us have just read about it or observed it in our friends, the following non-parent (and Kidfree Survey respondent) actually wrote a thesis about how marriage quality can suffer with the presence of children. Not surprisingly, she found plenty of research to support her premise:

I am a sociologist and behavioral science student. In the course of my research for my senior thesis, I found a body of existing social research, which supports the idea that the presence of children is detrimental to marital quality. Simply stated, childfree couples are happier and more likely to stay together than childed couples. This is a scientifically proven fact, which is more than enough justification for me to remain childfree. —Tonya Mertens, 33, Mission Viejo, CA

There are myriad ways a romantic relationship can suffer by raising children, and this chapter attempts to highlight just a few.

## Dad Becomes a Distant Third

I enjoy the company of my husband
and don't want another person spoiling our relationship.
—Jo Jager, 42, Kent, England

*I listen while Mike continues to tell me he feels like "persona non grata" in his own home and wonders if some hormonal change occurred in his wife during childbirth to remove all feelings of affection toward him. "She has plenty of love for the baby, but none left for me at the end of the day."*

Even though I am female and it's typically the father that gets cast aside into what a co-worker of mine called a "distant third" position, I didn't want to be that woman who suddenly dumped Brian for the new ten-pound love affair in my life. And even if I consciously fought such tendencies to place the safety and comfort of my child above my husband's, studies have shown that it is a naturally occurring—one might say *instinctive*—process that takes place in most human mothers.

One such mother, in an online article titled "I wanted to be a full-time mother…but I hadn't reckoned falling out of love with my husband," confessed that she pushed her husband away:

> Oscar was *our* son—but Jamie was, in effect, out of the picture. Without realizing what I was doing, I began edging him out of the triangle. Everything I said was either an instruction or a criticism. I couldn't remember what on earth we used to talk about, let alone laugh about.
> ~Anonymous, *Times Online, UK*[2]

The husband or significant other can no longer count on being number one in the eyes of his mate after the first child comes home. Or, as our former neighbor once put it, "I went from being king to pauper."

### Rearing Raises Conflicts

My husband and I were raised very differently and would have
a hard time agreeing on how to raise our own—
causing totally avoidable marital conflict.
—April Houston, 22, Jackson, TN

"Avoidable" only by not having kids. At age 22, April (above) is wise before her time. Most of the arguments I can remember between my mom and dad centered on us kids, especially on how to raise or discipline us.

"You're being too hard on the kids, Dick." "They won't learn if I don't punish them, Suzie." My dad believed in ruling by discipline, and my mom believed in letting us learn by our own mistakes. Both are viable ways to raise kids, but not in tandem.

After years of quarreling about whether to take the strict or lenient path toward parenting issues, my parents grew distant from each other.

What's worse is that on the rare occasion when mom really *did* think we needed punishment, she would leave the dirty deed to my dad by saying, "Wait 'til your father gets home!" And when he did get home— after a trying day at work—he had the unwelcome task of having to lecture and/or spank one of us.

As the sole disciplinarian, my dad (unfairly) became the "bad guy," and my mom became the "cool mom." I learned that if parents don't agree on how to raise their kids, there will be much conflict—not to mention anger and resentment—in their relationship. Some don't want to risk it:

> I don't want to ruin my marriage by raising kids. (Pretty sure we would if my husband and I had any kids. We were raised so differently.)
> —Kana, 32, Panama City, FL

I don't want the possible conflicts with my spouse over how to raise them, discipline them, etc. Or the biggest horror of all, single parenthood!
—Ginger, 40, Boston, MA

Notice how Ginger cleverly connects the dots between *conflicts with how to raise children* and *single parenthood*. As with my parents, the disagreements and disillusions can finally lead to divorce—followed by the custody battle to determine who will do most of the single parenting.

### Why Ruin a Good Thing?

My husband and I are so happy now, and even parents agree that everything changes when you have a kid. Why throw a bomb into Eden?
—Serenity, 32, Nova Scotia, Canada

In their article "When Husband and Wife Become Mom and Dad," Drs. Les and Leslie Parrott (parents of two boys and authors of several books on marriage) warn that, no matter how ready you are for parenting, "the birth of each child signals a serious and permanent alteration in your marriage."

While they say this alteration is "deeply enriching," they add "for the majority of couples it is also somewhat confusing if not downright challenging."[3] Here are excerpts from their article:

Studies show that when baby makes three, conflicts increase eightfold; marriage takes a back seat; women feel overburdened and men feel shoved aside. By the baby's first birthday, most mothers are less happy about their marriage and some are wondering whether their marriage will even make it.

Baby-induced marital meltdowns are not uncommon. In the year after the first baby arrives, 70 percent of wives experience a precipitous plummet in their marital satisfaction. For the husband, the dissatisfaction usually kicks in later, as a reaction to his wife's unhappiness.

How can something as good as a little baby turn a marriage so bad? We could point to a wide range of reasons: lack of sleep, feeling overwhelmed and unappreciated, the awesome responsibility of caring for such a helpless little creature, juggling chores and other economic stress, and lack of time to oneself, among other things.

The root reason, however, is no big mystery. In plain language, children take time and attention away from a marriage. They suck all the hours out of the day and fill up every spare cell in your brain. Being a parent is wonderful, only somehow, it's made being a spouse…different.[4]

"Being a parent is wonderful" is an opinion. But the fact that it changes your relationship is a *truth*. Many of us like our relationships the way they are now, and do not wish to complicate them with a third party (other than maybe a pet).

## The Newly Neurotic Mother

If I remain with my current partner, our ideas about parenting
are very different and will likely result in conflict.
—Sofia Blackthorne, 18, New Orleans/Boston

We have a friend—I'll call him "Tom"—whose wife "Cindy" was so overprotective of their toddler that the husband wasn't trusted to be alone with him for a minute in his first three years. Cindy's world revolved around "little Justin" and his safety 24/7, and the husband was treated like an incompetent lummox around said child.

When the family came to visit us and Brian took Tom and his boy out to the patio while I stayed inside to bond with Cindy, the woman was beside herself with anxiety. She ran to the window to watch her boy on the patio. She did not look at me once, nor did she let that child out of her sight for a second. I could see she was nervous and not listening to a word I said, until she could no longer hold herself back and bolted out the door.

What happened? Had Justin hurt himself with two grown men watching him? I walked outside to see Cindy sweep her child off his feet. "You let him get too close to those stairs!" she snapped.

"Those stairs are ten feet away," Tom pleaded, "He wasn't going anywhere." He shook his head and slumped away like a wounded pup.

He later confided to Brian that his wife had transformed into a different person from the day they brought the baby home. She became a neurotic worrier, obsessed with the child's safety, and totally distrusting and disdainful of her husband. My heart goes out to men in this situation.

Obviously, Cindy is an extreme example. But I wonder what would have been had I had children? Would I succumb by default to becoming the domestic, doting, daft mother that I dreaded? Constantly distressing over every danger that could befall my darling daughter? Draconian to my husband? And would I wind up damaging the very marriage to which I was once devoted? Alas declaring divorce? The prospect is very disturbing.

I think that I would be a neurotic parent. Not necessarily a "bad" parent, as I'm very nurturing in my way, but I also crave my alone time. Also, I worry about EVERYTHING, and don't feel that this would be healthy for a child.
—Tiffany Lyman-Olszewski, 35, Easthampton, MA

I like my relationship with my husband and fear ruining it with kids. I know I would be a great mom, but perhaps at the expense of my marriage and part of myself. —Robin, 35, Portola Valley, CA

## "You've Lost That Lovin' Feeling"

It's no surprise that the physical act of love between parents gets thrown out with the dirty diapers, is it? As our anonymous mother that we earlier quoted puts it:

> Having children drives an enormous, invisible wedge between the sexes. Little chores that used to be acts of love (pairing his socks, preparing him a nice supper) became venom-loaded. As for the physical act of love, it just didn't happen. Aside from the exhaustion, neither of us felt loving enough. All the kissing was for chunky-thighed, gap-toothed Oscar.
> ~Anonymous mother, *Times Online UK*[5]

Aha! So it's more than being overworked, sleep-deprived, exhausted and lacking privacy that causes sex-deprivation in new parents. It's also that they plain old don't feel loving toward each other.

Many non-parents cherish the romance they share with their mate and would not welcome giving that up for offspring.

> I like to keep my sex life!!! —Heather, 32, Vancouver, BC, Canada

When hearing about the book I was writing, a childfree friend of mine, William, ordered me a giant customized fortune cookie. Inside, the fortune read:

> Confucius say: Woman or man who have no child...have much time to be wild.

## Three's a Crowd

> I have become a little selfish; I don't like sharing my partner.
> —Karen, 41, London, England

Kudos to Karen for admitting the inadmissible: We don't want to share our partner. This may sound selfish, but it's honest. The fact is, when two becomes three (or four or five) the dynamics of a relationship change.

It's not just the father who becomes the third wheel. I've seen many a mother become threatened by her husband's close relationship with a daughter. I was closer to my father than my mother, and had I been an only child that might have created an imbalanced triangle, leaving mom out in the cold. But, as it was my sister and brother were closer to our mom, so if anything my dad was in the minority. (Sound like Congress?)

The truth is, once a family of two becomes a family of three or more, the one-on-one romance is gone, the alliances form, and the politics begin!

## Having a Child Won't "Fix" a Bad Relationship

Our relationship was a bit rocky at the time,
and we didn't want to bring kids into a potential mess!!
—YMA, 54, Surrey, BC, Canada

It's bad enough when a good relationship falters by throwing a kid in the mix. How about people who have a child hoping to fix a bad relationship? Yikes, don't try it folks! Just as when people get married to fix a bad relationship, it won't work. Surprisingly however—"To improve our marriage; to bring us closer together"—was cited in a 2003 study by Coreen Beth Gray as a reason parents give for having children.[6]

In *The Complete Idiot's Guide to the Perfect Marriage*, the question is asked, "My spouse and I are having difficulties in our marriage. If we have a child, will that bring us closer?" The author's answer is:

Many people think that having a child will fix a troubled marriage. But, in fact, once you have children, you will need to work harder to keep your relationship strong. Ideally, you should work on and improve your marriage before you have children.[7]

Now this may seem obvious, but we see people making the mistake all the time: The wife who thinks fatherhood will make her husband either kick his bad habits, become a loving family man, or bring them closer together; and the husband who thinks his wife may become less angry and depressed if she had a baby to care for. Don't count on it!

As author and father Joe Sindoni states, "Your marriage problems are not caused by being childless. And making a baby will not fix them." In fact, your problems may get worse:

Once you have a child, you will have even *less* time to work on these issues and more stress to compound them. And, you can add to that the hormonal changes that occur in many women during and after pregnancy. ~Joe Sindoni, "Can Having a Baby Save Your Marriage?"[8]

Enough about you and your spouse, what about the child? Those with any sense of duty or responsibility will not lay this burden on their child.

If children come into the world with the burden of saving a marriage—as many do—they sense it. When problems continue—as nearly all do—children try and fix them. When the marriage dissolves—as it likely will—children feel responsible for it.[9]

Thus, it is not only unrealistic to expect a child to fix a bad relationship, but it is irresponsible to expose them to one in the first place.

## Children Trumped by Chores

"Poll: Fewer People See Kids as Key to a Good Marriage"
~*Santa Barbara News-Press*, 2007[10]

The above headline hit my local newspaper the month I started writing this book. *How apropos*, I thought! Finally, the truth was revealed in a national survey of parents that kids are not the key to a good marriage.

The Pew Research Center study[11] compared the answers to their 2007 poll on marriage and parenting with those from a poll by World Values in 1990 and found that: The percentage of Americans who consider children "very important" to a successful marriage had dropped sharply since 1990. In fact, *children*—who once ranked third in importance—now rank *eighth* on a list of nine factors that people associate with "successful marriages." They were trumped by such issues as: faithfulness, a happy sexual relationship, shared interests, and even household chore sharing.

In less than two decades, "Sharing chores" went up by 15 points and "Children" went down by 24 points. In fact, "Children" beat out only "Agreement on politics" as key to a successful marriage. These findings show that either people are now *more realistic* about what makes a relationship tick, or are being *more honest* with themselves and others about the fact that offspring do not improve a relationship. Here is a chart ranking the nine factors Americans see as key to a successful marriage: [12]

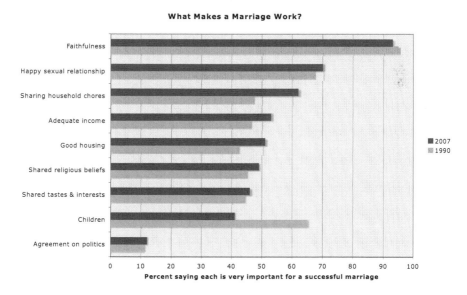

**What Makes a Marriage Work?**

Percent saying each is very important for a successful marriage

## We Are Not Lacking For Love

I was struck by the beauty and clarity of the following quote in my survey by a woman from Kansas. She captures the way I feel:

> Someone told us "I feel sorry for you, because if you don't have children, you'll never experience unconditional love." My response to that was "I feel sorry for you, that you have not experienced that love *without* having children, because I *do* have that with my husband, and that will always be enough. I don't need to have a child to know love." —Angela, 37, Kansas

Some of us are lucky to have unconditional love in our romantic relationships, and know that it is not exclusive to the parent-child bond.

Yes, we've all heard of a mother's unconditional love for her child— even in relation to mass murderers and such. However, the fact that more than 200 women kill their children in the U.S. every year[13] proves that not all mothers love their kids unconditionally.

Conversely, one may ask, "Do all kids love their parents unconditionally?" Well, if the fact that one child kills a parent almost daily in the U.S.[14] (300 killings per year) is any indication, I guess not.

## We Are a Family of *Two*

We are each other's big kid! And very happy with it.
—"The Rabbits," 45, Walnut Creek, CA

This is the way Brian and I feel about it. We are each other's kids, so why do we need another one? Although usually said with tongue in cheek, it seems to be an issue for non-parents who are annoyed by a society that says a "family" has to be made up of parents and children.

While these semantics don't bother me, I agree that two childless people living together—with or without pets—can be considered a family. Especially if, like Cass below, they don't have a void to fill:

> I always tell people that I am very happy with the company of my husband and don't have a void to fill. —Cass, 40, Sydney, Australia

I can relate to 44-year-old Christie from Santa Barbara, California, who endearingly says, "My Husband is my kid!"

\*    \*    \*

In the end, it all comes down to *energy*. I have thought long and hard about what I call the Energy Equation, and believe it is a big reason I'm happier living kidfree. We human beings have a finite amount of energy to give to others and to our interests. The more things we expend energy on, the less energy available for each. The same equation can be applied to *time*.

Many non-parents are aware that if we have kids, we would not be able to focus as much time or energy on our significant others. And, like Ellen below, we like having *all* of each other:

> I don't want a baby because I know the kind of love that must take and I don't want to share... I like having all of her [De Rossi] and she likes having all of me, and we have freedom, and we have time.[15]
> ~Ellen DeGeneres, TV host, comedienne

Why change it?

# CHAPTER 14

## Pets & Surrogates Are More Fun
### *(Even Better Than the Real Thing!)*

We longed for the patter of little feet, so we got a dog.
It was cheaper than a baby and it had more feet.
~Rita Rudner, Comedienne

Question: Does one have to biologically reproduce in order to enjoy the benefits of parenting and nurturing? Answer: No. In fact, many of us enjoy spending time with other people's children—be they our siblings' kids, our friends' kids or our students—as long as we can give them back at the end of the day.

And even more of us—the vast majority of kidfree—revel in our roles as parents to our fine furry four-legged friends, our pets.

The myths—which we'll discuss in Part II—that the childfree are somehow *cold selfish child-haters* like Ebenezer Scrooge in *The Christmas Carol*, or fastidious clean-freaks like Howard Hughes, simply don't hold water when you look at how many are teachers, loving aunts and uncles and/or pet lovers.

Sure there are non-parents out there who do not like spending time with nieces and nephews, but they are a minority. Only one in five survey respondents admitted this.

Likewise, there are non-parents who—like Hughes—would not relish a hairy animal running through the house. But the truth is, nearly nine out of ten non-parents are either pet owners or pet lovers.

## Our Pets Are Our Kids!

I have a baby! He just has four legs and lots of hair!!
–Pip, 30, London, England

The childfree give new meaning to the term "animal-lover." When categorizing the thousands of childfree quotes from my survey, I literally ran out of space tallying all of the pet quotes. In addition to hundreds of comments regarding pressures to procreate and reasons not to, one of the most quoted topics from non-parents in the Kidfree Survey was regarding their beloved pets. And—drum-roll please—here is the most popular:

If I want to hear the pitter-patter of little feet, I'll put shoes on the cat.
—Eve, 41, Raleigh, NC

The above quote and variations thereof—including the substitution of boots and tap shoes—is widely used among the childfree. And, although the original author is unknown, this quote can be found on bumper stickers and T-shirts, and has led to alternative versions from dog-lovers:

If I wanted to hear the pitter-patter of little feet, I'd put shoes on the bulldogs! —Eileen R., 29, Baltimore, MD

As noted earlier, one truism of non-parents is their propensity to own pets. We all know pets are popular. Australia has the highest pet ownership in the world at 63% of all households,[1] while the U.S. is a close second at 57% of all households;[2] in Canada it's 53%,[3] and in the UK pet ownership is only 43% of all households.[4] But for Kidfree Survey respondents, the numbers are up to 24% higher in these countries. Here are the findings:

### Non-Parents Who Own Pets:

| | |
|---|---|
| United States | 74% |
| Australia | 70% |
| United Kingdom | 67% |
| Canada | 65% |

Interestingly, pet ownership is on the rise in countries where childfree are on the rise. According to this expert dog trainer from Austin, Texas:

As the number of childless women and couples in Japan has increased, so has the number of dogs, which are being coddled and doted upon in place of children, experts say. In the last decade, the number of pet dogs in Japan has doubled to 13 million last year—outnumbering children under 12—according to Takashi Harada, president of Yaseisha, a publisher of pet industry magazines. "Households with few or no children are turning to dogs to fill the void," he said. "For a dog to be part of the family, it has to be unique and have character, like a person." [5]
~WillaWoman, a disabled trainer of wheelchair dogs

Many non-parents consider their pets to be their children, and take the responsibility of training, raising and caring for them extremely seriously. Hardly a day goes by on the childfree network that pets are not mentioned. Akin to a blog for new mothers sharing information about baby formulas and health risks, the childfree network discusses everything from pet food recalls to rare diseases and health conditions in their four-legged friends. (And with the number of PhDs and animal experts on our list, the fountain of knowledge for treatments is forthcoming and qualified!)

On the lighter side, like the mommy blogs, we too boastfully link to photos of our new pride and joy, but instead of baby Britney, it's shots of our new Springer Spaniel, Siamese or Quarter Horse! Recently childfree network members discussed how they have to spell out certain words—like w.a.l.k. or t.r.e.a.t.—in front of their dog or cat. The funny thing is, one woman said her dog has learned these spellings! (I bet you can't say that about a human baby.)

Not all non-parents have the ability—in their current situation—to own and raise a pet even if they want to, so I put a third answer under Do you have pets?—"No, but I'm a pet-lover." Another 17% checked this answer. (I'm in this category, since the loss of our beloved tabby, Buddy.) That means that 88% of us either *own a pet* or are a *pet-lover*.

### Preferring Pets to Pipsqueaks

People used to say I would make a good mother. My reply was always,
"No way. I would much sooner have another dog!"
—"Houndwoman," 53, Birmingham, England

Whether it's a biological trait or an acquired behavior, many of us are simply more attracted to a furry feline or a fluffy puppy than to an infant human being. Like this Brit below, we may gravitate toward a stranger's puppy more than to a stranger's baby:

My sister's friend had twin boys. We popped in to see them. As I entered the house, there were two babies laying on a sofa to my right, but on the armchair immediately in front of me, was an 8-week-old Jack Russell pup! I ran to the pup cooing, much to my sister's annoyance, and blanked the babies, until I realized what I'd done. They don't do anything for me! My sibling's kids are a very different matter though. I ADORE them!!
—Karen, London, England

Notice how she qualifies her statement, by saying that her sibling's kids—her nieces and nephews—are a different matter. I feel this way too.

Other than my sister's and brother's children, I have had no attraction to infants and babies for as long as I can remember. But give me an orange tabby kitten or a Golden Retriever puppy and I melt.

In addition to our physical attraction to pets over pipsqueaks, there is also that underlying knowledge that pets are oh-so-much easier to train and raise than a human being. Plus, they don't talk back to you:

> Having pets is better than kids—you don't have to save for college, they don't talk back, and you can put them in a cage without being arrested. —Sidhewlf, 44, Gloucester, VA

Parents may protest this comparison of pets to people, saying that the burden of a human child is worth it, because it is so much more rewarding. But have you ever experienced the unconditional love and loyalty of a dog? As Carrie Van Ness of Colorado—a member of our CF group—says, "Look at dog love. If that isn't beloved, I don't know what is."

There can be a lot of heartbreak and disappointment raising a child who becomes a disrespectful teen, but a dog will put you on a pedestal and always be grateful for your love and attention. As this English woman puts it so succinctly:

> When people complain about their kids, I always say, "That's why dogs are better than kids." They don't answer back, they don't go out and get pregnant, they don't start smoking or do drugs, you don't have to pay forcollege fees, and they never say "I hate you"—their love is unconditional. —Sproggie, 29, Surrey, England

### Crazy for Cats or Canines?

I like the bumper stickers: "Dogs, Not Sprogs" and "Cats, Not Brats."
–Roxanne Brennan, 38, Estell Manor, NJ

Do you consider yourself a cat person or a dog person? (Or neither?) It was hard to decipher from all of the quotes whether non-parents are more cat lovers or dog lovers. So, I launched an impromptu survey of 100 childfree, and here are the results.

It appears cats are king (or queen?) with the unchilded. Two thirds of pet owners (66%) I surveyed own cats, while 43% own dogs. And when asked if they had to choose, 60% said they'd rather own a cat, and 34% a dog. Since these numbers are inverse of the national statistics (46% own dogs, 38% cats), I attribute this to a cat's low maintenance being more conducive to an active kidfree lifestyle. It's been found that cat owners are more educated than dog owners, and—according to a scientific survey of pet ownership in Great Britain—"People with cats are more likely to have university degrees than those with dogs."[6]

But if you cat lovers think it's due to the superior intelligence of felines, you're mistaken. Rather, it's because cats don't need to be walked and require less time per day than dogs, appealing to educated people who work late and are home less often. This brings us full circle to kidfree people who are active and travel more.

Here's a sampling of frequent quotes from the "cats are king" camp:

Cats, Not Kids! —Toryn, Charlotte, NC

Cats, Not Brats! —Christina, Columbia, SC

Kids are for people who can't have cats. —Justine, Ronkonkoma, NY

And from the "dogs not sprogs" camp:

I Would Rather Have a Dog Than a Sprog!
—Suzanne Schneider, Aviano, Italy

I like dogs—they'll never tell you to go to hell. —Claire, St. Louis, MO

To me, a warm puppy and razor teeth are so much more rewarding than crying and vomit! —Female, 40, Boston, MA

But we're not just about cats and dogs. It turns out, one in three childfree pet owners surveyed own at least one of these other animal types: birds, horses, rabbits, reptiles, rodents, ferrets, fish, frogs, snakes, ducks and even a couple sheep!

Whether you're crazy for cats or canines, horses or hares, rabbits or reptiles, fish or ferrets—the consensus seems to be that pets are preferred to "kids," "brats" or "sprogs." And, according to one CF, if you word your preference correctly, you won't even offend those inquisitive breeders:

When asked about whether or not we have kids, we've always had a good response to a lighthearted "We chose to stick to the four-legged variety!" That often brings "Good choice," "I wish I could have made that choice back in my day," "Yeah, I love my dog too," and other positive comments. —Janet Thew, 45, Loomis, CA

## Students & Surrogates Suffice

Children are wonderful as long as they are someone else's!
—Joann R., 47, Casselberry, FL

It's amazing how many childfree—both from my online groups and my two surveys—work with kids. From teachers of tiny tots to professors of college students, these people work with kids daily and are often relieved that they don't have to come home to more of them at the end of the day.

In the interest of confidentiality, I did not ask for respondents' professions in my survey, as I didn't think it relevant at the time. However, having a career where one teaches or works with children is relevant, and luckily dozens of people volunteered this information through their telling quotes and comments like these:

> As a teacher, my head is full of children, all of whom I care about enormously... but at night, I let it all go. You do your best, and then you go home. Ultimately their parents are responsible for them, and my students themselves are responsible for their own lives. I am happy to serve as a teacher but I love going home to my quiet house. No wailing after what I lost here—I go back every day! —Katie, 38, Los Angeles, CA

> I love children. I especially love it when it's time for them to go home. (Usually said with a smile after a long day teaching children.) —Nature Chick, 36, Racine, WI

Being a teacher and liking kids does not predispose one to want to raise their own from infant to adult. In fact, many teachers and childcare workers find they enjoy working with only one specific age group. In my teens, I visualized being a teacher someday, but preferably for middle school, and certainly never—like below—for toddlers or tiny tots.

> I am a primary school teacher and used to cover the nursery class once a week. I have little idea of how to entertain 3 to 4 year olds and just find them generally difficult to interact with. Thank heavens for nursery nurses!! Anyway, sometimes our paths would cross and she would catch me with some horrified look on my face at the child with snot all down its face or the one who'd just wet themselves. She would give me a *knowing* look and say, "You wait until you have your own!" This, despite the fact that I'd told her on numerous occasions that I had no desire to have kids. —DazzleDust, 31, London, England

Yet many teachers adore the young innocent ones, and couldn't imagine teaching hardened high school kids. Either way, I have found that schoolteachers often come to their decision not to have kids due to their firsthand experience with children. And those who did not choose, but are kidfree by *circumstance*, often find themselves thankful in hindsight that they don't have more kids to be responsible for the second half of the day.

One doesn't have to be a teacher or childcare worker to get their dose of surrogate kids. Besides relatives—which we will discuss next—many of us have friends, neighbors or co-workers with kids whom we can see often, and perhaps even develop a bond with. You may be one of the 27% of non-parents who like kids so much that you gave them a "7" or greater on a scale of "1 to 10" and you seek out relationships with them, in spite of the fact that you don't want your own. This can be rewarding, with very little downside, as "D" from Florida boasts:

> Don't get me wrong MOST kids are good, but the best is to spoil them and then give them back to their parents. That's my role. I am always the favorite with the kids and have lots of fun, but I don't want to take them home at the end of the day. That makes me more special sometimes than their parents. —D, 30, Altamonte Springs, FL

Or, as Annie Appleread from Alma, Arkansas (with an alliterate alias, I might add) says: "I like other people's children. I can play with them, read to them, have fun with them, and then I get to GO HOME."

Another way the childfree or childless can get their kid-fix—and help the world at the same time—is by becoming a volunteer mentor to a child. One time this subject came up on our childfree list, and I was amazed—and somewhat ashamed of myself to be quite honest—at the amount of CFs who said they volunteer at organizations to help kids!

Two organizations that come to mind are Big Brothers Big Sisters and CASA (Court Appointed Special Advocates), both of which likely have a chapter near you if you live in the U.S.

### Nieces & Nephews Will Do Just Fine

Happiness is being an uncle. —Brad, Dayton, OH
I tell people I'm a great aunt. —Yonmei, Edinburgh, Scotland

Do your siblings have kids? If so, do you enjoy spending time with them? I'll bet the majority of you answered "yes" and "yes" with qualifications. According to the Kidfree Survey, over 55% have nieces and/or nephews, and of those who do, over 30% answered "Yes" to enjoying spending time with them, and another 47% said "Yes, in small doses." This may surprise those who peg us as child-haters, but it doesn't surprise me.

I have five wonderful nieces and nephews that I cherish dearly, and although I don't spend as much time with them as I would like, when I do it is an enjoyable experience. This is not only my chance to bond with them, but to see into the world of a child and all the quirky little things they do (that only kids will do!). It can be quite entertaining, and—at any rate—it is a refreshing break from my daily adult world.

These kidfree women echo my sentiments about being an aunt:

> I play with my sister's children and have fun playing with them, but I don't have to deal with the pressures of being a parent.
> —Female, 23, North Carolina

> I want to be the favorite aunt and not the bitchy mom. —Heidi, 34, Ohio

Now don't get me wrong, it's not that I don't like children, I do...BUT...
I don't want any of my own and I am very content with being an aunt.
—Cherie Collins, 34, Orlando, FL

An aunt or uncle can be an important figure in a child's life. They can introduce kids to new hobbies, teach them new things, or simply show them a different way of life besides "mom and dad's way." A bond can be built over a lifetime, and often an aunt or uncle will outlive his or her siblings and become the sole remaining adult relative in the child's life.

One of my kidfree-by-circumstance friends, Lori, is longing for her little sister to have a child, because she loves kids and can't wait to be an aunt. She is even considering uprooting her entire life—and moving from the West to East Coast—if and when this happens. Of course, it also takes a lot of pressure off us CFs when our siblings have them for us, right? (Then the parents won't whine about not becoming grandparents!)

Although I love the outings with my niece and nephew or the time I spend playing with the neighbor's kids, it's comforting knowing that—after a few hours of kiddie stuff—I can drop them off at their parents' and go back to my quiet, peaceful kidfree home. As Cathleen says:

The best kinds of children are the ones I can give back.
—Cathleen, 24, Issaquah, WA

\*　　\*　　\*

Whether we spend time with someone else's children or our own pets, most non-parents are far from "missing out" on the pleasures of nurturing an innocent creature. With the vast majority of us enjoying either our friend's or family's kids and/or our fine furry friends, it is safe to say we have found ourselves some significant surrogates to surround ourselves with, stroll with, secretly spoil, or simply be silly with.

# —PART II—

## ISSUES WE FACE
### *The "Not-So-Lovin' It" Side of Non-Parenting*

# CHAPTER 15

## Our Four Biggest Fears
### *Of Not Having Children*

Nothing in life is to be feared. It is only to be understood.
~Marie Curie, Nobel Prize in Physics 1903

Who will take care of me when I'm older? Will I be lonely? Am I missing out on something in life? Will I lose my friends who have kids? Will I regret not having them once it's too late? These are just a few of the unknowns that many of us—who don't have children—ponder.

"Fear" might be too strong a word, because most of us non-parents (except those who are still on the fence) have made our choice in spite of these unknowns. Nonetheless, we may still have those nagging questions.

Are these obstacles really as ominous as we make them out to be? Or, as Marie Curie implies above, do we fear them because we don't understand them? A good number of respondents to my survey—37%— checked "I have no fears about not having children." Congratulations! You fearless ones have either become wise enough to conclude that these "problems" don't hold water, or you have found solutions to dealing with them—and you may now skip this chapter if you like.

For the other 63% of you, we will explore each of these fears—or issues if you will—in hopes that doing so will bring the unknown into the light. We will reveal that some of these scary creatures are just figments of our imagination, while others are quite real, but manageable. Either way, if you believe Ralph Waldo Emerson's aphorism that "Fear always springs from ignorance," it will benefit you and me to sort through each issue.

## FEAR #1: That I'll Regret Not Having Them Once It's Too Late

I worry that I will regret it when I am even older.
—"firstmatelisa," 45, Venice, CA

What if I change my mind? What if I get an epiphany at 50 that I really do want kids? What if I regret not having them? Ah, the fear of the unknown. According to the Kidfree Survey, the mysterious "what if" question mark looms over almost one in three non-parents, and is our most cited fear.

For many respondents who checked this answer—"That I'll regret not having them once it's too late"—it was the only fear they checked. But for some, like this female from Ireland, in time they grew out of their fear:

I used to be afraid of regretting not having them, but over time I realized that I'd rather regret *not* having them than regret having them.
—"Irish girl," 30, Dublin, Ireland

Don't worry about the possibility of regretting it later. Dreading the unknown is wasted energy, and is certainly not a good reason to have kids. Here are four reasons why…

### Rebuttal #1: Better to Regret *Not* Having Them, Than Regret *Having* Them!

I'd rather regret NOT having children than regret having them.
—Princess Kessie, 35, Perth, Australia
—John R., 34, Washington, D.C.
—Lisa, 38, Chicago, IL

The above statement—although credited to only three people—is one of the most quoted in my survey. Hundreds of childfree around the world are spreading this nugget of wisdom to those who are worried they'll regret not having kids: "It is better to regret *not* having them than it is to regret *having* them."

What could be more logical? And what could be worse than having children because of various fears and pressures, only to find you are not cut out for the job?

In viewing the online responses to a recent childfree article in Australia, I found this revealing confession from a mother of three:

Here it is Mother's Day and I am a 56-year-old mother of three and grandmother of two writing to say that I wish I'd never had kids.

At least you don't have to spend your life regretting your decision. I certainly do. I didn't have my first until I was married at 27. I had a good career and I had to give it up. I went and did a uni degree after my third was born and I haven't really been able to pursue that career either. I think there is too much of a taboo about this parent thing. It isn't all good. I hated it and I'm stuck with it.

My daughter sent a text today to tell me what a great mum I have been to her. I responded with "don't ever have kids—it's not what it's cracked up to be" and she was offended. Herein lies the problem: if those of us—who have had kids and *wouldn't* if we could do it over—speak out, then we hurt our kids feelings.

I asked around at work recently whether others would do it again and out of ten middle-aged mothers only *one* said she would and that she enjoyed being a mother. ~Anonymous mother, Australia

Only one in ten would do it again? Wow, those are bad odds! But who would know the real odds of childbearing regret, when parents are afraid to admit it for fear they'll hurt their kids' feelings or look like a failure?

For those of you who are afraid you may regret not having children certain times of year—like family holidays—this childfree from Canada puts a new twist on the popular regret quote:

I'd rather regret not having a kid a few hours a year, than regret having one 300 or more days a year.
—"Childfree Writer," 36, Winnipeg, MB, Canada

Sure there may be times—especially for those with fond childhood memories—when we wish we had kids to help decorate the Christmas tree or Easter eggs, but let's not forget these are a few days of joy out of 365!

### Rebuttal #2: It Turns Out, We *Don't* Regret It Later

I did worry that I would regret not having children once I was in the menopause; thankfully I have *not* regretted it.
—Kathy W., 58, London, England

While one in three of us worry that we might regret it in the future, I have yet to find in my field research any older men or women who actually have regretted it. I'm sure they're out there, but they are not among the childfree groups I belong to.

No, the vast majority of non-parents I have come across are kidfree. Remember, my definition of "kidfree" is: one who has no children—whether by choice or by circumstance—and is, in hindsight, glad about this fact. Some—like myself—even rejoice at the freedom and experiences not having kids has brought them.

I had these concerns before, but I don't have these concerns as much, and have no regrets how my life has turned out. —Female, 48, Goleta, CA

I too once had the fear of future regret. But now, I can honestly say the only regret I have is the time I wasted worrying I might regret it!

### Rebuttal #3: We Feel More *Relief* Than *Regret*

> Those *were* my fears, but I'm starting to care less and less about what others think. I also am realizing that I will not regret not having them.
> —Janelle, 42, Montreal, QC, Canada

Another reason we may not regret having them later, is that we are going to be happier in older age than our childed friends. According to a study of 13,000 U.S. adults published in the Journal of Health and Social Behavior: not only are parents more depressed than adults without kids, but even empty-nest parents are not happier than adults who never had children.[1] (There goes the theory that it's only 18 years of drudgery!)

I find that as I get older—and seemingly wiser—I feel a sense of relief more than regret that I don't have children. I see what my friends, siblings and co-workers go through to parent, and I feel fortunate to have avoided that stress.

### Rebuttal #4: And if We Do, We Can Always *Adopt*

> My "fear" of possible regret later is minimal. If my wife and I truly feel like we HAVE to have kids someday (extremely unlikely) we agreed we'd adopt. —Keith, 37, Sacramento, CA

In the unlikely event that you *do* regret it later, you can always look into adopting a child. As mentioned earlier, adoption—for the huge number of children out there who need to find homes—is a good thing.

Many people in childfree groups are pro-adoption for several reasons. Not only is it good for world population to help a child that already exists, but it is also proof that you possess a strong desire to do so for reasons other than producing a "mini-me."

Also, adoption usually involves a rigorous *qualifying* element, which means adoptive parents are likely qualified to parent—(although the system's not perfect, so there are exceptions to the rule).

My sister and her kids are an excellent example of how wonderful adoption can be. She and her husband tried for years to conceive, until finally they adopted their three children. These children—now grown—had a happy and healthy upbringing and are sources of joy to their parents.

If you find yourself regretting you don't have children, and you have the desire and means to go through the process, adopting a child can be a worthwhile and gratifying option.

## FEAR #2: Who Will Take Care of Us When We're Older?

The only things I fear are: that my husband won't have anyone to look after him after I die and that we will end up in a nursing home and be mistreated because we won't have anyone to check in on us (but who says our children would've anyway?).
—Female, 34, Cincinnati, OH

Have you ever had that fear of just rotting away in a nursing home with no one to visit you, like the woman from Cincinnati above? I have; and apparently many others have too. When asked, "What are/were your fears (if any) about not having kids?" more than one in four of us (28%) checked "Growing old with no one to care for me/us." Some feel that having children would bring them a general feeling of security.

General fears of losing my faculties, my money and having to be dependent on others. Having children will give some sense of security whether or not the likelihood of children caring for you in old age is doubtful. —Eveline How, 32, Singapore

It is perfectly normal to feel insecure about growing old and being alone with no one to care for us when we're older. And, yes, there are still offspring in this world who invite their parents to move in with them when they're ill or frail and do their best to take care of them. But let's not delude ourselves, many will not. There are many arguments against this reason to bear children, and here are just four of them...

### Rebuttal #1: There Are No Guarantees

But there is *no guarantee* that they would be around to care for us in our old age, so why bother with it all?
—Debby McMichael-Delo, 46, Big Lake, AK

For some respondents like Debby (above) "growing old with no one to care for me" is the only fear they checked. Yet even Debby knows the reality of that plan: You can't count on it. That's why having kids so they can take care of us when we're older is not only a selfish idea, it's a misguided idea.

One has only to look in the overcrowded nursing homes to see that offspring do not take care of their parents the way they used to. These days, "taking care of them" often consists of paying for the assisted caregiver, not actually *being* the assisted caregiver.

Who wants to be a burden on their kids anyway, especially if they have their own children to raise? It would be nice to have them come and visit, but even *that* may be too much to expect these days, as the following survey respondents wrote in:

> Originally in my early 20s, the only reason I could see for having kids was maybe someone to take care of you when you're old, but now that I'm in my late 30s I know that's not true. After all, I moved 3,000 miles away from my own parents. —Monica, 36, Seattle, WA

> People kid themselves about having kids to take care of them in their old age. Most kids don't even live near their parents and all their focus is on THEIR kids. What a joke. —Female, 46, Michigan

> I have no fears about getting old without children. I think there a lot of people that think their kids will be there. Then the kids move 1,000s of miles away. They are in the same boat. They don't even know their kids as adults. So all that sacrifice in their life is gone.
> —Shelby Richardson, 49, Oregon, WI

As these non-parents realize, there are no guarantees that your kids will take care of you or even visit you when you are older. There is even a small chance that—like Brian's grandparents who lost both their kids in mid-life—you will outlive your offspring before you even need elder care.

### Rebuttal #2: Sometimes They *Take* More Than They *Give*

I have a pitiful story about elder abuse by an offspring that I must share in this section in order to prove that not only might a child not take care of you in old age, but might actually take from you. There is a well-to-do family we know of wherein the son's addiction to drugs and alcohol has caused great turmoil in the family and great fear to his one surviving parent—his 92-year-old mother.

This seemingly "normal" family lived in an upscale area of white suburbia America, and tried to raise their kids the best they could. The daughter—now a successful businesswoman—did well in school and graduated Phi Beta Kappa from a top university. The son, however (we'll call him "Damien") ran amok in his teens and never came back. He is now in his 50s, a severe addict, jailed several times, no job and no money other than what he's obtained either from handouts or—you got it—illegally.

He and his junkie girlfriend "Dee" (who, by the way, never sees her own kids she lost custody of) moved in with Damien's mother under the pretense of taking care of her. Well, between visits to the drug rehab, his "taking care of his mother" consisted of constant drugfests in her home, dealers coming in and out, personal items (such as heirloom jewelry) being stolen and sold, and the forging of his mother's checks.

To make an ongoing saga as short as possible: After the sister found the mother dehydrated lying on the floor while the son partied in the other room, she put her mother in a nursing home, kicked Damien and Dee out, and put a restraining order on the son. The couple then turned to the last surviving parent they could take from: her father who has Alzheimer's.

These "kids" are in their fifties, draining their parents and everyone around them financially and emotionally. This is not a case of bad parenting. This is a case—and there are more out there—of selfish children who never grew up and never stopped taking from their parents, even when those parents were elderly and needed them most.

### Rebuttal #3: We'll Cultivate Our *Own* Friendships and Family Ties

Having kids is no guarantee that they will take care of you...I prefer to cultivate meaningful friendships (and have extra money from not having kids so that we can take care of ourselves!).
—Female, 38, Colorado Springs, CO

Who says it has to be our own children to take care of us in old age? Most assume this, but they shouldn't. How about your own spouse or significant other? I plan on keeping mine so healthy he'll outlive me. And there's no one I'd trust more to take care of me, anyway. We are not burdens to each other; we are blessings.

But what if we outlive our partners, or have no partners to begin with? Like the CF from Colorado Springs (above), we can cultivate *friendships.* (In fact, it is smart for us to do this long before we get old.) Besides the proverbial bridge group we might form as we get older, companionship can be found by reuniting with an old high school buddy or striking up a new friendship with a lonely neighbor.

There are numerous ways one can meet new people at any age, including joining book or travel clubs, taking up new sports or activities, joining health and fitness clubs, attending special events, or just walking your dog.

Are you close to a niece or nephew? As we mentioned earlier, many children feel a special connection with a particular aunt or uncle that can carry through a lifetime. And it's possibly that those of you who enjoy spending time with your niece or nephew now, will not go unnoticed by them when you are old and perhaps in need.

In this village we call Earth, there are always people out there looking to help the elderly. And if it's not your relatives or friends and neighbors, then perhaps it's a helpful stranger through an organization like Senior Services, Neighborly Care Network or Meals on Wheels.

### Rebuttal #4: We'll Have the Money to Care For Ourselves

> I'm a saver and I don't expect people to take care of me when I'm old.
> I'll have the money to take care of myself so that's not a problem.
> —Zellie, 23, Charlottesville, NC

How many of you want to be a burden on others in old age anyway? I don't relish the idea of being dependent—financially or otherwise—on others, and I certainly don't think it's fair to dump it all on one's offspring. Perhaps if you invest some of that half-of-a-million-plus you'll be saving by not having two children, you can be independent enough in old age to choose by whom you want to be taken care of and where.

We have a wonderful upscale retirement community nearby—that resembles a five star resort more than an "old folks home"—in which I would feel privileged to live out my sunset years (finances willing).

> I have never understood the argument (thrown at me regularly) that I won't have anyone to look after me when I'm old. I intend to plan for my old age and not rely on family who may or may not end up being there for me.
> —Jo, 32, Christchurch, New Zealand

And, like Jo above, "plan" I must if I hope to live in a place like Casa Dorinda. But with the money saved from not having children, I will more likely be able to afford this posh retirement community. Then, at that point—with in-house physicians, a medical center, a bevy of activities and dozens of social events per year at my fingertips—my fears of loneliness and no one to care for me will vanish in one fell swoop!

## FEAR #3: Loneliness

> I have problems about loneliness and no one to care for me,
> but "fear" is too strong a word with regard to kids, because
> it was *so* not a good enough reason to have them!!
> —Patricia, England

I think most people—whether they have spouses, children or no one at all—wonder if they'll be lonely in old age. After all, we could outlive our loved ones, and humans are basically social creatures who need interaction with others. Perhaps those of us without offspring have an even higher propensity to worry about loneliness than most.

With more than one in five checking "loneliness" as a fear of not having kids, it was the third most prevalent fear out of ten on my survey.

For those who currently have no partner, it is more of a real and current issue than a fear of the future. In fact, for respondents who are "single" (not married or in a relationship), "Loneliness" was their second

highest fear, right behind "Growing old with no one to care for me."
Here are two single women's responses regarding loneliness:

> I'm divorced and an only child...when my parents die, I'll be completely alone. —Roxanne Brennan, 38, Estell Manor, NJ

> I am alone. If I'd had a child, as least someone would care what happens to me—as it is, no one does. —Ellen, 54, Rochester, NY

But this fear of loneliness is not unique to just single men and women, as several with spouses expressed concern, if not for themselves then for their spouses. It is common for many of us to worry what life will be like when one of us goes:

> That my husband will die first and I will be all alone.
> —Female, 37, New York, NY

> I don't worry about being lonely as long as my husband is alive. I fear that if he died I would regret not having a part of him, yet the idea of raising a child myself sounds even worse. —Pamela Burns, 38, Cherry Hill, NJ

> My wife's loneliness is my concern if I die first. I'll be fine alone, I think. —AKD, 36, Illinois

> I do sometimes wonder what will happen when I'm old—will I die alone, etc. But that's the choice I've made. —Anne Mears, 42, Yeovil, England

**Rebuttal #1: Ensure You're Not Lonely (Cultivate friends and furry things)**

While loneliness is a legitimate concern of the unchilded, we have the power to be less lonely. Whether you're involved in a serious relationship or totally single, it behooves you now to start cultivating lifelong relationships. To put a twist on an old cliché, "put lots of eggs in your social basket."

I hearken back to Rebuttal #3 under the fear of "Who will take care of us when we're older?" One answer: We'll cultivate our own friendships and family ties.

Another great way to keep loneliness at bay: Get a fine furry friend, if you don't already have one! The connection between my 80-year-old dad and his beloved Jack Russell Terrier, Annie, is human-like. Between the twice-daily walks, the non-verbal communication, and the loyal companionship he has with Annie, he is not living alone.

My late mother—who lived alone for years—had a similar relationship with her two little mutts, Sister and Baby. (I know.)

You've probably heard the studies that show just the act of petting a dog or cat raises the level of serotonin (the happy drug) in our brain. It's a good thing then that three quarters of all non-parents have their own pets!

### Rebuttal #2: Your Kids May Not *Want* to Come Around Anyway

A part of me feels that I'll be lonely when I get older, with no one to spend the holidays with me. But, a part of me sees the frustrated parents who've dedicated their lives to children who want nothing to do with them and show up once a year out of a sense of obligation. I don't know which is worse. —Aris, 34, Denver, CO

Remember the song "Cat's in the Cradle" by Harry Chapin? First, the father's too busy to spend quality time with his son, and then when the son grows up—and the father wants to spend time with him now—the son is too busy for him. "When ya comin' home, son?" "I don't know when, but we'll get together then, Dad." The fact is: By the time you're old, your child may be so ensconced with a wife and kids of his own, that he will barely have time to visit you during the holidays, even if he wants to.

Brian has a widowed client—Tom—in his 90s who actually confides in him about his unloving children. They hardly ever visit him (not even Christmas this year), and yet recently they've attempted to take over his finances and move him into a nursing home. While Brian doesn't detect any dementia, the kids are purporting that he is no longer mentally capable of running his own affairs, and would like to take over as conservators.

While Tom finally gave in—after a struggle—to their wish to move him out of his beachfront condo to a nursing home, he told Brian he does not want to let them take control of his finances and his entire life. He is afraid and I don't blame him. They aren't treating him with respect and, in fact, are trying to abscond with any remaining control he has of his life.

It seems odd that offspring who were too busy for years to pay him nary a visit, suddenly want to take over his life and finances against his will. We've all seen cases where the heirs wait around like vultures for a parent to die. There is no guarantee our children will have our best interests at heart when we are old and feeble and near the end.

This isn't humor, but it really helped in my decision not to have kids. People always say "Oh who will take care of you when you get old if you don't have any kids?" Well my grandpa's brother, Uncle Herman, had a wife and child. He is 92 now. His wife passed away of cancer and his son (who was gay) died of AIDS at the early onset of AIDS in the 80's. Herman is not lonely though. He lives in an assisted living community, plays golf, makes homemade wine, has quite a few girlfriends and generally lives it up. I realized that it doesn't matter if you have kids or not, you could still end up with no family at the end. But Uncle Herman proves you can STILL HAVE FUN. :) —Desert Girl, 33, Phoenix, AZ

### FEAR #4: That I Will Lose My Friends That Have Kids

I've already lost all my friends. They are having kids left and right, and I feel like I don't have anything in common with them anymore.
—Bob M., 39, Milwaukee, WI

CF couple Doug and Tina used to get together with Bill and Karen most weekends for fine dining, wine tastings or movies, but now they are invited to kiddie parties, zoo outings and pizza parlors with their new son.

Once he was delivered, all Bill and Karen could talk about was "little Willy," and their world now revolves around him 24/7. This bores Doug and Tina, who miss the stimulating conversation and activities they used to have with their favorite couple.

Like the three survey respondents below, they find it hard to relate to the changes their friends have made since having kids:

Definitely the biggest problem is that when people have kids, that becomes their world and I have very little to relate to them about anymore. I see their personality disintegrating into "mommy mentality" and all their stories are things I'm not interested in, all their woes are woes I avoided in the first place, and I hate people complaining about something they chose to get into. —Zellie, 23, Charlottesville, VA

As I get older I find it harder and harder to relate to people my age because most have families, so our context and priorities are usually completely different. —Deborah Sullivan, 44, New Hampshire

My friends who used to brag about being "DINK (Double Income No Kids) are already planning for their second. They insisted their lives would not change at all, but they are completely different people now!
—Leslie Hunter, 35, Chandler, AZ

Growing apart from our friends who have jumped on the baby bandwagon is a fact of life for most kidfree, and one we must deal with.

Along with the two following, almost one in five (19.2%) survey respondents checked "That I Will Lose My Friends That Have Kids" as a fear of remaining a non-parent:

Losing the friends was not a real strong fear, but for the most part it did in fact happen, but mostly because we just didn't have much in common with them. —CC, 54, Florida

It is very difficult at my age (36) to make new friends, especially with other women, because I have very little in common with the majority of them who have children. Especially because I am uninterested in discussing kid stuff all day. —Female, Long Island, NY

Losing friends with kids was a very small fear—I don't really feel "fear" is a good word. —Female, 57, St. Louis, MO

I agree that "fear" is too strong a word. Although it may be a concern for those whose friends haven't yet started procreating, it becomes more of an issue one deals with—say in their 20s and 30s—when everyone starts popping them out and we're bombarded with baby shower invites. Later in life, when our friends' kids are grown, it is less of an issue.

But for almost one in five of my survey respondents it is an issue they are concerned with. Non-parents suddenly find their friends consumed with *breeder blab* about such riveting topics as Connor's first crawl and how to best burp Brendan; and some lose their weekend sidekicks or travel buddies, as these three lament:

> When a travel companion of mine and her husband told me they were expecting a child, I laughed "You are not only ruining your life but mine also, as we will no longer have those great vacations together."
> —Dwight van den Hoek, 44, California

> I do find it awkward at my age to be one of very few of my friends who do not have kids. To my knowledge, I am the only one of my friends of childbearing age that does not plan to have children. It's tough to find activities with friends on a Saturday night that won't be kid-centric sometimes. —Kelly, 32, Winnipeg, MB, Canada

> "I have nothing to offer you." A quote from a once acquaintance of mine after she had her child, and when I invited her to go out shopping with me and bring her child with us. Needless to say, we parted ways.
> —Cheryl S. Levinson, 62, San Jose, CA

This last quote from Cheryl incenses me a bit. This new mother no longer felt a need for her unchilded friend (who was trying to be inclusive of her child) so she just dumped her *tout de suite*. Good riddance, I say!

### Rebuttal #1: Learn to Adjust *(and make lemon bars!)*

> My relationships with some of my friends have changed since they had kids, but that's just a natural part of the situation, not something to fear, in my opinion. —Patricia, 43, Warren, MI

So, what do non-parents like Doug or Tina do when their friends turn their lives into a year-round Chevy Chase vacation? They learn to adjust. When life throws us lemons, why not make lemon bars?

Before you dump your friends, redefine your relationship with them. Perhaps you can learn to enjoy the family outings in small doses, and become the great observer of the modern American family. Better yet— and because you'll never have your own—perhaps you can develop a bond with one or both of the kids, much like an uncle or aunty role in the family.

My brother and his wife have a friend, Paul, who is over 50 with no kids. Over a decade ago nearly all of Paul's friends got married and had kids. He never followed suit. Suddenly the group getaways to spots like the Caribbean went from adult getaways to family vacations, planned around school breaks. Did Paul dump his friends? To the contrary, he bonded with the kids, and has become "Uncle Paulie." In fact, he comes to my brother's for most holidays, and my niece and nephew love him.

Even if you don't jump in with both feet like Uncle Paulie, you can try to establish a new routine with your childed friends that may consist of a compromise between family events and adult events.

### Rebuttal #2: Find New Friends!

Even though I'm not as close with some of my friends that have kids, I find myself friends with other CF'ers. —Denise F., 38, West Virginia

What if you're simply not into being around kids, especially your friends' noisy, unruly chillun? Your friends can't return their kids, so you may have to say "bye-bye for now" to them. It's time to settle in to the childfree world and make some new friends. (I know, easier said than done.)

But, if about one in five of us will never have children, there's got to be a few of us out there for you to meet, no? If you turn to my Kidfree Resources in the back of this book, you'll find many ways to meet like-minded people in the U.S. and around the globe.

There are groups—like Childfree Meetups and No Kidding! in cities around the world—where non-parents get together for monthly events and activities. If there isn't one in your town you can start your own. And, if you don't mind cyberspace friends, there are dozens of childfree blogs in which to connect with others.

I started to realize that I had no real social group, and understood finally that it was because my female peers are completely wrapped up in childrearing and a parenting lifestyle. When I started to identify with being a "childfree by choice" married woman, I realized I needed to reach out to other active women without children (some of whom are younger than I am but equally active). This has helped me form friendships, and at the same time I have let go of the need to explain myself to my peers/friends who do have children. —Joy, 44, Mammoth Lakes, CA

Like Joy, if you feel your social life fade away from you as your friends morph into modern moms and dads, just realize there are others like you in the same situation. Find them; reach out to them; befriend them.

\*     \*     \*

As you can see, our biggest concerns of being "without child"—whether real or imagined—are nothing we can't deal with. And, perhaps now that we've examined each, our fears will dissipate.

In any case, as inspirational author David Joseph Schwartz once said, "Do what you fear and fear disappears."

# CHAPTER 16

## Pressures To Procreate
### And Follow the Norm

Without deviation from the norm, progress is not possible.
~Frank Zappa (1940-1993), musician

"*What a cute romper, Sue, it's perfect for her,*" *her sister-in-law says as she puts the box on the floor and wads the Christmas paper into a ball. "You know, we're saving all these baby clothes for you when you have your kids!" she beamed. Not knowing what to say, Sue smiles and nods nervously. "Oh jeez," she thinks, "I hope she's not going to save boxes of clothes for years, only to find I'm never having kids!"*

...And so it went for several birthdays and holidays. Sue didn't blame her sister-in-law for assuming she'd have kids. So did her brother and father and probably her sister and mother. How could they not? Sue had even thought she would someday. She just hadn't gotten around to telling people that "someday" wasn't going to come anymore. She and Robert had decided parenting wasn't for them.

How do you tell your family and friends that you're breaking one of society's biggest social paradigms? You know, the one where everyone gets married and has children? Will it offend them that you don't want to join their club? Or will it just disappoint them?

More than 17% of those surveyed cited, "Disappointing my parents and/or siblings" as a fear of not having children. Not surprisingly, the same amount checked "That I won't fit in with family or friends" as a concern.

Pretty sad how much I care about what loved ones think about my decisions, but it's the truth. —Kathleen, 29, Chicago, IL

And why shouldn't we care about what others think? It's only natural. From the not-so-subtle hints dropped by family members to the constant questioning of "when" from friends and co-workers, the pressure to follow the norm and bear children is pervasive throughout society.

Why do these people care so much about your procreation plans? There could be many reasons: A mother wants to become a grandparent; a sibling wants cousins for their children; a friend wants you to join her in parenting; co-workers want you to attend kiddie events with them, etc.

Notice these "wants" are not necessarily what's best for *you*, but what's best for them. In fact, many non-parents believe their childed friends are jealous of their lifestyle and want them to join in their misery:

> I honestly think that many (not all) are jealous—they see through us that they too could have made a different choice, but now are stuck. So to feel better they turn it around, like we are the ones that are missing out.
> —Amy, 40, Averill Park, NY

> My favorite childfree quote is "Misery Loves Company!" I am convinced that most people want others to have children so they can "see what it's like." —Elena Izquierdo, 35, Miami, FL

On the other hand, many people may have no agenda at all. They simply ask "When?" because they *assume* you are going to have kids some day. Most people do it, why should you be any different? Well, because you *are* different, you have thought it through and you know it's not for you. End of discussion, right? If only it were that simple...

### Pressure From Parents
*AKA: Nurturing, Needing and Nagging*

We all know of the proverbial pushy mother who can't wait till her progeny gives her grandbabies that she can spoil and buy baby booties for. These are usually the maternal types that miss the mothering they did more than two decades ago. Unfortunately (for mom), you may not have inherited her knack or need for nurturing. Not understanding this, she continues to nag once you're engaged, once you're married, yada yada...

> After being proposed to at a romantic beach setting in Hawaii, I rang my mother to tell her we were engaged, and the details behind it. Before I could go into details, she said: "Why? Are you pregnant?" Fast forward 2.5 years: After a two-month honeymoon through Cuba, Mexico, the U.S., Cook Islands and the Caribbean, I rang my mother to tell her how fantastic a time we had. Before I could open my mouth, she said, "Are you pregnant yet?" And she hasn't stopped since!
> —Tash Watts, 33, Sydney, Australia

This type of mother must be told early—and adamantly—that you have no interest in parenthood, lest she continue to carp until your clock goes kaput. Luckily, not all of us have mothers like this. In fact, many of us are blessed with moms who understand or are supportive of our choice:

> My mom has come to terms with my childfree status and has been very supportive for many years now. —Ruth, 37, Santa Cruz, CA

> I think my mum would love to have grandchildren, but thankfully she is selfless enough to allow me to choose my own life no matter how badly she might want grandchildren. —Hapa Honey, 22, Toronto, Canada

> I told my mom when we were at the beach one day that I never wanted kids. She replied, "I sort of gathered that." I was 16. She's been supportive ever since and I'm now 55. —Denise, Montana

According to dozens of comments on the survey, it's often *dad* who has a problem with our kidfree status more than mom. Perhaps this is because mom knows better than dad what the day-to-day tasks of childrearing entail, and thus understands your trepidation.

> My mother is resigned to the fact that I don't want children; my dad still doesn't really understand that I won't be having kids.
> —Marie, 24, Los Angeles, CA

> My Dad is pining to be a grandfather. A couple of years ago he exclaimed that he had brought up a family of DINKS (my two brothers and myself). —
> Felicia Davis-Burden, 42, Staines, Middlesex, England

Another cross some have to bear is being an "only child"—the only one to pass on the bloodline or the family name. What's worse is you are also the only hope for your parents becoming grandparents.

> I am an only child, so my mother is CRAZY for me to start having kids.
> —"On the fence" in Pennsylvania

Although there are families where all kids remain childless, it is rare, and the odds are that *four of five siblings* will produce offspring, taking an enormous strain off of those who don't. Luckily, I have two siblings who gave my parents five grandchildren to enjoy, like this childfree male:

> There are currently 5 grandchildren, so we don't have a lot of pressure right now. —Male, 29, Omaha, NE

Then there's the "Don't Ask, Don't Tell" group that doesn't know where their parents stand on the issue, either because they haven't yet broached the subject or the parents are hiding their feelings on the matter:

> I think they'd like a grandchild someday, but we don't really talk about it.
> —Kayelle, 27, Antwerp, Belgium

> I'm sure my mom and dad secretly wish they were grandparents.
> —Erin, 31, USA (city and state unspecified)

## Self-Serving Siblings

My brother actually yelled at me once that we were selfish for not having children, and that "Everyone should have children, because everyone needs a little misery in their lives." Yes, he actually said that. And he thought that would convince us?
—Paul Dolce, 43, Fort Collins, CO

Sometimes siblings put more pressure on us to procreate than do our parents. This may be in part because—like Paul's brother above—misery loves company. It might seem unfair to a parent that his or her sibling chose the less demanding path of "childfreedom."

My sibs, I have four, would like me to suffer along just as they do under the guise of "bliss." —BdRonald, 44, Center Line, MI

Our choice may also make them examine the validity of their *own* choice to bear children, once it's too late. The anger Paul's brother has toward his decision not to breed shows that he may not be happy with his own situation. Some siblings don't even bother to hide their self-serving reasons for wanting us to have children:

My sister told me I was being selfish—that because of me, she wouldn't get to be an aunt. —Double L, 24, New York, NY

Which sister in the above scenario is being selfish? The one who won't have a child to appease her sister, or the one who is pressuring her sister to have a child so that she can be an aunt?

Other siblings may choose guilt, religion or morality to sway us:

My brothers often comment that I should have children. One even said to me that life's purpose is to go forth and multiply.
—Boxer Babies, 34, Geraldton, Australia

Fortunately, most siblings, including mine, are not as pushy as these. Some may try to hide their disappointment, but you know it's there. I believe my brother and sister-in-law—who live nearby—would have loved it if I had given their kids some cousins to play with. No doubt the family get-togethers would have been more plentiful, we would have exchanged turns babysitting, our house would have been childproofed, and we would have shared hand-me-downs. I can relate to how these women think their sister and brother (respectively) stand on the issue:

I think my sister (who has kids) wishes I would have kids so I could share the experience. —Lyondi Arr, 28, Indianapolis, IN

I know that my Dad always wanted me to have kids, but the worst part was disappointing my brother and his wife who couldn't *wait* for me to give their kids some cousins nearby to play with! —Jennifer, 46, San Diego, CA

## Other Unrelenting Relatives

My parents are fine with my choice, but my in-laws are baby-crazy.
We avoid the topic when we are around them.
They cannot accept our views on this issue.
—"Happy & Free," 29, Georgia

The pressure doesn't always start—or stop—in the nuclear family. Even when mom, dad, sis and bro come to accept (if not understand) your choice not to procreate, there is inevitably someone among the couple's two clans who will stick their nose into your childbearing business.

Literally, within 5 minutes of getting married, my auntie asked me when we were having children. I said we weren't, so she asked me why we bothered getting married! —Danielle Gail, 33, Brisbane, Australia

I was visiting my aunt and uncle in Florida about a month ago. I was holding my cousin's new baby when my uncle asked, "How long have you and your husband been married?" I replied that we had been married for ten years, as of September. He then asked, "So you do know by now what causes babies?" I retorted, "WANTING babies causes babies!" It's just another example of the often very rude and intrusive questions that we child-free people have to put up with. —Kristen D., 37, Eugene, OR

In other cases, they are not particularly pestering us, but we are sad that we will not be able to give our relatives what they want:

My biggest disappointment about not having children is that my grandparents will not be great-grandparents. —Jennifer, 29, Dallas, TX

## Prodding from Peers

My fears all revolved around the societal pressure that everyone
wants or should want children. That there must be something
wrong with me if I don't want them.
—Su, 38, Santa Barbara, CA

While families are often dysfunctional guilt factories more than love nests, our friendships are supposed to be our safe harbors for support and understanding. Or so they say. Sometimes it is our friends themselves who overlook our desire to follow a different path, if it isn't the path their on.

I had a friend who was convinced I would change my mind about having kids. She was the only one of my friends or family that didn't really respect my decision to be childfree. Once I became an aunt, and proudly announced the news, my friend said to me, "Oh, you're going to love being an aunt, so much so that I bet you change your mind about having kids." I looked at her and said, "I love you very much, but when you say things like that to me, it is no less hurtful or disrespectful than if I say to you, 'I know you think your daughters are really fun and fascinating right now, but in about 10 years, you're going to wish they were never born.'" That effectively closed the topic and she's never said anything since.
—Cool Aunt Molly, 36, North Hollywood, CA

Even if not meant in malice, many have no idea how disrespectful it is to try to change a person's mind about this life-altering decision. One way to let them know, like Molly above, is to tell them it truly hurts you or give them an example of what it would feel like if you pushed your opinions on them. Or, you can always use a little shock value to shut them right up:

> At a recent party attended by many couples with kids, my husband and I had to hear so many times that night, "You guys need to have babies." Any time either of us would hold a kid's hand or get them a soda, or play in their little games, people would give us that "Aaaahhhh...." look. All the adults were seated around a fire pit chatting and a woman looked directly at me and said loudly, "Cyndi—we all want you and Ed to have kids." All the other conversations stopped and everyone looked at me. I looked right back at her and said, "Why do you want us to have kids so badly?" Her husband piped right up, "Because" (as if that's an answer). I looked incredulously at him and said, "Because? Because why? Because misery loves company?" Everyone's mouths dropped open, and magically the conversation quickly changed. —Cyndi Holbert, 28, Pocatello, ID

Touché! How many of us wish we could come back with a snappy, jaw-dropping zapper like that? But seriously folks, even if you lack Cyndi's chutzpah, you do have the final say. Many "friends" may try to sway you during your childbearing years to jump on the kiddie carousel with them, but stand your ground firmly with what you feel is best for you.

> Most of them always say I'm wrong for wanting to live child-free, and that I'll have a hard time finding someone that shares my desire to remain that way. They say I'll change my mind. We'll just have to see about that!
> —Corey, 21, Baton Rouge, LA

### Military Mom Mongers

Army, Navy, Air Force, Marines—if you find yourself living in a military community with no kids, and no plans to have kids, you may find yourself shunned and alone, like these women:

> I wish I had some humor to contribute, but the sad fact is that I am constantly put down and shunned in our community (Marine Corps) because I dislike children. I am accused of being unnatural and "not right in the head." One particularly religious breeder told me that women are meant to breed, and that throughout history that has been their exalted position. Personally, I don't see that, historically, women had been given much choice, and it saddens me that modern women are thus brainwashed. —Anne Walsh, 25, Camp Pendleton, CA

> My husband and I have been married not even two years and already we're sick of hearing the question "So when are you two going to have some little ones?" Having friends in a young military community means having friends with babies and children. I've never understood why, but it's the "norm" as a young military couple to pop out a couple kids right off the

bat. It just doesn't make any sense to me! Don't these couples want to spend their blissful honeymoon years alone? Do they like being broke, tired, and tied down? My husband and I say NO, and we're waiting at least five years to make a decision about children. —Katie P, 22, Virginia

When asked about her fears of not having children, one respondent replied:

That I won't make many friends in general that do not have children. It's extremely difficult, especially in the military (in our case Navy) community. People get married young and have kids young as well. Not everyone, but most seem to. We got married young (my husband on his 21st birthday and me five days from turning 21), and I just don't feel that kids fit into the equation anywhere after that. —Female, 27, St. Mary's, GA

What is it about military communities that make women want to bear children? Is it their conservative bent, or simply because they are bored? Childfree Karyn Johnson was excited to move to Germany with her husband who is in the Air Force, but surprised when "all the military wives surrounding me treated me like I had a disease." In her compelling essay, "Childfree in a Military Community," she states:

Most of them were young wives who had married fresh out of high school and began having kids shortly thereafter. They knew no other way of life, so the concept of being childfree was completely foreign and unnatural to them. Of course, I got the types of responses that we childfree folks use to play Bingo, but I also heard one that struck me as being the most ridiculous thing I ever heard: "You have lots of free time while you're stationed here, so you might as well have a kid to give you something to do." What? Please tell me that is not a reason people use to justify having kids while they're here. ~Karyn Johnson[1]

### Church Vs. Childfree

Another group that might have difficulties with your childfree choice is the Church. After all, doesn't the bible tell us to "Go forth and multiply?"

My father point-blank told me it wasn't possible to be a childfree Christian. The subject hasn't come up with my oldest brother, but I am sure he would chastise me from a "Christian" point of view. My sister-with-kids accepts that it's my life to live, and my youngest sister encourages me since she doesn't want kids either. —Sarah, 22, Mountain Home, AR

There are many practicing Christians who have chosen not to have children. In fact, there are several blogs and websites for childfree Christians, including:

"Childfree Christian" on Childfreechristian.blogspot.com
"Childfree Christians" on livejournal.com
"Life as a Childfree Christian" on wordpress.com
"The Cyber-Church of Jesus Christ Childfree" on eilertech.com

In fact, "The Cyber-Church of Jesus Christ Childfree" website reminds us that Jesus had no descendants by fleshly means. Still, the fact remains that Christian dogma states: sex is an act reserved for procreation, birth control should not be used, and God put us on this earth to reproduce.

The following story from a childfree survey respondent reveals how having children is a *given*—not a choice—to most Catholics:

> I went to Catholic school from 1st through 8th grade. When I was in 6th grade (12 years old) our teacher went around the room and asked everyone how many kids they wanted. (I don't remember how this got started, but hey, it was Catholic school!) I knew then I didn't want any, but I was also smart enough to know that I didn't want to give THAT answer in a Catholic school. The boy sitting in front of me said "three," so I did as well. —Madchen, 39, Fort Collins, CO

Notice how it's not "if" but "how many?" And notice too the social pressure is so great she wouldn't even consider telling the truth. The bible is full of references to fertility, maternity and reproduction. As shown here, it equates children with blessings, and barrenness with punishment:

> "As for you, be fruitful and increase in number; multiply on the earth and increase upon it." ~Genesis 9:7
>
> "You will be blessed more than any other people; none of your men or women will be childless, nor any of your livestock without young." ~Deuteronomy 7:14
>
> "He maketh the barren woman to keep house, and to be a joyful mother of children. Praise ye the LORD." ~Psalm 113:9
>
> "I will therefore that the younger women marry, bear children, guide the house, give none occasion to the adversary to speak reproachfully." ~1 Timothy 5:14
>
> "[...] For Adam was formed first, then Eve. And Adam was not the one deceived; it was the woman who was deceived and became a sinner. But women will be saved through childbearing—if they continue in faith, love and holiness with propriety." ~1 Timothy 2:9-15
>
> "Sons are a heritage from the LORD, children a reward from him. Like arrows in the hands of a warrior are sons born in one's youth. Blessed is the man whose quiver is full of them. They will not be put to shame when they contend with their enemies in the gate." ~Psalm 127:3-5

Perhaps it's the authoritative ring of the ancient tongue in which they are written, but these passages from the bible can make even a non-believer feel like a heal for not bearing children. These sentiments have been propagated over the years by church leaders like Martin Luther who said:

> Maternity is a glorious thing since all mankind has been conceived, born, and nourished of women. All human laws should encourage the multiplication of families. ~Martin Luther, founder of the Lutheran Church

In addition to Christianity, most religions—including Hinduism, Judaism and Muslim—refer to the importance of marriage and children in their scriptures. When asked about the importance of childbearing to the Hindu culture, one male member of the childfree network said:

Children are considered a "necessity" in this part of the world, culture and religion conspiring together in this regard. There is the classic "children are a gift from God" belief. Some scriptures say that a son is essential to help the parent's soul on its onward journey after death, and many religious rituals are prescribed for this purpose. —P. Srivastava, 39, India

The wrath of the church can be felt in modern Florida as well:

Five years with someone, great relationship, dumped because his church and family told him a woman who didn't want children was "ungodly" and unfit to be a wife. —Kathleen, Florida

Regardless of our religion, when a parent tells us that our god would not approve of certain behaviors, it may leave us with a stigma of guilt or shame. But when Olivia grew up she could see the irony in the preachings:

My mom says that "God wouldn't approve," yet she is somebody who truly should have been childfree. I'm not saying she was a terrible mother, but she constantly complained about what she couldn't do because she was "stuck" with the kids. Never could figure out why she went and had six of us! I guess it's a Catholic thing! —Olivia Smith, 37, Ohio

## Go Ahead...Break the News
*(You may be surprised!)*

My parents were proud of the fact that I chose not to have children.
—Candy Lake, Founder of the Charlotte, NC Chapter of No Kidding!

The good news is: There are friends and family out there who will respect your decision not to have kids, no matter how worried you are to break the news to them. When asked, "Do your parents or siblings wish you had kids?" about 40% answered "Yes," and a lucky 25% said "No" they don't. However, 36% were "not sure" how their parents or siblings feel about it. I'll bet many in this "unsure" group have not dared to share their decision yet, for fear of the negative reactions they may get.

You may be surprised to find out it won't be as bad as you thought. Before my mother died she told me it was *no biggie* that I might not have children, because it's a huge lifestyle change that I may be happier without. She admitted she had kids because "that's what you did back then," but in today's world she might not have. My dad and siblings may have been *slightly* disappointed initially, but have been supportive ever since.

There are those who say it's nobody's business and you don't have to reveal your decision to be childfree, but it might not hurt to get it out in the open. This way, you will get it off your chest, people might stop asking, and you may even find a supportive response, as these three did:

I felt greatly relieved when my late grandmother told me it was "no big deal" that I didn't want to have kids. It was the single most comforting moment of my life. —Janet, 29, of Ledyard, CT

I've talked with my mom about my decision, and she's very understanding. She also believes in this day and age, she wouldn't want to bring a child into this world either. —Female, 35, Iowa

Actually, my family is OK with my choice, and my sister has said she loves her kids, but if she had it to do again, she may not have had kids. —Patti, 45, Bel Air, CA

One of my favorite "breaking the news" stories is from Keith and his wife in California:

I've been married for ten years. My wife and I went on a trip to Disneyland with her wonderful parents. We decided we would "break the news" to them during our vacation that we had scheduled a consultation appointment for a vasectomy procedure. We had always been clear on the fact that we didn't want kids, but we recognized the "virtually permanent" aspect of the surgery, so we were a little concerned about how they might take the news. Fortunately, they were very understanding, and although they were slightly disappointed that we would not make them grandparents, they were clear in saying our happiness was top priority. It's great to have their support in our decision. On the plane ride back home, a young child was screaming during the flight. My father-in-law, who was seated several rows ahead of us, shouted back to me, "Hey Keith—thanks for getting a vasectomy!" The burst of laughter that followed drowned out the sound of the screaming child! —Keith, 37, Sacramento, CA

That's one cool father-in-law you have, Keith!

\*    \*    \*

Although society seems more kid-centric than ever, the silver lining to the modern world may be that people are more tolerant of those who are different, and thus more open minded to alternative lifestyles.

As English psychiatrist and author Anthony Storr (1920-2001) once said, "Originality implies being bold enough to go beyond accepted norms." Living outside the box takes courage, but if you are forthright in your convictions you will probably find that people not only tolerate—but actually revere—your uniqueness of being.

# CHAPTER 17

## "BREEDER BINGO"
### And Creative Comebacks

*It is easier to develop your quips than to rely solely on a quick wit.*

S o, what are all these relatives, friends, co-workers, military moms and churchgoers saying to make us feel guilty—if not *foolish*—for not following the norm? "It's human nature to procreate." "You're not a real adult until you have kids." "What if your parents never had children?" "Don't you *like* kids?" and so on...

The queries and clichés never stop coming.

Although newly married couples in their prime reproductive years are the biggest targets, all of us fall victim to breeder comments—called "bingos" by childfree—once we divulge our uncertainty about childbearing or our decision to remain kidfree.

This propensity for parents to push their purported wisdom like procreation pundits has spurred the invention of "Breeder Bingo." Although I first came across two links to bingo cards on the *Happily Childfree* website, its hosts say they did not create the card or the term "Breeder Bingo," nor do they know who did.[1] Nonetheless, it's a fun little game to play for the kidfree—and all non-parents—in order to prevent the pressure from getting us down.

I've created my own Kidfree Bingo card with what I've found to be the top 24 questions or comments directed at us when we inform a parent we *don't have kids* or *aren't planning to have kids*.

There are many more "bingos" that could be included—which we will outline later in this chapter—so feel free to create your *own* card after you complete this one. In the back of this book, you will find an extra Kidfree Bingo Card with a blank bingo card on the backside for your own creation—to tear out and take with you.

As each statement from a breeder comes up, just smile and "X" off another box until…BINGO!

# KIDFREE BINGO CARD

| When are you going to have kids? | It's Human Nature to Procreate | What if your parents never had children? | Don't You Like Kids? | Who will take care of you when you're older? |
|---|---|---|---|---|
| You're Not a Family Without Children | You Were a Child Once Too | Your child could grow up to cure cancer | Aren't you curious what they would look like? | What about carrying on the family name? |
| You'll Change Your Mind! | Don't you want to give your parents grand-children? | KIDFREE PARKING | Your Biological Clock is Ticking! | You aren't a real adult until you have kids |
| It's Selfish Not to Have Kids | You would make such a good parent | The only reason to get married is to have children | If everyone chose not to procreate, the human race would die out | Parenthood is the most important job in the world |
| It's All Worth it! | My kids are the most important thing in my life | It's Different When They're Your Own | You aren't a real woman until you experience childbirth | You'll Regret it Later! |
| **WHY** | **DON'T** | **YOU** | **HAVE** | **KIDS?** |
| **B** | **I** | **N** | **G** | **O** |

# CREATIVE COMEBACKS
## *...to common "Breeder Bingos"*

So, what do we say to those who are so interested in our procreation plans? What is the proper protocol (or not) toward such prying into our personal lives? Whether it's an assumptive "When are two having kids?" or a more terse "Don't you like kids?" we oftentimes find ourselves speechless as our mind races to formulate a fitting response. Don't let it happen again. Be prepared next time with your own creative comeback, or one borrowed from others in your situation.

Here's a list of 35 common questions or comments you may receive from family, friends, co-workers or even strangers regarding your parenting plans (or lack thereof), followed by quick, cool and creative comebacks developed by the childfree. Though some are my creations, most have been garnered from survey respondents and childfree groups over the years. Note they range from lighthearted and laughable to downright curt and crude, with a blank space after each for your own creation...

**1)  Do You Have Kids?**

Don't have any, don't want any. —Male, 48, Clifton, N.J.

Don't have 'em, don't want 'em. —Female, 21, Syracuse, NY

No, I have money and a life. —Jeremy Matties, 21, Fairport, NY

I have kids, they just have fur.
—Rosanne Maitland, 40, Edmonton, Canada

"Oh, I can't bear children," I respond, without qualifying whether I can't *physically* conceive/carry a baby, or whether I just can't stand to be around them! —Hyde, 25, St. Louis, MO

I simply respond, "I'm a non-breeder." Or I answer "Not that I know of," which draws blank stares, as I am a female. —Ziji, 40, Alberta, Canada

We got rid of kids, the cats were allergic. —Ed, 50, West Warwick, RI

Kids? No way! I'm having a life instead. —V, 28, Chile

*Your own:* _____

**2)  *When* are you going to have kids?**

When people ask *when* (never if) I am going to have children I say "I am waiting for UPS to deliver." —Loving zebras, 58, Springfield, VA

Here are my two favorite responses to those questions on occasions when you don't want to be rude back to the inquirer, despite their rudeness in asking: "We're still practicing." or "We're too selfish." (Excellent for dropping jaws when said *by* the childfree rather than *to* the childfree!) —Cheryl, 39, St. Charles, MO

[My cousin] would not take, "we're not going to have kids" as being the end of the discussion. So, after one of her, "you must have kids" speeches I told her in front of our entire family that, "we'll have kids when the condom breaks." The entire room erupted in laughter. Even my grandmother was rolling on the floor. Guess what, she has never said anything about it again. —Keith Zimmerman, 36, La Salle, IL

A couple years after dating my DH, I finally met one of his sisters and her family. Not even 15 minutes into our meeting her husband said, "So when are you two getting married?" "Well, later." Then his next question, "So Carma, when are you going to start popping out babies?" EH? I smiled sweetly and told him "as soon as DH could carry one to full term." —Carma, 38, Des Moines, IA

I quickly reply with, "We aren't, we are having dogs instead." I get a variety of responses from, "Oh, are you sure? Kids are so wonderful," which usually makes me respond with, "Some kids are—not all" to "Good for you for knowing. Raising kids is a hard job and if you don't want to do it, then don't." —Molly Ray, 35, Seattle, WA

*Your own:* _____

## 3)  Why don't you have kids?

I like to respond with "Just lucky I guess"...Love the facial expressions! —Rebecca, 33, Melbourne, Australia

Why have kids when you can have a life! —Miya, 42, San Francisco Bay Area, CA

I need a kid like a fish needs a bicycle. —Jennifer, 36, Frederick, (U.S. state not specified)

My favorite comeback? "You don't want me near children" is usually good for strangers. They pretty much leave you alone after that! Retorts that are appropriate for well-meaning family/friends are much harder to find. —Kathleen, 29, Chicago, IL

Why don't we have kids? The critters did the math and we can't afford 'em. The cats say they are allergic to toddlers! —Anne M. Geffert, 41, Coweta, GA

*Your own:* _____

## 4)  Why don't you want kids?

When someone asks me, "Why don't you want kids?" I say, "Why don't you want a root canal?" That shuts them up. —Yordanka Penton, 28, West Palm Beach, FL

When people ask why we don't have kids, my husband always says, "Because they might turn out like you" to the asker. —Brenda, 35, Fort Collins, CO

When people ask, "Why don't you want to have kids?" I immediately ask "Why would I (or you) WANT to have them?" In my mind, there's just no good reason. Nothing about it seems appealing in the least. —Carol H., Seven Hills, OH

When anyone gives me the third degree, I just reply "Why is it so important to you personally?" And somehow they can never give an answer...Guess that says it all. —Kalinka, 37, Bavaria, Germany

When someone asks me why I don't want children, I ask them why they don't want a horse. Horses are beautiful creatures, faithful, fun to take out. OK maybe it costs a lot to feed them and the mucking out is stinky and you have to tend to them every day for years and years but you get so much back. No, they say, they're not convinced. They just don't have that need for a horse no matter how wonderful I say it is. Well that's just the way I feel about children. And I don't have a horse either!
—"Limeygirl of U.K.," 44, United Kingdom

*Your own:* _____

### 5) It's Different When They're Your Own

Yeah, you can't give them back and you're stuck with them!
—Jayne Claire Ochoa, 39, Dallas, TX

I tell people I don't like kids and they never fail to answer back, "You'll like your own!" I just can't help responding back, "You say that, but there is always some lady who drowns her kids in the bath tub, and I'll be damned if it's going to be me." They either laugh and drop the subject, or they are so outraged by my taste-less joke they stop talking to me. Either way it's a win-win situation. —Kate T., 24, Orlando, FL

*Your own:* _____

### 6) Parenthood is the most important job in the world

It may be for *you,* but it's not for me.

*Your own:* _____

### 7) What if your parents hadn't had children?

While I was doing a radio talk show, a listener phoned in and said, "Where would you be if your parents had decided not to have children?" I answered, "I wouldn't be here, and you'd be talking to yourself."
—Jerry Steinberg, Founding Non-Father Emeritus of No Kidding!

If your parents never had children, chances are you won't, either.
—Marlana Dear, 21, Wintersville, OH (quoting Dick Cavett)

*Your own:* _____

### 8) Don't you want to give your parents grandchildren?

That's what my siblings are for!

My husband and I were sitting down for dinner together one evening when the subject of The Duggars came up (the family with 16, no 17, no 18 children that have their own reality show). My father made the comment, "Well, I would settle for just one grand-child." To which I replied, "Call them, maybe they'll give you one of theirs." My husband found the comment amusing—not my parents. —J.K.E., 34, Alexandria, VA

*Your own:* _____

### 9) Who Will Take Care of You When You're Older?

I always hear "Who will take care of you when you are old?" Just because you have children, doesn't mean that they will take care of you when you're old. —Mary, 40, Ontario, Canada

When I'm asked, "Who's going to take care of you when you're old?" my response is, "The same robots that will be taking care of you in the nursing home." —Juls, 49, Cincinnati, OH

*Your own:* _____

### 10) You're Not a Family Without Children

That depends on your definition of "family." My spouse and I along with our pet(s) are a happy family, thank you very much!

Since I got married at 35, co-workers seem to think I'm in a hurry to "start" a family, not realizing you can be a family of two! I must have been irritated at several months of questions, so finally I just said, "So I can be miserable like all the mothers I know?" which, in hindsight, wasn't the nicest thing to say, but that's kinda how I feel. —Jenny, 35, Milwaukee, WI

*Your own:* _____

### 11) You Were a Child Once Too

Yes, and even *then* I didn't like being around them.

"How can you not like kids? You were a child once too, you know." "Yes I was, and when I finally grew up and stepped into the world of adulthood, I found it infinitely preferable." —Female, 43, California

When people find out I don't like children, they often respond with the tired old line of: "But you were a child yourself once!" I've taken to countering that with the fact that I also used to live near Detroit; does that mean I have to like the people there? Nobody ever seems to have a comeback for that one. —J. Asher Henry, 25, Marquette, MI

*Your own:* _____

### 12) Your Biological Clock is Ticking!

I took the batteries out of my biological clock and put them in my vibrator. —"Childfree Chick," 28, Phoenix, AZ

If I do have a biological clock, someone stole the batteries. —Susanne, 37, Sydney, Australia

I sold my biological clock at a yard sale. —Jen, 35, Frederick, MD

*Your own:* _____

### 13) You'll Change Your Mind

No, I'm perfectly happy with the one I have now. ~Happily Childfree website, happilychildfree.com

I am so sure I will never want kids I am currently selling my womb on eBay! —Louise "Louppy" Hart, 24, U.K.

*Your own:* _____

**14) You would make such a good parent**

But they would be influenced by other bad parents and their kids.

Not if I have a child I don't want, and then resent it.

*Your own:* _____

**15) Don't You *Like* Kids?**

I like children—*fried.* ~W.C. Fields

I love kids, *other* people's! —M.R., 45, Lake Geneva, WI

I love children—especially with BBQ sauce on a spit!
—Gracie, 52, New York, NY

"Q: Do you like kids? A: On a case by case basis." From the Movie *Family Man* with Nicholas Cage. —Alysha, 24, Toronto, Canada

I like children, but I couldn't eat a whole one.
—Cool Auntie, 38, Sydney, Australia

We like children as long as we can give them back to someone else!
—"Mllang94," 44, Fort Mill, SC

I like kids, as long as they aren't mine! —T, 37, Simpsonville, KY

*Your own:* _____

**16) The only reason to get married is to have children**

I'm sorry to hear that. I got married because I love my husband/wife.

*Your own:* _____

**17) Aren't you curious what they would look like?**

Yes, but this is one of the shallowest reasons I can think of to bear children.

*Your own:* _____

**18) What about carrying on the family name?**

Now *there's* a good reason to screw up my life for 18 years!

*Your own:* _____

**19) You'll Regret It Later**

I'd rather regret not having a child, than have one and regret its existence.
—Gwen Gillet, 47, Ontario, Canada

I'd rather regret not having kids than regret having them.
—Lisa, 38, Chicago, IL

*Your own:* _____

**20) It's *All* Worth It!**

It may be worth it to *you*, but it's not to me.

*Your own:* _____

**21)  You aren't a real adult until you have kids**

I know plenty of immature parents.

*Your own:* _____

**22)  Children are a woman's greatest achievement**

I wonder what Florence Nightingale would say to that?

*Your own:* _____

**23)  It's Selfish Not to Have Kids**

When people suggest that being childfree is selfish, I tell them I think it's selfish for someone to create another human being to amuse themselves. —Phoena from happilychildfree.com, Texas

To parents who feel people are selfish for not having children: Can you tell me why you became a parent without saying, "I wanted?"
—Gil, 44, Austin, TX

When I am told that I am "selfish" for not having/wanting kids, I like to smile real big and say "Yep, I sure am selfish! So isn't it good that I am not having kids?" —Kara, 33, Dayton, OH

Kid free is not selfish; it's so very unselfish. —Tamroc, 40, Lancaster, PA

*Your own:* _____

**24)  It's human nature to procreate**

That's debatable. It's *animal* nature to procreate, and humans were given the ability to *choose*.

It's also human nature to be greedy. Does that make it right?

*Your own:* _____

**25)  Don't you want to *make* something together with your spouse?**

Concerning people who have children because they want to "make something together" I once read the perfect comeback: "Then write a book together!" —Female, 26, Dayton, OH

*Your own:* _____

**26)  Don't you want to hear the pitter pat of little feet?**

If I wanted to hear the pitter-patter of little feet, I'd put shoes on my pets. —Zoe, 31, Huskisson, Australia

*Your own:* _____

**27)  You're not a real woman until you experience childbirth**

Then I guess I'll have to be a fake woman.

*Your own:* _____

**28) It's not *normal* to not have kids**

When I'm accused of not being "normal" because I don't want children, I use a comeback I picked up on a CF site: *"Normal* is a setting on a washing machine!" —Kate, 37, London, England

*Your own:* _____

**29) My kids are the most important thing in my life**

That's because you've made them the *only* thing in your life.

*Your own:* _____

**30) Your child could grow up to cure cancer**

Do you think Charles Manson's parents said the same thing?

*Your own:* _____

**31) But we could raise our kids together!**

Why, because misery loves company?

*Your own:* _____

**32) There's nothing better than the smell of a new baby.**

Yes but that's only one year out of eighteen!

You need to get out more. ~happilychildfree.com website

*Your own:* _____

**33) Are You Infertile?**

I think when one is asked if they're childless by choice or if it's a fertility issue, CF people should not become offended—see it as an opportunity to explain your choice. Educate the childed. "Look around; do you really think we need more people in the world? Is your DNA that important?" I honestly think that so many people never even thought that you didn't *have* to have kids—it's just what you do next." —Female, 46, Michigan

*Your own:* _____

**34) Children Are The Future!**

Well, the future's not looking good enough to put any of my kids through it!

*Your own:* _____

**35) If everyone chose not to procreate, the human race would die out.**

Is this a *bad* thing?

With over 7 billion people in the world and about four babies born per second, I don't think this problem is imminent.

*Your own:* _____

\*    \*    \*

## Never Fear... Just Prepare!

If you're like me, you wish you were quick-witted enough to come back with a clever quip when someone floors you with a cliché comment or rude remark. Later the bell goes off in your head and you recite the perfect retort. You kick yourself, because you're already home sitting on the toilet!

Never fear. You are not alone. Just be prepared next time. Starting in your twenties and into your forties, you'll hear plenty of people pontificate and preach about the pleasures, piousness and profundity of parenting. Remember, these people are simply trying to persuade you to their perspective. Do not grit your teeth or let your heart palpitate in anger...

Take a deep breath and "X" off another square on your Kidfree Bingo card. Then, politely (or not) present your previously prepared quip with poise and purpose!

# CHAPTER 18

## "Stunted Souls"
### *And Other Childfree Myths*

Crude classifications and false generalizations
are the curse of organized life.
~George Bernard Shaw (1856-1950)

A re you a shallow, selfish, child-hating curmudgeon? I didn't think so. Perhaps one of the most difficult aspects of being kidfree—or part of any non-conforming group for that matter—is being the brunt of misconceptions, labels and generalizations.

Humans fear what they don't understand, and thus are constantly trying to make sense of their world. Unfortunately, many do this by categorizing and labeling, much to the chagrin of the misunderstood group.

There are several myths about the childfree that have developed over the years, many of which—empirical evidence shows—have little or no basis in reality. And, when they do, they only apply to a small percentage of us, not the majority.

This chapter examines four major myths about the childfree, in order of prevalence, and gives a short rebuttal to each.

## Myth #1: We Are Selfish

Selfishness is not living as one wishes to live,
it is asking others to live as one wishes to live.
~Oscar Wilde (1854-1900)

Of all the generalizations about people who choose not to have children, this one baffles us the most. The fact that we are considered "selfish" by parents because we choose not to have children is a widely discussed conundrum among childfree groups. Merriam Webster defines "selfish" as:

1- concerned excessively or exclusively with oneself: seeking or concentrating on one's own advantage, pleasure, or well-being without regard for others; 2- arising from concern with one's own welfare or advantage in disregard of others <a *selfish* act>.

Is it a selfish act not to have children? While the first half of the definition "arising from concern with one's own welfare or advantage" may be true of many kidfrees (myself included), the latter half of the definition "in disregard of others" is where the comparison ends.

Who are the childfree in "disregard of?" Are we being selfish to the unborn child by not conceiving or bearing it? If children that are not yet conceived have souls and rights, the pro-life community is going to have a field day! But no, the truth is, there is no child yet to be selfish against.

You can't be selfish about something that doesn't exist.
—A.M., 26, Cocoa Beach, FL

Are we being selfish to the friends and family who want us to have children? Gwen Gillet (47) of Ontario, Canada, points to Oscar Wilde's above quote and says "it is selfish of them to want us to live the way they want us to live, instead of the way we wish to live." I think Amanda would agree:

My grandmother told me I was selfish because SHE wants great-grandbabies. I said, "How is wanting kids and getting what you want any less selfish than not wanting kids and getting what you want?" She had no answer. I also added "I'm selfish because I won't give YOU the great-grandbabies you want? What?" Jeez, it's not like my uterus is some wish fulfillment station. —Amanda, 26 (American living in South Korea)

Who is being selfish here? Amanda or her grandmother?

Perhaps the childfree are being selfish to society in general. This revisits the question: Is it bad for nations to decline in population? Many argue—for reasons set forth in Chapter 7—that population declines are a good thing. But national leaders concerned with GDP extol the virtues of population gain.

According to a study conducted by Georgia State University economist Ben Scafidi, single mothers cost U.S. taxpayers more than $112 billion a year, including the cost of federal, state and local government programs and lost tax revenue at all levels.[1]

Is it not more selfish to have a child to receive government handouts than to refrain from having one? Many survey respondents point out that procreating is selfish in that it is often about what a parent can *gain* from it:

> People say I'm selfish not to want kids. Hey, Mother Teresa and Florence Nightingale didn't have kids. Were they selfish? Besides, isn't it just as selfish to have kids "because you want them" or "to have someone to care for you when you're older" or to "carry on your genes?"
> —Kathleen, 35, Florida

> One of the most infuriating accusations leveled at the childfree is that we are "selfish" for not having children. Likewise, the claim that parents are selfless is fundamentally flawed. Ask any parent why they had children, and nine times out of ten the reasons will stem from what they gained from the experience, i.e. fulfillment, unconditional love, etc.
> —Kathy, 38, London, England

Visions of "octomom" Nadya Suleman—the one who chose to have eight babies in addition to the six she was unable to care for—come to mind when the word selfish comes up. Who is hurting society more? The woman who chose to forgo parenting and pursue other interests or a woman like Suleman who—by her own admission—chose to have a litter of (health-risked) children to make up for her loneliness and lack of siblings as a child. Single and jobless, she knew she couldn't afford—let alone care for—those 14 children, without others subsidizing her.

So, she burdened everyone around her, including the California taxpayers (who foot her enormous hospital bill) in order to gain attention and validation—and arguably to land a reality show. In the ultimate selfish act, she filed for bankruptcy in 2012 to evade over $1 million in debt she owed to more than 20 parties.[2] (Luckily, the case was thrown out of court.) Obviously, Suleman is an anomaly and not indicative of the typical parent, so it should be stated that she is an *exceptional* case. We only use her as an example of how people can procreate for highly selfish reasons.

Earlier we examined other selfish reasons—besides attention, validation and greed—that people procreate, and these include ego, power, status and self-aggrandizement.

> Many parents accuse the childfree of being selfish, but really, what's more selfish than reproducing yourself? —Kristyn, 46, Los Angeles, CA

There are non-parents, however, who *do* buy into the "selfish" label:

> I'm selfish, and I freely acknowledge that. I think all children should be wanted and loved and I know I could only be resentful about having to subjugate my needs to them. —Juanita Marquez, 40, Cincinnati, OH

Ironically, Juanita's choice not to have a child that would be unwanted and resented is not only a smart choice, but an *unselfish* one. Many feel it would selfish to procreate when we don't want to change our lifestyle:

> I know that it would be selfish of me to have a child, when I'm not prepared to make any changes to my lifestyle. I know I can't have my cake and eat it too. —"No I won't change my mind," 25, El Paso, TX

Perhaps it's a matter of semantics. The term "self-centered" might better describe at least some of us. We are concerned with our own happiness, but *not* to the detriment of others. Brian and I are self-centered in that we like our peace and quiet, we don't want to be responsible for a child's well-being, and the purported rewards of having a child are not worth the sacrifice. One might also label that "self-aware."

## Myth #2: Our Souls Are Stunted

> I read an article that choosing not to have kids to focus on me is a sure way to stunt a soul... Stunt a soul? I guarantee my soul isn't stunted at all, but this is the kind of reaction childfrees get to our choice or circumstance. —"Childfree in Charlotte," 31, Charlotte, NC

While the "Selfish" myth is largely unfounded, the "Souls are Stunted" accusation is a cruel and hurtful one. As one who has always taken great interest in the soul, its purpose, and the ultimate meaning of life (and who has read many books on the topic), I take exception to people—like author Betsy Hart—who say that being childfree is a "good way to stunt a soul."

In her response to the article, "Does Fatherhood Make You Happy?" by Daniel Gilbert, Hart expounds her opinion that even asking such a question shows the selfishness of our American culture, and that the selfless act of raising children is so "noble" it need not make you happy. She goes on to say:

> Web sites and books for people who choose to never have children [...] have boomed and a new term was coined for the phenomenon in the 1990s: "childfree." Again and again, these resources celebrate people, especially married couples, who say they just want to live life on their own terms, and do what they want to do when they want to do it. Yeah. Whoopee. In the end, that's a pretty good way to stunt a soul—and it's no accident it's a growing American trend.
> ~Betsy Hart, "Ain't this America...The kid trap"[3]

This statement outraged the childfree community, which condemned the ignorance of such a visceral blanket statement. Is she suggesting that a soul is not complete without the pain and hardship of parenting? Do other hardships in life—like the death of a parent in childhood—count?

It was not just non-parents who were appalled by Hart's conjectures. Even mothers shot back with responses like this:

> [...] I don't think people who did not want to have children are stunted souls. What an awful thing to say. Some people know they don't have the means to be parents, whether it be physical, emotional, financial, or spiritual means. Some people can't have children. Some people choose to give themselves to something else that calls them: marriage, the church, charity, etc. To generalize and call people without children stunted souls is ignorant. —Posted by "Vodkarella" on the troll-baby.com website

It's nice to know some parents understand us. Ironically, Hart's sarcastic tone of "Yeah, Whoopee" smacks of defensiveness and jealousy, which makes her soul seem stunted.

What drives the need to attack the childfree? Is it fear baked in ignorance and sprinkled with a little envy? Like any new movement in society, it takes time to first become understood, and then—hopefully—accepted. But to say that people who have taken the time to carefully consider parenting, and find that it's not for them, are somehow "less evolved souls" is absurd.

As we will discuss in the chapter on Purpose, there are many ways to lead a meaningful life that don't include bearing and raising children. In fact, some childfree argue that we are more evolved souls. One male respondent, when asked, "What are the reasons you think your friends and family had kids?" answered:

> Ignorance. I believe the birth/death cycle keeps man on the carnal level. To break free and achieve the spiritual, we must be spiritual. This doesn't mean you can't "- - - -," just stop procreating!
> —Trafferd Pryce, 52, Santa Barbara, CA

There are indubitably non-parents out there with stunted souls, just as there are parents out there with stunted souls. I guess the dispute would be: Which group has the higher percentage? That is difficult to measure, and would depend on one's definition of an *evolved* vs. a *stunted* soul.

One thing we do know is that the childfree are thinkers. According to my survey findings and field research, non-parents tend to be well-educated (94% college educated) and well-read individuals.

Online childfree groups are full of passionate people who enjoy discussing and learning about human nature, different cultures, and the meaning of life. Although we don't always agree, we debate issues from how to solve current world problems to simply how to cure the ailments of our beloved pets. Shallow, stunted souls we are not.

Again, not all parents think non-parents are less evolved. Author and mother Anne Lamott has the following to say about parents who label the childless as unauthentic or *un-evolved*:

> Let me say that not one part of me thinks you need to have children to be complete, to know parts of yourself that cannot be known any other way. People with children like to think this, although if you are not a parent, they hide it—their belief that having a child legitimizes them somehow, validates their psychic parking tickets. They tell pregnant women and couples and one another that those who have chosen not to breed can never know what real love is, what selflessness really means. They like to say that having a child taught them about authenticity.
>
> This is a total crock. Many of the most shut-down, narcissistic, selfish people on earth have children. Many of the most evolved—the richest in spirit, the most giving—choose not to. The exact same chances for awakening, for personal restoration and connection, exist for breeders and nonbreeders alike. ~Anne Lamont, author, *Grace (Eventually)*

Thank you Anne. That pretty much says it all!

### Myth 3: We Are Child-Haters

"We don't hate kids, or your kid...We just don't want kids!"
I'm a midwife, so it's not like I don't like babies! I'm just really
not interested in having any of my own!
Natalie, 26, London, ON, Canada

If we don't want to have children, it follows that we must not like children, right? Wrong! (At least for most of us.) This is an incorrect generalization that bothers the childfree community greatly.

> I think there is a certain amount of disdain for the childfree among us from parents. By choosing not to have kids we have been branded everything from unnatural to sad, with a few less pleasant terms in between! Child-hater is one that makes me laugh most, as I'm sure that must identify some insecurities in the parents that have had kids and feel they need to comment on those who don't!
> —Richard Lindley, Nottinghamshire, England

Yes, there are childfree folks (as shown in Chapter 8) who hate kids, but it's a small percentage. According to my survey, when asked, "On a Scale of 1 to 10 (1 = Hate them, 5 = Neutral, 10 = Love them), how do you feel about kids in general?" only about 6% answered "1/Hate them." About

55% answered between 5 and 10, revealing that less than half non-parents surveyed do not like kids. Almost 3% rated their love for kids a full "10!"

Of course there are those among us who bash kids, some to the point of giving the rest of us a bad name. The problem is, these people offend not only the childed, but often their childfree cohorts, like Heidi here:

> I was on a childfree website where I thought I could meet some cool childfree singles, but after reading their emails they were just plain mean about people with children, calling them "breeders" and the kids being called "sprogs." It talked about how awful it is to be around kids, so I opted out of that website altogether. I love being kid-free, but I also like kids (in small doses and when they belong to another person). That's almost the definition for Grandmother (ha ha). And I think that needs to be said, because I don't want to be portrayed as the "child-hater" just because I don't have them. —Heidi Newstrom, 31, Minneapolis, MN

In defense of the terminology Heidi mentions, the term "breeder" is meant only to describe bad or inept parents (not all parents), and the term "sprog" finds its roots in the UK, where it is slang for "child." Nonetheless, there are blogs and groups that use such flagrant anti-child/anti-parent tones that they turn off even the more resilient among us.

The stigma of being "child-haters" was brought up in one online CF group. Do the neighbors think that, because we chose not to have children, we might somehow be nasty or mean to kids on Halloween night? As much as we enjoy it, would we be better off skipping the scary costumes or haunted house, to spare ourselves from fulfilling the neighbors' fears that we might somehow be abusive to their little ones? Even if much of it is imagined, this is a powerful stigma carried by many childfree, as reflected in this post from Childfree Network member Kristel:

> I was discussing Halloween plans with a coworker, and he said he was planning to make a haunted house in his front yard and scare all the neighborhood kids. The thing is, he has three kids all boys and all at an age to have fun with that. He was trying to convince me to make a haunted house too. I said I can't, because it wouldn't come across the same way. It would come across as the "neighborhood-child-hating-creepy-Halloween-lady," since I don't have kids. In any case, I wasn't planning to make a haunted house. But I thought it was interesting, if you HAVE kids, it would be viewed as OK, but if you DON'T have kids, it would be taken as "mean people scaring little kids." —Kristel, Phoenix, AZ

Many people chimed in that they too fear certain actions may peg them as a child-hater, because they don't have kids. Not only do many childfree like kids, but quite a few are actively involved with children and their causes.

Kristel posed the question to our group: "How much involvement do the rest of you have in kids around you even though we are all CF?"

You'd be surprised at some of the responses. Yes, there were those who have little or no involvement with kids and like it that way. But this was fewer than one third of the respondents. There were several who said they have moderate involvement, mostly with nieces and nephews. But over half of those who responded had substantial involvement with kids in their life, including working with them and helping their causes.

First there is Marina who adores spending time with her four-year-old niece and is also a "very active volunteer with the foster care system." (Which she says she wouldn't have time for if she had her own kids.)

Then there's Amanda, who is an elementary schoolteacher for Korean children learning English, plus she has plenty of children in her taekwondo class. When her family asks why she likes being around kids, she says, "I like kids. I like sending them home at the end of the day, too."

Amy, another CF on our list, is very involved in the birthing process and has been a "birthing partner" for co-workers and friends, plus she has just become a "big sister" through Big Brothers Big Sisters organization.

A good percentage of non-parents are around children in their daily work—often in a capacity of helping them—like schoolteachers and children's doctors or nurses. Others enjoy one-on-one outings with nieces or nephews to get their "kid fix." As stated earlier, when survey respondents were asked if they enjoyed spending time with their nieces and nephews, nearly 80% answered either "Yes" or "In small doses."

Perhaps it's a case of mistaken identity. If there's anything we don't like about children, it's their parents. This fact was illustrated on Question #17 of my survey asking, "Why don't you want children?" More than 53% answered, "I don't like the way kids are being raised today."

I don't dislike children, I just don't particularly want to be around their parents. —Kguy, 49, Conroe, TX

Thus, if one need generalize about the childfree, it would be more accurate to label us *parent-haters* than child-haters (although even that would be stretching it). When asking for final comments on my survey, a surprising number of respondents stated it quite simply:

I like kids. I just don't want any. —Tabatha S., 28, Springfield, IL

## Myth 4: We Are Cold and Unloving

Just the stigma of being childfree. I like kids and consider myself one. I actually had someone tell me I was cold hearted mainly for the fact I don't want kids. Or I get the look of "what, you don't have kids? I don't get why."
—Heidi, 31, Illinois

OK, so if we're not child-haters, we're at least cold and un-nurturing—"sterile" perhaps—in that we don't want to bear and raise cute little rug rats, and let them drool all over us and mess up the house, right? Maybe so, for some. I think it would be futile to be a fastidious clean nut while trying to raise kids. But again, the myth that we are cold, bitter and/or unloving is another sad perception. And I was guilty of perpetuating it once.

I grew up next door to a woman who lived alone and never had kids. I am ashamed to say that I don't know her name or anything about her, other than the neighborhood kids deemed her "Miss Crab Apple." She was never mean to us, but kept to herself, and tolerated us being mean to her. We played many pranks on the poor woman, including leaving "dog doo" on her doorstep, ringing the bell and running off snickering, and actually one time throwing eggs at her when she answered the door.

She never told our parents the horrible things we did to her or her yard. Was she afraid that she'd come off like the bitter old maid? (Much like I'm afraid to complain to the staff about the screaming children in our tennis club?) You see, we just assumed Miss Crab Apple was mean and bitter, because she didn't have kids like everyone else on the block. But was she? Perhaps she was an introvert who just wanted peace. I'll never know, but I do know now that we shouldn't have pegged her unknowingly.

Even if she didn't like kids, did that make her cold and heartless? Perhaps she—like so many kidfree—preferred nurturing animals more than humans. She always had a cat, and I'll bet that cat was well loved by her.

When asked what she fears about not having kids, Danielle—who has both pets and a husband—answered:

That others will see me as cold and heartless, selfish even, just because I choose not to have a child. —Danielle, Salem, IN

With the childfree, it's not so much that we don't want to nurture, but that we don't want to nurture a *baby*. Almost 60% surveyed are married, another 20% are in a serious relationship, and more than 70% of us have pets. Perhaps it's our *partner* or our *pets* we want to share our hugs with.

Here's someone who doesn't like kids, but has pets, and has gotten over the stigma of being "evil, cold or strange" by finding others like her:

> About three years ago I found the online childfree communities and realized that I wasn't alone in my dislike of and not wanting children. After that, I became totally comfortable with my choice and realized that I wasn't abnormal, evil, cold or strange. That's what made me the happiest. That, and I'll never have to get up at 2:00 in the morning to take care of a screaming baby who just had a poop explosion out of the top of its diaper.
> —Maggie, 32, Michigan

No doubt many of us don't feel we were born to hold an infant in our arms. But give us a soft animal to cuddle and we feel right at home!

*   *   *

Clearly, when you choose to walk the path less traveled there are consequences. One of those is to be misunderstood and falsely classified by those on the main path. If we choose the path of non-parenting, our task is not to begrudge the childed for their misconceptions of us, nor is it to lash out in defense of our choice.

Rather, we should understand that this is human nature, not be hypocrites by in turn labeling all parents, and give ourselves a pat on the back for daring to make the right choice for ourselves!

# CHAPTER 19

## Stigma and Status
### *In a Kid-Centric World*

Your child doesn't have to be the center of everyone else's universe too.
~Andy Heidel, "Stroller Manifesto"

*" Kids are to be seen and not heard," Dad would say while entertaining adults. "That's right, this is adult time," Mom would follow up. "You kids go out and play." And off we went, to the yard or beyond, only to return if beckoned for dinner or bedtime. It was a win/win situation for both the parents and kids. But that was the 1960s...*

Fast forward to the 1990s, and the pendulum had swung in the opposite direction. Kids are not only invited to most gatherings, they are the center of most gatherings, and are indubitably seen and very well heard. Now, more than ever, we live in a kid-centric society, where parents kowtow to kids rather than visa versa.

Whether this child-centeredness has sprung from modern parents' desire to reverse the way they were brought up, or whether it's due to a glut of new literature and media focused on how to be the perfect parent, is hard to say. But ironically—or perhaps fittingly—it is happening in conjunction with a growing childfree trend.

Many choose not to parent due to this hyper-focus on parenting, but we still have to live day to day in a world that appears to be revolving around the pinkies of modern day babes. Even as society seems to be accepting more lifestyle choices, so is society inundating us with reminders that our choice is not mainstream.

## Abby-Normal We *Are!*

I'll be judged by others as having something "wrong" with me.
—Chloe, 49, New York, NY

Nearly one in five respondents to the Kidfree Survey said they fear they "won't fit in with their family and friends" if they don't have kids, and almost as many fear they "won't be respected in society."

While these may sound like unfounded insecurities, they have much basis in reality. Often parents do bond better with their kids who give them grandchildren. Often couples with children are given more respect than the childless. And, often non-parents are given strange looks when they say they don't want kids:

> One of the things that does bother me when we do tell people we aren't having kids is the horrified look they get, like we have a disease. And it's such a completely foreign idea to them that we're too strange to be around. Or, the pity look when they think it's because we medically can't. Also, when they immediately assume we hate kids.
> —Jeremy Kessens, 28, Waterloo, IA

> It does not change my mind about having kids, but I get so sick of the look I receive when we tell people we don't want to have kids. We are labeled "Different." —Female, 22, Dallas, TX

Are we "weird" for not having kids? Well, if you look at the numbers (4 out of 5 people become parents), it's not "normal" to not have children. But why be normal? I pride myself on being what Igor from *Young Frankenstein* calls "abby-normal." Fitting in with the norm is not always the responsible choice to make, and—to some—the choice can be "reprehensible" when it comes to bearing and raising children:

> The choice to take another life into your hands is an enormous responsibility, and doing so merely to fulfill others' desires for you to have children or some perceived social or religious directive is reprehensible.
> —Mishka L. Rogers, 26, Oxford, NC

It begs the question: Does following the norm render happy results?

> I often wonder why "society" thinks it is perfectly normal to have a couple of kids, be divorced (at least once), remarry, etc. But if you are a married couple, both with college degrees and good incomes, or even a single person with the same, you are "weird" or "there must be something wrong with you" if you have no children or aren't actively pursuing marriage and children. To me it is the more responsible decision to not have kids or marriage if, for whatever personal reason, you are not willing to make the sacrifices necessary to make that choice a success.
> —Leah, "kidfree by choice" in Ohio

Although it's not always easy to be the only one in your clan with polka dots when everyone else has stripes, try not to take it personally when they ask, "Where are your stripes?" Remember, the test of tolerance comes when we are in the majority, but the test of courage comes when we are in the *minority*.

## Second Class Status

I do get tired of being treated like a "second class" citizen.
—Wendy W., 46, California

Several respondents to my survey actually wrote of their fear and/or disdain of being treated like second-class citizens for forgoing parenting. We know it doesn't take a rocket scientist—or even a high school diploma—to procreate. But, for whatever reason, there is usually more respect shown to those with offspring.

My only real "fear" is of always being treated like a second-class citizen, and not being respected for not contributing to overpopulation.
—Phoena, 32, Texas

Our relatives—whether consciously or not—may treat us like we're not as important as our childed siblings:

My husband's parents have been close to their grandchildren and my husband's brother and his wife, as the kids seem to have brought them closer together. Whenever we're all sitting as a group for a family dinner, I really dislike the way I always feel like the least important person at the table. I think it's because I'm not a blood relative and I haven't provided any children yet (in doing so I guess I'd be more accepted). They just babble about the grandchildren, which is fine up to a point (I am their auntie after all), but they don't seem to take any interest in my/our lives. I guess they think I can barely have one since I don't have kids!
—Dairylea, Edinburgh, Scotland

We may even be openly criticized by a society that does not respect or understand our position on childbearing.

I have already had plenty of criticism for not having/wanting kids. People who have children seem to be personally offended that I don't want children, and I think it's stupid that they can't respect me.
—Rachel, 21, Indianapolis, IN

But, we should not let that stigma change who we are:

However, I really didn't want to just pop the kids to be acceptable to others. Why should I have to have kids to be acceptable to be friends with? —DJ, 48, Sydney, Australia

## The Career Conundrum

It clearly is an obstruction at work.
Executives only promote married people with kids.
—Jose Fritz, 32, King of Prussia, PA

Although illogical, some say that not having kids can hurt your career. Both male and female respondents wrote of this setback on their surveys.

I worry that not having children will be an impediment to my career. In sales, you're expected to connect on a personal level with other people, and women with children find it hard to believe that a woman without children could ever possibly relate to them.
—Jessica Donahoe, 25, Columbia, MO

I did encounter prejudice when dealing with clients who had children. Some would opt to advertise with the publisher who had kids in the same school as their kids, and one even admitted it was why they were choosing my competitor. What could I say? "That won't attract diners to your café!" Nope, when the parent bond trumps logic, there's no convincing them.

While some see non-parenting as a clear handicap on their career path, others just fear a general stigma at the office:

Thinking that co-workers may think I'm "weird" for not having kids.
—Dahlia, 40, San Francisco, CA

One researcher found that childless women can even be "vilified" by bosses. Dr. Caroline Gatrell of the UK spent six years researching women in the workplace, and found that women who explicitly choose career over kids are often vilified at work and face enormously unjust treatment.[1] She said that bosses believe they are "cold, odd and somehow emotionally deficient in an almost dangerous way that leads to them being excluded from promotions that would place them in charge of others."

It seems incongruous that people with more time and energy to devote to their jobs are unjustly hindered by clients, co-workers or bosses based solely on their lack of parental status.

## Issues By Gender
### Kidfree Mars vs. Kidfree Venus

The stigma you may feel about never having children may be quite different than the stigma your partner of the opposite sex feels. There are definitely issues women face for choosing not to be mothers that men do not have to contend with, and visa versa. Let's explore a few of these issues on both sides, starting with ladies first...

## *Kidfree Venus:*

There's a reason why more than 80% of respondents to my survey were women. The task of bearing and raising children has historically fallen primarily on the female gender, and still does. Hence, it's no surprise that women who choose not to breed in their lifetime encounter more grief than the men who make the same decision. This grief comes mostly in the form of being misunderstood, labeled and treated differently.

> Sometimes it seems that not having kids puts a woman in 2nd place in society. It's as if we don't have an excuse for our bodies to age.
> —"HyderabadChick", 42, Hyderabad, India

### Non-Mothers are "Self-Absorbed"

In her article, "Child-Free Isn't Too Risky," Philadelphia Sex Advice Examiner Robin Cooper, says:

> There is a stigma about women who do not want children, somewhat reminiscent of the woman who is so self-absorbed that she simply doesn't have time for dirty diapers, whiny requests and play time. But, there is a difference between not liking kids and not wanting to give birth.
> ~Robin Cooper, "Child-Free Isn't Too Risky"[2]

Childfree women are often labeled self-absorbed for choosing not to raise and nurture our own children, even if we nurture other people or animals. Many have jumped to the conclusion that career must be my sole reason for opting out of parenting, even though it's not. I doubt childfree men share the same stigma.

### Childless Females are "Not Natural"

One of the worst stigmas a childless female faces is that she is not *natural*. Perhaps because we are given equipment we don't use in our lifetime (i.e. a womb to carry a child and breasts to feed them), we feel we are not viewed as real women.

In a world that reveres motherhood, some struggle with the stigma of being different. When I asked what they feared about not having children, here's how some women responded:

> That I'll always have to explain why I don't want them. People don't consider childless females "real women."
> —Cynthia Shepherd, 27, Asheville, NC

> I was socialized to believe that being a woman meant getting married AND having children. I am struggling to create my own definition of what a woman is outside of marriage and children. —Robin R., 49, Vacaville, CA

> Not understanding the experience that everyone says you don't know 'til you give birth... —Debra, 41, Elkridge, MD

It is true that we will never feel something alive and kicking inside of us, nor will we share stories about labor pains or breast-feeding methods with our girlfriends. While many CFs could care less, some do, and some have ways of dealing with it. One woman on the childfree network said she is fascinated with pregnancy and childbirth, and—since she will never experience it firsthand—chose to become a maternity nurse.

Many women think it's time to stop idolizing motherhood as the be-all end-all in a female's life. One respondent quoted author Kathy Lette (herself a mother) about the need to end this fallacy:

> "The myth that motherhood is the ultimate fulfillment for a female is the last great sacred cow, and it's time to whack it on the barbeque."
> —Esley, 43, Portland, OR (quoting author Kathy Lette)

### Increased Risk of Cancer

Some kidfree women are aware that not giving birth to a child can increase our risk of some types of cancer. When asked what she fears about not having children, Sonia from Canada replied, "Increased risk of breast cancer." And her fears are not unfounded.

According to Dr. Martee Hensley, "women who have been pregnant appear to be at a lower risk for breast cancer, endometrial cancer, and ovarian cancer. Women who have had children, particularly if they also breastfed following pregnancy, have a lower risk of breast cancer." But the good news is, women who have used the birth control pill have a reduced risk of ovarian cancer, whether they've had children or not.[3]

When weighed against the risks and complications of pregnancy and childbirth, kidfree women will take their chances. As one childfree puts it:

> Having children to lower your cancer risk is sort of like burning down your house to get rid of termites... LOL! —Sherry, Childfree Network member

### Fighting the Female Fertility Issue

Many kidfree women feel that—when it comes to women's health issues—society focuses too much on *fertility*. How will this or that condition or drug effect fertility? From the medical pundits to our very own physicians, the emphasis is always on *fertility*. Here's one of several posts about it:

> Every health decision your doctor makes is predicated upon how it affects your fertility. Every time I turn on the Discovery Health channel there is a breeding show—as if there are no other women's health issues. I am overweight and I get that keeping your weight down is good for your long-term health, but my doctor bugged me about it not because I am at a greater risk for heart disease or something, but because it could affect my fertility. —Therese Lee, Chicago, IL (post on Childfree Network)

The other way the female fertility issue rears its insistent head is by doctors trying to bar women from permanent sterilization. Many physicians are opposed to giving tubal ligations to women without medical cause. Some are convinced a woman in her twenties is not mature enough to make this permanent decision not to have children—even if a woman says she has been 100% sure she doesn't want kids since she was a child. Many young women on our Childfree Network have searched far and wide for a doctor who will perform a tubal on them, and some are still looking. I would imagine that at age 18, Sofia would find it nearly impossible:

> My only concern about not having children is convincing other people and/or a doctor that I should be able to get a tubal ligation/Essure procedure, and my current (and/or future) partner that I'm serious.
> —Sofia Blackthorne, 18, New Orleans/Boston

Doctors deliver babies for women in their teens and twenties on a daily basis. So, it begs the question: If a woman is deemed mature enough to make the decision to give birth to a child and raise it, why is not a woman of the same age mature enough to decide *not* to give birth to a child and raise it?

### *Kidfree Mars:*

Women aren't the only ones who feel the stigma of being a non-parent. Men too often feel like a pariah in a posse of papas. Remember the military wife, Karyn Johnson (Chapter 16), who wrote about being childfree in a military community? She further observes that it's not only military wives who face the stigma; it's *military husbands* too. In fact, they may get it even worse, according to an excerpt from her essay:

> But I'm not the only one who gets harassed about my childfree status. My husband actually gets it worse than I do. I've been told that I'm not a real woman unless I'm a mother, and apparently, my husband is not a real man unless he can prove the power of his seed. Frequently, he comes home from work, irritated because one of his colleagues gave him a hard time about not wanting to be a father.
> ~Karyn Johnson, "Childfree in a Military Community," UnscriptedLife.net[4]

**Non-fathers are not "real men"**

One reason it could be worse for military men is the stigma that you are not a "real man" until you've fathered a child. First, there is the misguided connection between *physical virility* and the *number of offspring* a man produces. This myth is often present in cultures where machismo is a coveted trait. To not father children in such cultures is to be misunderstood or pitied—as if there's something "wrong" with such men. Even in this "civilized" era, male machismo is alive and well, and a large brood is the most visible way to flaunt it. When asked about his fears, one male said:

> The constant gossip from others wondering what's wrong with me.
> —Matthew Ford, 45, Victoria, B.C., Canada

**Only fathers attain maturity**

The second way fathering children purportedly makes you a "real man" is that it matures you. Many non-fathers feel the prejudice from society that their growth must be stunted since they have not taken on fatherhood.

> The expectation/assumption that one will have children is so great that it seems those that don't are thought either to be selfish, lazy or weak.
> —Bruce, 46, Syracuse, NY

In fact, one survey respondent—Vic from Los Angeles—said he fears he is "not mature enough to be a good father." Ironically, this insight along with his ensuing decision not to procreate shows more maturity than one who jumps into fatherhood unprepared and fails miserably.

**Missing out on father-son stuff**

Like women, kidfree men fear losing their friends who become fathers and focus on their offspring. This "bragging about my boy" can also remind childless men of what they might be missing: a rewarding father-son relationship. When asked what he feared about not having children, Ryan pointed to not being able to do the father-son stuff:

> I admit the idea of having a son to do all the cool stuff I wanted to do with my dad but never did is appealing. I also realize that I'm more like my emotionally absent father than I want to be and would probably ignore the kid most of the time. Also, the kid may not want to do the stuff I want to do, which would kill the fantasy. Plus, it's an ego-drive reason. So no matter what, it's a stupid reason to have a kid. —Ryan, 34, Buffalo, NY

Brian sometimes misses that he can't be involved with a son's sports. But, like Ryan, he realizes that may have become an unfulfilled fantasy. We know so many fathers whose sons do not share their interests.

**Not continuing the family name or bloodline**

Twice as many males as females have an issue with not being able to carry on the family name or bloodline. Almost one in five males surveyed— when asked what they feared—checked "that nobody will carry on the family name or bloodline." Although more women are keeping their surnames, it is still largely incumbent upon the male heir to continue the family name.

> My family name is so unique (6 persons in this country), it would be a shame if it would not continue. —Male, 43, Lahti, Finland

> Comment on "nobody will carry on the family name": It irritates me that I feel this way. It's foolish, but nonetheless it nags at the back of my mind from time to time. —Max, 35, Milwaukee, WI

I think many of us—male and female alike—can relate to the wonder of replicating ourselves into the future, like Steve here:

> Not a fear, but a bit of sadness: there is a sort of magic in putting yourself into the infinite future. —Steve, 57, Santa Barbara, CA

**Not being able to find or keep a partner or spouse**

As we will examine in a later chapter, finding a mate who shares your desire to remain childfree is not an easy task. Single males are particularly aware of this. Although I didn't list it as an answer option in my survey, about one in three of all single male respondents who checked "Other" wrote in that they are worried about not being able to find a partner who shares their desire to remain childfree. When asked their fears about not having kids, many males echoed this concern:

> That it would be difficult and/or impossible to find a romantic partner who feels the same way. —Brian, 36, Saginaw, MI

Ironically, those who have found a wife or partner are apt to worry about disappointing or losing her for not having children. In fact "Losing My Spouse" is the only fear M. Toohey of South Carolina says he has about not having kids, and others share this concern:

> That I will end a great relationship (my current one) due to her desire for kids. —Rob, 31, Saint Augustine, FL

> That my wife would regret later. —Shannon Wagner, 38, Brooklyn, NY

> That my partner will grow to resent me for not having kids with her. —Chris, 27, Melbourne, Australia

We can thank our baby-crazed society for keeping these fears alive in men.

**Too young to qualify for a vasectomy**

On a practical note, men (like women) need to contend with laws and customs that may prohibit their attaining permanent birth control. Sterilization procedures like vasectomy are hard to come by for a male in his twenties whom doctors believe may be too immature to make such a life-altering decision.

> My only regret is that the theocrats that make the laws discriminate for sterilization procedures based on age. Too young for a vasectomy, not old enough for lazy sperm. —Russell Tidwell JR, 26, Las Vegas, NV

## Navigating a Kid-Centric World
*Is No Easy Task*

Sometimes being unchilded in a child-centric world feels like paddling a canoe amid a lake full of noisy powerboats and jet skis buzzing all around us. We paddle one way to escape the noise, only to find another boat buzzing us with its big wake. We seek a quiet cove, but can't find one. Finally, we row for shore to retreat to the safety and serenity of our own homes.

Whether or not you feel the pressures to procreate, there is still that little issue of having to live alongside parents and their progeny for the rest of your life. In other words, you may be happy with your decision not to parent, but you still have to deal with those that didn't share your decision.

In an era where they now produce business cards for babies, we are constantly reminded that "kids come first"—and it is politically incorrect to think otherwise. Following are the Top Ten Signs that the axis of the world now spins (however precariously) around the spine of the child...

### 1)  First Question Asked

A much-maligned proclivity of parents is to ask couples if they have kids. In fact, it's often the first question out of their mouths. As if it's the most important asset a couple can have, total strangers are compelled to ask, "Do you have kids?" What's worse is the feeling that we'll disappoint them when we say, "No."

> My husband and I moved to our neighborhood only a few years ago. Most of our neighbors introduced themselves to us and every first question that came out of their mouths was "Do you have kids?" Once we said "No," we were viewed as outcasts and the neighbors now only say "Hi" to us. We are never part of any social activities or parties, as they all revolve around the kids. —Jenny4dogs, 35, Oxford, MI

Strangers don't approach us and ask personal questions like, "Do you have a job?" So, why do they feel it's OK to ask if we have procreated?

### 2)  Strollers on Steroids

The modern day stroller is analogous to the invasive powerboats mentioned earlier. Bigger and brawnier than ever, these "prams" as the Brits call them, are piloted by bold and brazen mommies now more righteous than ever.

Now that kids must be allowed *everywhere*—and since the modern mother is wont to continue her prematernal lifestyle—we see strollers of all shapes and sizes in all public places, no matter how obtrusive.

The "moo" (mother operating offensively) will use said stroller to cut in line when necessary and has no qualms about taking up half a coffee house with her buggy. But that's not the worst place you'll find the mother-baby-stroller trio...

**3)   Babies in Bars**

In point of fact, the modern day mother doesn't mind bellying up to the bar with her baby and buggy. Unfortunately, she also doesn't seem to mind if you mind. I first witnessed this about ten years ago. A single mother brought her hyper young boy to a crowded local bar during happy hour. It was standing room only, and while many were waiting for a table, someone felt they should offer theirs to the mother-child duo.

To make an annoying story short, the bored child disturbed the clientele by running under each table squealing; the mother proceeded to bring him "gifts" to calm him down. First, it was the entire bin of colorful plastic monkeys and marlins (that garnish tropical drinks) spread on the table, then floor, and now rendered unusable. Second, the bartender's bin of cherries was sacrificed for the now-whining boy. Third, I don't know, because I exited with my friends to find a more peaceful establishment.

The trend of babes in bars continues to grow in towns across the U.S. Even bars in tony hoods—like Park Slope in Brooklyn—are not immune to the righteous moms with their demanding offspring. In fact, it's what led one frustrated bartender there to post the infamous "Stroller Manifesto":

> Listen, if you're a parent now, your child doesn't have to be the center of everyone else's universe too. Get a babysitter if you want to go out to a bar, or buy a bottle of wine and invite your friends over, just stop imposing your lifestyle on the rest of us in our sanctuary of choice. You made the decision to have a child and now, like a responsible adult and parent, you have to change your lifestyle as well.
> ~Andy Heidel, Brooklyn, NY, "Stroller Manifesto" [5]

Thank You, Andy! I'm glad someone had the nerve to voice the thoughts of adult bar goers across the country. But, of course, it was not without a protest from parents. This manifesto opened up years of "stroller wars," which are still alive and spirited online.

**4)   "Kids-Only" Christmases**

I'm sure I will tick off a few of my friends when I say, "Please don't send us a holiday card with only your kids' photo on it!" Yes, we love to see how they are growing, changing and achieving, but—remember—we like you too! Last I checked, you are human, you are important, and you are our friends. We miss you! We know your kids are the center of your world, so you don't need to prove it to us. Include yourself in your family mug shot, lest we conclude you've vanished, as does this peeved CF:

> What did we all learn from the Yule-time letters and Christmas messages? I learned people have mysteriously vanished from pictures sent once they have children. —Post on Childfree Network

But what should we care, since we don't have kids anyway? That's what some parents think when it comes to holidays: that they must mean nothing without children. One childfree blogger protested such nonsense:

> A child-free friend of mine had a typically annoying experience this week. She was talking holiday plans with a group of friends at work, when a woman with children said, "Well, Christmas probably doesn't mean much to you, since you don't have kids." Excuse me? I love Christmas! It's my favorite time of the year—and you surely do NOT need to own a rugrat to appreciate the joy of the season. ~RamonaCreel.com[6]

### 5) Birthday Bashes for Babes

When and why did birthdays for tots become such complicated and expensive extravaganzas? When we were young, one or two mothers might take the birthday kid and friends to a pizza or ice-cream parlor one year; the park or zoo the next. They were simple events, planned in a pinch.

Now, parties for pipsqueaks—some who don't yet walk or talk—are orchestrated weeks or months in advance and often entail paid entertainment, catered food, a rented venue, kiddie amusements, lots of kids, oh, and...lots of adults! Yes, in this dangerous day and age, at least one parent of each child is expected to attend the bash—making them *adult* affairs too—which could explain the need for snazzier entertainment. (We have to impress the other parents, don't we?) These bashes for babies are often ranted about in childfree groups.

> **Post on Childfree Network:**
> This is somewhat of a rant about "first birthday" parties for a baby. I never knew it was a big deal, but in my wife's family it's a huge affair where extended family [...] are all invited, and it has even involved renting community or church halls on occasion to accommodate all the people. I just don't "get it" though—a year-old baby doesn't know when its birthday is, or understand why all the fuss is going on, and it certainly won't remember anything that happens or anyone that's there. It seems like it's more of a "show-off" for the parents and adults. (Of course, little Joey's party simply *must* be a huge extravaganza, since his cousin, little Johnny, had this big blowout where they had clowns, dancing bears, etc. And we can't look like our side of the family can't keep up...LOL).

**Response by Andrea:**
I've ranted here about this very thing! My younger sister has a son, and his first b-day was reasonable...only family, a small affair. Then his 2nd b-day came, and she went nuts! Wound up spending close to $1,000 on the party...go figure! I don't get it. All I can say is that I think it's a "keeping up with the Joneses" thing, and it's totally for the parent's benefit of, "Look what I can do!" Jessie had fun, but he also has fun banging on pots and pans, and all he really cared about was the cake and the cheezies!

Speaking of cake, some parents now spend a fortune on their kids' birthday cakes. According to a news story in Australia, "competitive parents are spending as much as $2,500 on edible creations for kids' birthday parties." [7] Are these pricey parties for the sake of the *children* or the *adults*? Even non-parents don't get an escape clause from such affairs, because all nearby adult relatives of the birthday prince or princess are expected to attend.

**6) Only Kids' Lives Matter**

Does it seem there is nothing more important to society than the life and death—and health—of a child? Well, that's because there *isn't*—to most. Only parents and their offspring appear in Life Insurance ads; only "Baby on Board" signs are used to make us drive safer; and the first account in any disaster is how many children were wounded or killed.

Honda has a radio commercial that says that there is one good reason to take your Honda into the dealer for maintenance, then a kid says, "Hi Mommy! Hi Daddy!" Which leaves me thinking, "So, only kids' lives matter?" —Jerry Steinberg, Founding Non-Father Emeritus of No Kidding!

Whether out of political correctness or true concern, the message is, "the safety and lives of children are more important than that of adults." After an earthquake in central Italy, one member from our childfree list quoted an Italian newspaper in her online post:

Pope Benedict XVI prayed "for the victims, in particular for children," and sent a condolence message to the archbishop of L'Aquila, the Vatican said." (From Republica World). So once again, per the media and those they quote, the deaths of adults—old or young—are just not as important. —Brenda, Childfree Network member

Why couldn't the Pope pray equally for *all* the victims? Why does he have to qualify it with, "in particular for the children?"

**7) Pandering to Families**

Tired of politicians and world leaders referring only to "the families?" You're not alone. For more than two decades, the Clintons, the Bushes, and the Obamas have—from campaigns to state of the union speeches—

continually referred to "the families" as their focus. It's as if single and childless adults are not even citizens.

In my Child-Free Zone Australia group, these pandering sound bites—especially "for the working families"—are frequently ranted about, in this case regarding then Prime Minister Kevin Rudd:

> But Rudd is still trumpeting his withered wreck of a catch cry, "Working Families." Which means that the market research is still telling him that there's still enough greedheads out there who respond to his cheap tactics. —Post on Child-Free Zone

In addition to politicians pandering to parents, there are continually new laws enacted that revolve around the purported safety of children—at the expense of all others. Two inane examples are: 1) Limiting building heights, so potential pedophiles could not look down upon a schoolyard,[8] and 2) Ordering park attendants to "stop and interrogate anyone who is not accompanied by children" in the park.[9] Aren't we going a bit far?

### 8) Modern Kids Must "Express Themselves"

How about the newfangled need for kids to express themselves at the expense of others? Screaming, yelling, stomping, throwing food, banging things, running around like wild animals…These were all once considered rude behaviors, at any age. Somewhere in the past two decades these became—according to many parents—acceptable behaviors in a child. After all, the child is merely "expressing himself."

> I have a friend who has a child. This child is spoiled and my friend and her husband think this child is the second coming. Every time I'm on the phone with her, the kid starts doing something like throwing food on the floor or screaming and crying. My friend says she lets her kid "express himself." I absolutely hate it when parents think that their kid is the last birth on the planet. Am I wrong to feel this way?
> —Post from female on Child-Free Zone

No, we all feel this way. I turn—once again—to our "tennis club-turned-daycare center" with a little story of my own:

*One day, while Brian and I were quietly playing tennis, two young boys decided to quit terrorizing the people at the pool and venture out to the tennis courts. The kids were yelling (seemingly to hear their own voices) and started throwing rocks at each other and beyond. We gently "shushed" them. They looked at us in horror like they had never heard "shh" before, but started in again yelling and throwing… We had to stop our game after several rounds of this, rocks even rolling onto our court. We walked over to ask them to go play elsewhere, when an irate mother came storming up. (Finally! Where had she been?) When she realized we were waiting for her to discipline the kids, she shot a nasty look at us and blurted, "little boys need to express themselves!"*

### 9) Every Step an "Amazing Milestone"

At one time, a "milestone" was a major accomplishment or turning point in one's life. Usually limited to a handful in a lifetime, a milestone might include: learning to walk and talk, high school and college graduations, marriage, and/or a scientific discovery or invention in one's field.

Children now have several milestones a year. Did you know that the first day of nursery school and kindergarten—and graduation from both—are now each "milestones" in a parent's eye? Quoting an announcement sent by a parent in an online newsletter, one childfree shared her disdain:

> "Today my son started his first day of school in his kindergarten class. It was a very bittersweet moment for me as a mom. On one hand, I am just so darn proud of him and that we have made it to this amazing milestone in our life." My jaw just dropped as my anger surfaced. An "AMAZING MILESTONE?" What is wrong with these parents?!
>
> This is the same attitude that made me constantly on edge and angry when I was teaching in the U.S. These parents of the last 10 or 20 years just think that every little step their kids make is "AMAZING." I am sorry but a cure for cancer or AIDS or the like is AMAZING. Also, Kindergarten is NOT a milestone. It will be amazing, indeed, if I make it to age 50 without going insane what with all the pro-kid garbage a CFer has to deal with on a daily basis. —Rachael in Ireland, Childfree Network member

I put this pandering to progeny in the same category as rewarding kids for losing. Today's adults feel a need to give every child on the team a trophy, no matter how poorly they perform, to "protect their self-esteem." What will happen to these kid's self-esteem when they are adults and—rather than rewarded—they get fired for performing poorly on the job?

### 10) Hollywood Baby Craze

It doesn't help that our media glorifies motherhood. Kate Gosselin, Nadia Sulemon and Michelle Duggar have each given birth to more offspring than the average litter of rabbits, and have capitalized on this fact to achieve fame and fortune.

Our society makes heroines out of celebrities for having even one baby, and celebrities out of non-heroines for having a litter of babies. We are so baby-crazed that we have created wealthy stars out of disreputable characters just because they are raising more children than they ought to.

Just when we thought it was safe to browse the newsstand, the celebrity bump watch rears its ugly head—or rather stomach—again. Between Demi's pregnant debut on the cover of Vanity Fair in 1991 and Italian star Monica Bellucci's copycat pose on the same cover in 2010, there has been a parade of pregnant poses on magazine covers for 20 years.

Can't the tabloids spare us all and come up with something original? The answer is: Yes, but they won't, because bare bodies about to bear babies sell magazines. We non-parents may never understand why tabloids document the monthly progression of a starlet's growing bump and are willing to pay the Pitts $11 million for photos of their newborns; or even why actresses and singers are lauded for popping out kids between films and gigs, and leaving the bulk of childrearing to nannies.

Apparently, it all appeals to the masses in our pro-natal world.

*   *   *

In a Communications course at UCSB years ago, the question posed to us by the professor was a chicken and egg analogy: "Which comes first? Does media *change* society by what it portrays? Or, does media merely *reflect* society as it is?" Good question.

Does media make society more child-centric by glorifying pregnancy and parenthood? Or, does media merely *reflect and report it* to an already baby-obsessed culture? I believe the answer is *both*. The human function of procreation—however base and primitive—still intrigues our natalist tribes into gawking at it in the media. In turn, the media packages it, glorifies it and sells it in a way that the masses want to emulate.

The unchilded will never totally be part of this kid-centric craze. But—as we'll see later—the pendulum may be swinging the other way. In the meantime, we can learn to live alongside it as best we can. We can interact with the buzz when we choose, paddle to a quiet cove when we seek serenity, or…simply retreat to our kidfree sanctuaries!

# CHAPTER 20

## Breeder Entitlement
### *And the Unfair Baby Bonus*

History cannot look kindly on a nation that can protect its parents and children only by demeaning its childless citizens, by creating one set of rules for those who breed and a different set for those who do not. Freedom and equal rights for one group can never be purchased or guaranteed at the expense of another.
~Elinor Burkett, author of *The Baby Boon*[1]

"All men are created equal," according to the U.S. Declaration of Independence. And much to the credit of our founding fathers and lawmakers since that was written in 1776, the United States has been honing its laws of freedom and rights to ensure its citizens are all treated equally. But are we?

Now that all races and genders have been given basic civil and political rights—freedom of speech and expression, freedom of religion, freedom to assemble, right to vote, right to a fair trial, etc.—politicians have been busily creating new laws that benefit certain groups over others, often at the expense of others. Why? Usually because it looks good to the voting majority, and thus generates votes.

The childless are a social minority, and the majority seeks to protect and perpetuate itself. Thus, those who have children and those who are planning to have children get top billing. With the new laws and tax benefits implemented in the past two decades, it's no longer "women and children come first," but rather "parents and children come first."

Unfair tax credits, baby bonuses, government subsidies, extended time off work, and downright cosseting and coddling, are all given to those who have chosen to be parents, as opposed to those who have not. This is what we call "Breeder Entitlement." And—although some childless are impervious to these inequities—they are a growing concern, and childfree groups rarely go a week without discussing them.

## Work Entitlements
### *AKA: We Pick Up the Slack*

Coworkers with kids don't work nearly the overtime that childless people do—their excuse nearly always being the *children*. I'm complaining mainly about jobs, which are salaried, and the child-laden employees who are foisting work onto childless employees without compensation.
—Beth, 47, Oklahoma

Have you ever worked longer or less desirable hours to pick up the slack for a co-worker who has a child? Or, have you watched as they received preferential treatment that burdens the employer, the company and—ultimately—you? Then you're not alone.

Breeder entitlement in the workplace is a thorn with non-parents, and is an oft-discussed issue in childfree groups worldwide. Besides co-workers bringing their charming but chatty children to the workplace to destroy all hopes of focus for the day, we also don't fancy filling in for parents who suddenly drop everything to tend to the needs of their child, or—worse yet—to take extended leaves to bear a child.

One hot button is the issue of Parental Leave, how it is used and abused by employees, and how there is no fair equivalent time off given for non-parents. It's bad enough that employers must leave a position open for months while the parent is on leave, and that they are not required to increase compensation to those who work harder in their absence; but when we see that parents can—and do—so easily abuse the system, it irks us even more. Here's one conversation among many that have taken place in the online childfree community:

**Question posted on Childfree Network:**
What is the experience you have with maternity leave being abused in that they collect the pay for maternity leave but then "suddenly change her mind" about coming back to work? I've heard that this practice is being abused. —Female, Childfree Network member

**1st Response to post:**
In my experience it is abused. Of all the women who have taken maternity leave at my company only one returned. And it was only for 8 weeks because the company did have a policy where one on maternity leave HAD to come back. Otherwise, they'd be billed for their health insurance that was paid on their behalf while on leave. So she came back to pay it off and then gave notice. We saw it coming a mile away because she made no arrangements for childcare. It really is dishonest as the company keeps the job open and then has to scramble around to hire a replacement. —Sherry, Childfree Network member

**2nd Response to post:**
Paid leave or even unpaid leave could only be fair if everyone got such a leave, but that would really cause employers problems! I'm against women getting time off, paid or unpaid, for breeding. They should plan for any amount of time past normal vacation time they feel they will need. Save up the money so they can afford the time.
—Aimee, Childfree Network member

That's what working women did back when our moms bore children: They planned, saved and asked for a short time off. They didn't complain, because they knew they were choosing to have it both ways. Now that the government has told moms it's their *right* to take a substantial amount of time off work and that their employer should pay them for that time plus leave the job open for their return, they've come to expect it.

No matter how unfair the maternity statutes are for the childless, and how burdensome they are on our business owners, they are only worsening in countries like the U.S., Australia and the UK, as we will now examine.

**Maternity Leave**

Maternity Leave laws in the U.S. underwent a significant change in 1993 with the passage of the Family and Medical Leave Act (FMLA). These Federal regulations require covered employers to provide up to 12 work weeks of unpaid leave during any 12-month period for the birth and care of a newborn child, among other family medical provisions. The law also states that the job must be fully restored for the employee upon return. The law, however, did not provide equal time off for those without children.

In another unfair boon to government employees lately, the U.S. government has introduced the Federal Employees Paid Parental Leave Act of 2011 (H.R. 616). This bill will allow federal employees to substitute *any available paid leave* for *any leave without pay* for either: 1) the birth of a child; or 2) the placement of a child with the employee for either adoption or foster care. Basically, it's a bill to spend more of your tax dollars to increase the parental leave for childbirth or adoption.

Each state in the U.S. also has its own statutes regarding parental leave, often more generous than the Fed's. Federal and state lawmakers are—in effect—treating pregnancy and childbirth as disabilities to be covered by the employer. But many argue that procreation is a *choice*, not a disability, and one that should be planned for by parents.

The inequities to the unchilded are even worse in the United Kingdom where, according to the UK's *Telegraph* Consumer Affairs Editor Harry Wallop, "statutory maternity leave has become increasingly generous over the last decade. Mothers are now entitled to a full year off work with 39 weeks of paid leave." In his article titled "Women without children should be allowed maternity leave," Wallop discussed a study of 2,000 women done by *Red Magazine*, which found that 74% of women would be in favor of being allowed to take a six-month break, or even longer, as mothers are allowed to do when they give birth.[2]

And, although these employer-sponsored bonding sabbaticals are hurting business's bottom line, another article came out the same year in the same newspaper touting that "New fathers should get eight months paid paternity leave," according to Britain's equalities watchdog. "The Equalities and Human Rights Commission claims extending paternity leave rights significantly would make parenting more of a 'team effort' and give children a better chance in life," correspondent Martin Beckford wrote.[3] While this may be true, I wonder if this Human Rights Commission considered the childless rights in this case? We are human, aren't we?

### Flexible Work Schedule (for parents only)

Another hot button in the childfree discussion groups is the assumption that we non-parents will adjust our schedule in order to accommodate mommy's or daddy's new sporadic work schedule. Most working stiffs have dealt with the child-laden co-worker who has to leave early to take their child to the doctor or practice.

Who will fill in? By default, it will likely be he or she who doesn't have children of his or her own to tend to. Well, the Australian government didn't want to leave it to the employer or employees to work out. So, they decided to force flexibility upon the employer instead. In January 2010, the National Employment Standards (NES) replaced the non-pay rate provisions of the Australian Fair Pay and Conditions Standard. Under the new NES, in addition to 12 months unpaid parental leave, eligible employees have a right to request "flexible working arrangements" to assist them to care for their child.[4] This "flexible working arrangement" basically allows the employee to ask the company to rearrange all the logistics of their job, including:

- Changes in hours of work (including reduction in hours)
- Changes in patterns of work (i.e. split shifts/job sharing)
- Changes in location of work (including working from home)

And this flexibility not only applies to those with newborns, but also to parents with a child under school age and those with a child under 18 with a disability. The message from the Australian government is: If you become a parent, we will kowtow to your every need. They call this the Fair Work Act 2009, but unchilded Aussies fail to see the "fair" in it at all.

In their discussions of workplace inequities, some non-parents have proposed progressive ideas to curb the unfairness, such as the following:

There should be FAIRNESS LEAVE or EQUITY LEAVE that allows leave for other reasons such as helping out others, education, traveling, whatever the individual selects, but NOT maternity leave only. That is unfair and untenable. A democracy should strive for fairness to all.
—Brenda, Childfree Network member

I think this is a brilliant idea, as did others in my childfree group: an allotted amount of time for each employee to use for caring for children, pets, elders or spouses—or whatever one chooses. Upon reflection though, I see problems that could make the program difficult to implement and sustain. The number one glitch: How much time do you allow? Let's say the average number of offspring per female is around two. That means countries like Australia and the United Kingdom would have to allow every employee up to two years leave.

It gets more complicated when you factor in that some women only have one child where some women have three or four. Working mothers may go up in arms over the fact that they can no longer take maternity leave for their third, fourth or fifth child (even though the policy makes sense and would definitely curb overpopulation!). Politicians know all too well how hard it is to take away handouts that people have come to expect.

Furthermore, this wouldn't even address the issue of Paid Leave, which is another growing trend in governments today that are trying to sustain falling populations. How much paid leave can you allot every employee in your country? And is this on the employer's dime? (I can see small businesses laying off workers as I type this!)

225

## Government Entitlements
### AKA: We Pick Up the Tab

Hey! Choosing to have a child is a lifestyle. I don't ask the parents
to pay for *my* lifestyle. Why should I pay them for *theirs*?
—Beth, Child-Free Zone member

Are you tired of hearing politicians continually use sound bites like: "It's our job to protect the families," "We need to help the working families," etc? It wouldn't be so bad if they considered you, your spouse and your pet a family, but they don't. "Family" in poli-speak simply refers to parents and their minor children, and they are the chosen group to receive government rewards and handouts.

This coveting of families by politicians is more vexing to the childless than I was aware of before conducting my survey. When I asked survey respondents, "What are your fears of not having kids?" quite a few wrote of their concerns about unfair treatment from the government and society. Here's a sampling:

Discrimination at work, through government programs, socially, etc.
—Phoena from happilychildfree.com, 33, Texas

My wife and I are the constant target of society's "status quo." We are prejudiced against by the taxing governments, as well the very right to refer to our collective selves as a "family." To which neither society nor the government feel we qualify (as a family).
—"Bad Ronald," 44, Center Line, MI

That I will be taxed to the hilt, or face the wrath of a natalist government.
—"Othello Cat, Brizzie," 39, Queensland, Australia

That I will be discriminated against in the workplace, and I won't get huge tax breaks. —Amanda, 40, Houston

Being taxed more than others who have kids without any benefit going to my causes (pets, home, hobbies, etc.).
—SprogFree 4 Life, 38, Oakland, CA

I truly fear the day when the bias against unchilded people (especially women!) becomes so bad that we are denied Social Security and other government assistance, not to mention housing and employment. We already carry more than our share of the overall tax burden, and are subject to other forms of blatant discrimination in the workplace.
—Female, 43, California

An excellent book written on the subject of unfair policies toward non-parents is Elinor Burkett's *The Baby Boon: How Family-Friendly America Cheats the Childless*. In it, Burkett reveals how in the 1990s America saw the most massive redistribution of wealth since the War on Poverty—"this time not from rich to poor but from non-parents, no matter how modest their means, to parents, no matter how affluent."[5]

## Child-Care Tax Credits

President Clinton started his "family-friendly" campaign in 1997, when he launched a massive middle-class tax break totaling more than $5 billion a year. The problem is, it was delivered as a *tax credit for children* and left the taxes of the childless unchanged, shifting the national tax burden more heavily onto the childless shoulders.

This handout was shortly followed by a tax credit for college tuition, given to parents with college-age children. In her book, Burkett outlines the inequities as follows:

> A professional couple in suburban Boston with a six-digit income receives a $1,000 tax credit for their two younger children, a $960 tax credit for childcare because the wife works two evenings a week, and an additional $1,500 tax credit because their daughter is in college, on top of five standard dependent exemptions. But a nonparent in poverty can receive only three months of food stamps every three years because he has no kids, and a nonparent earning as little as $10,000 a year receives a maximum Earned Income Tax Credit of $341—while an adult with a single child in that same income bracket can claim up to $2,210.[6]

That is absurd. Two adults earn the same income, and the one with only one child gets more than six times the tax credit as the one with no children? Even if you believe in subsidizing parents for their choice to bear children, these numbers don't make sense. Are the living expenses for one child six times more than the expenses for one adult? Or is it just a stealth way for government officials to win votes from the majority while propagating the next generation of taxpayers?

The situation has only gotten worse since Burkett wrote her above analogy. In 2010, both the Obama Administration and the House of Representatives proposed bills that would nearly double the Child-Care Tax Credit. The House's plan "would allow a family with two children making $50,000 to claim a tax credit of up to $2,100 for child-care costs, while under current law the same family could receive a maximum credit of $1,200."[7] The House bill also would remove current income limitations, so that *all* parents regardless of income could receive the maximum credit amount on their taxes.

Thus, in the midst of one of the country's worst recessions, the federal government would hand out tax credits to those who don't need them, simply because they reproduced; and, in so doing, add an estimated $2.1 billion to the $3.5 billion annual cost of providing the credit. In addition to being unfair to the childless, does this make sense on any level?

## Unemployment Insurance Benefits

In 1999, non-parents got another whack on the head with a baby bottle when Clinton's congress authorized states to extend unemployment insurance benefits to parents who want to stay home with their newborn. In other words, non-parents pay the same premiums as parents toward unemployment insurance, but parents get more benefits. We only benefit if we lose our job, they benefit every time they procreate, as well as if they lose their job. Not only that, but when they do lose their job, in some states parents get a higher check than a non-parent, even though they pay the same premium. This is discrimination against non-parents. Either one should pay less to receive lower benefits, or they should pay the same and receive the same benefits.

## The Baby Bonus

Although the U.S. government has several furtive ways of rewarding parents in order to gain votes and perpetuate the population, other countries—like Australia, Canada and several less developed nations—come right out and pay parents to breed. Enter The Baby Bonus—an outright check written to parents each time they bear a child.

The Baby Bonus is nothing new to Australia, who led the path a century ago and who still hands out some of the largest checks per child in the world. It first introduced the baby bonus under Andrew Fisher's government in 1912 to purportedly "help mothers in time of need," but also to increase birth rates to ensure white Australians' control of the country.[8] The Federal Government introduced a more aggressive bonus in 2002, primarily to boost the falling fertility rate and mitigate the effects of Australia's aging population.

Much to the chagrin of non-parents down under, the amount of the bonus has increased rapidly since then—from $3,000 in 2002 to $5,300 per child in 2011. No wonder members of the Child-Free Zone of Australia are frequently posting about breeder entitlement programs in Australia.

In fact, it drove childfree Sandra Van Eyk of Sydney to write a post-graduate paper titled "Penalising the Deliberately Barren: An Evaluation of Australia's Pronatalist Policy." Van Eyk postulates that the unstated objectives of the Australian Government's pro-natalist policies have marginalized and stigmatized childless households at the expense of providing voter-driven middle-class welfare.[9]

Sounds bleak, but some childfree Aussies believe the Australian government could be headed for a backlash:

> It's just thinly veiled bribery of the breeders, so they will continue to vote for the party that throws the most money at them. But karma is a bitch; it will (and is) coming back to bite them.
> —Deb, Sydney, Australia (post on Child-Free Zone)

Canada's government sends parents a monthly check for around C$100 (depending on income) for the first child every month until he turns 18. Russia—which has seen its population fall 2.5 million since 2000—is placing TV ads to urge couples to have more sex. Prime Minister Putin plans to increase the population by promising mothers of a *third* child three gifts: better housing, $221 a month, and free kindergarten.

Singapore has a program—aptly titled the Baby Bonus Scheme—that would make a populationist's blood curdle. They pay parents 50% more per child for the third and fourth child, plus offer a "Matching Government Contribution" per child that is tripled for the fifth and sixth child![10]

We've discussed how these handouts are governments' way of increasing the population of future taxpayers—purportedly a "populate or perish" tactic. But is it working? Probably not for the highly educated, independent and entrepreneurial citizens (who appear to be moving from the childed ranks to the childfree ranks). However, these laws do give incentive to the lazier members of society who seek and expect handouts from the government and employers.

When asked, "Why did your friends and family have kids?" a surprising amount of survey respondents wrote that they did so for benefits and government support:

> They wanted welfare and government support instead of working for a living. —Julie Ann, 28, Colorado Springs, CO

> Marketing and Government pressure—we really don't promote an alternative. —Lisa Presland, 42, Cardiff, Wales

> My sister-in-law is 3rd generation unemployed on govt. benefits. (Her grandparents never worked, father had a mild heart attack at 31 and got on sickness benefits, mother worked 4 days as a waitress and then developed yet to be diagnosed "turns" at 18 and never worked again, sister neglected her children and now they are slow/ADD misfits, allowing her to receive a govt. pension to raise her OWN children—I know, it boggles the mind! The sister has also remained unmarried to the father, for increased govt. benefits). My sister-in-law was 13 weeks pregnant on a Tuesday and begrudgingly worked until the Friday of the same week. The children are now 14 and 12, and she still will not consider a job.
> —Danica, 33, NSW, Australia

While we wouldn't trade places with these sloths who siphon from society, we see that—as with Danica's in-laws above—these pro-natal handouts are urging the wrong people to procreate if they are looking for future taxpayers. They are more likely to create more of their own kind that *take* from the system rather than put *in* to it.

> There are too many stupid and/or "entitlement" minded people reproducing...We need to dilute the "idiot gene pool" with more intelligencia with IQs over 80. —Wolfe, 33, New York

If Wolfe's politically incorrect statement above reflects reality, one would conclude that government handouts to breeders are not the solution.

## Social Entitlements
### *AKA: We Kowtow to You*

> It seems most people with kids these days have this sense of entitlement, like everyone else should bow to their will just because they can reproduce. Here's a newsflash for those breeders:
> Just because you CAN reproduce, doesn't mean you SHOULD!
> —Shannon, St. Paul, MN

The above quote is from a survey respondent who wants kids and is experiencing "the prince and the pauper" pinch from those in society who feel their life takes priority because they are parents. Whether it's bringing little Willy to work in spite of her co-workers, cutting in line with her double-wide stroller, expecting unchilded relatives to work around her holiday schedule, or blaming someone's non-childproofed home for her toddler's mishaps, we see mothers operating offensively everywhere.

But they didn't develop these traits on their own. Modern society has been feeding them with unending entitlements. Besides the aforementioned rewards from governments and employers, and the special status given by friends and family members, entitlement is doled out to parents by our schools, our airlines and even our parking lots.

I am referring to "stork parking" of course—that preferred parking spot set aside for the precious pregnant few who can't bear to walk too far to get into the shopping mall. With modern health manuals touting the benefits of exercise while pregnant, aren't we taking a giant step backward to treat these women like invalids? How did our mothers ever manage?

And what about airline flight pre-boarding for parents with children? Why? Shouldn't the noisy, hyper children board *after* the adults? (Note: recently a few airlines did smartly eliminate the child pre-boarding policy.)

Now colleges reward students for getting pregnant straight out of high school. Many offer scholarships for single moms with few qualifications. It came up on a thread about "Discrimination Against Family Status" on the Childfree Network, as follows:

> I received my undergrad degree from the University of Utah. I have a very vivid memory of sitting in the financial aid office desperately working with the counselor to come up with a scholarship for which I might be eligible. There were quite a few scholarships I could have applied for IF I were pregnant or had a child. I was quite upset that, because at 19 years old I had made the responsible choice to not have a child, I did not qualify for a large portion of the scholarships. What a message to send to a teenager.
> —Female, Childfree Network member

Even high schools are propagating breeder entitlement. They encourage teen pregnancy by offering free campus daycare (on taxpayer dollars); and now teen mothers are asking for maternity leave from high school! Here's an example:

> Pregnant students in a Denver high school are asking for at least four weeks of maternity leave, so they can heal, bond with their newborns and not be penalized with unexcused absences.
> ~Jeremy P. Meyer, *The Denver Post*[11]

I suppose—in keeping with workplace Maternity Leave laws—these teen moms will not want their grades to "suffer unfairly" and will demand everything remain the same after they return to school. Soon, teen fathers will be demanding Paternity Leave from class!

## Non-Parents Need to Unite

It's ironic that, although often labeled "selfish" by the childed, non-parents are the ones left picking up the slack for parents at the office and picking up the tab for government tax rebates and baby bonuses to parents.

Most of us don't have a problem with the fact that we are taxed for schools, playgrounds, parks and programs for other people's children. We realize that the safety, education and well-being of children helps society as a whole. It's the subsidizing of the *parents*—often wealthier than us—who *choose* to have children in spite of the expenses that irks us.

Until politicians open their eyes to their growing number of childless citizens (and thus try to covet their vote), non-parents may have to band together to form a united voice against these unfair laws and statutes.

A few organizations have been launched as political spokesmen for non-parents, including Kidding Aside (The British Childfree Association) in 2000, and the World Childfree Association in Australia in 2003. The former has reverted to an online childfree forum and the latter is now defunct. Nonetheless, I am encouraged by new groups that are periodically being formed by those attempting to give non-parents a united voice, including the latest by a childfree man hoping to fight for the repeal of the Child-Care Tax Credit in the U.S.

I was surprised to find, however, that his bold idea was not greeted with 100% support from those in our childfree group. In fact, two made statements to the effect that it would "perpetuate the idea that CFs are selfish, immature, elitist and anti-family."

\* \* \*

This brings us full-circle to a key issue: Because we are a misunderstood minority, many non-parents feel the stigma of being labeled and not fitting in. Thus, we fear asking for equal treatment lest it cast an "Us vs. Them" aura over us. I wonder if women felt this way before asking for the right to vote?

The following Frenchman's perplexity at the paradigm that "parents rule" speaks for many kidfree individuals:

Why should life revolve around sprogs; why should work rosters revolve around parents' obligations; why should an adult feel more important when having a child in his arms? I strive to be honest with myself, strong against adversity and happy every time I get up in the morning.
—Gilles, 47, Marseilles, France

The good news is that—although parents may be given more entitlements in the form of freebies, handouts and special privileges—they can never take away our entitlement to *not* have children!

# CHAPTER 21

## Single & Kidfree
### (For Better or Worse)

I am sticking to my guns & will be CF forever,
even if I stay single forever. I just turned 40.
—Mikinator (female), Los Alamos, NM

A re you *sans children* and *sans partner*? Whether by choice or by chance, being a non-parent and a non-partner—basically kidfree and single—brings with it a new set of challenges. Whether free and fearless or frustrated and lonely, single adults who *do not have* and *do not want* children are a misunderstood segment of society, but a growing segment nonetheless.

At more than 100 million, there are now more single (unmarried) adults in the U.S. today than ever before.[1] More people are marrying late, divorcing or never marrying. Twice as many people today (27%) live alone than in 1960. And, according to the U.S. Census Bureau, the number of married people has fallen from almost two-thirds of the population in 1970 to just over half (53%) in 2010.

Although the number of currently unmarried adults who will never have children is not measured, it is estimated to be about 9% of the U.S. population.[2]

I conducted a second survey—the Childfree Dating Survey (CFD)—of 630 respondents, in order to explore issues that single non-parents contend with. Between that and the Kidfree Survey, I have examined more than 1,200 single non-parents. To deliver it to you from the horse's mouth, I have built this chapter around their quotes, stories and survey answers.

## Seeking Total Independence
### *"Freemales" and Free Males*

I love my freedom and being responsible only for my own life.
—Sandra, 34, Sydney, Australia

Not every singleton is looking for a mate. In fact, some prefer going solo, often for the same reasons they prefer not having children. Nearly one in five respondents to my CFD survey say they are "single, but not currently dating or looking for a partner," and—of this group—more than 90% are "Childfree by Choice."

A "freemale" is a recently coined term to describe a female who chooses freedom over marriage and motherhood. Cameron Diaz is one of many modern celebs who could be considered a freemale, as she chooses an independent life over that of wife and mother. To quote Miss Diaz:

> I love being alone and being by myself. And I'm really good at it, too. Not in a weird "leave me alone" kind of way, but I'm just much more comfortable when I'm by myself. ~Cameron Diaz[3]

My mother (who said she preferred living alone the last 20 years of her life and who confessed she might not have had kids had she thought it was an option back then) was a wannabe freemale born in the wrong era. Today, it's not only more acceptable to be a single woman without children, it's more feasible, due in part to higher education, better job positions and higher incomes for females.

The portion of women who are unmarried in the U.S. has increased more than 10% since 1970, and—as mentioned—the percentage who will never have children has doubled since then. Men—perhaps by default—have followed the same pattern over the years, with fewer opting to be husbands and fathers. I think the term "freemale"—although a play on words for "free female"—could just as well apply to these men who choose freedom over wife and kids. They are, after all, *free males*.

Since about one in four adults are now cohabiting[4]—or as my dad puts "shacking up"—a better measure of "singlehood" is not those who are unmarried, but those who are living alone. With more than one-quarter of all households maintained by adults living alone in the U.S., rest assured you partnerless people are not alone in being alone.

Many partner-free people believe the downsides of marriage or commitment outweigh the benefits, much the way the childfree feel about parenting. Katharine Hepburn, a childfree who—despite a brief tumultuous marriage—could qualify as a freemale, was often heard dissing marriage in her movies and real life quotes like these:

> Marriage is a series of desperate arguments people feel passionately about. ~Katharine Hepburn
>
> Sometimes I wonder if men and women really suit each other. Perhaps they should live next door and just visit now and then. ~Katharine Hepburn

In line with the desire for freedom from partners and progeny is the freedom from pets. One difference I found between single vs. married non-parents, is the ownership of non-human dependants. While almost 80% of married non-parents have pets, only 54% of single non-parents do. It may be that many singles don't have the time or resources to care for pets, or some may just generally desire more freedom and independence from all obligations—human and animal alike.

## The Pains of Being Partnerless

> The government is prejudiced against single people without children.
> —Female, 59, York, England

Whether you are solo by choice or by circumstance, there are challenges to being both partnerless and childless. Perhaps the worst of these are the pity and the proselytizing. People who think you want to have what they want or have will pity you for not having a spouse or child. They assume you are lonely or unhappy—pining for a partner—and might even succeed in convincing you that you are.

But more likely this leads to your defending your position and their pressuring you to change your position. "We've got to find you a man," or "Once you're married, you'll want children." These are common "bingos" that kidfree singles must endure.

Single people—whether childfree or not—are stigmatized in our society. The traditional stereotype of the never-married older woman as the unhappy spinster still lingers, and men feel it too. In fact, Bella DePaulo, author of *Singled Out: How Singles Are Stereotyped, Stigmatized, and Ignored, and Still Live Happily Ever After*, found—through her research on public perception of singles—the following:

> We found that the single people were viewed more negatively than the married people. For example, they were seen as unhappy, lonely, and self-centered compared to their married counterparts. (The one exception is that single people were consistently viewed as more independent than married people.)[5]

DePaulo and her colleague, Wendy Morris, also found discrimination against singles in the workplace and marketplace. They looked up the federal statutes and found over a thousand instances in which marriage was linked to federal protections and benefits. These bennies are further multiplied when you have children, as we saw in the previous chapter. (I've come to find that being unmarried and childless puts me in the highest category of discrimination for government taxes and programs.)

DePaulo and Morris also found that singles are the most discriminated against when renting a home. Realtors and others said they would "prefer to rent to married couples than to single women, single men, unmarried couples, or a pair of friends—even when they all had equally positive references and ability to pay."[6]

With all this unfair treatment from society, it's no wonder single people are reportedly less happy. Studies show that married people are, in general, happier than unmarried. In his book *Gross National Happiness*, Arthur C. Brooks reveals findings from the General Social Surveys that in 2004, 42% of married Americans said they were "very happy," whereas only 23% of never-married said this, and results are even bleaker for the widowed (20%), divorced (17%) and separated (11%).[7]

It's no surprise then that almost 70% of all singles surveyed in the Childfree Dating Survey are looking for a partner. And that brings us to the biggest issue facing most single childfree people: Finding a mate who does not want children.

### Finding a Childfree Mate
*Like finding a pearl in an oyster*

As a single, older male, I find it very difficult to locate, let alone date, unattached women who have no children, and do not want children.
—"Childfree Geek," 48, Olympia, WA

Our "childfree geek" above is not alone in his frustration. More than 60% of respondents to the Childfree Dating Survey rated "finding a childfree mate" anywhere from difficult to impossible. But we know—from our CF groups that are replete with married couples and from my Kidfree Survey of which 78% respondents are married or in relationships—that CFs do find each other and do hook up. The question is: how and where?

Even though one in five people in the U.S. will end up being childless over the age of forty, to a confirmed childfree man or woman in the dating world the odds seem closer to one in 12,000 (the odds of finding a pearl in an oyster). It's hard enough to find someone you have a lot in common with and are attracted to, but when you throw in the "no kids" element, you really narrow your options.

> While I don't want to have children, I would consider marriage, if I find the right person. But I am afraid that because most people do want children at some point in their lives, either (a) the right person will be hard to find, or (b) she might suddenly decide that she wants children, and an otherwise good marriage would have to end. —A.G., 26, Maryland

In fact, when asked, "What are your fears (if any) about not having kids?" Casey of Newlyn, Australia, echoed the fears of many survey respondents when he answered simply, "Not finding a compatible partner."

Single men in childfree groups often lament about how hard it is to find a woman that honestly doesn't want kids. One guy even informed the women on our childfree group that they are at a premium in the dating world, and solicited their advice on how to find them:

> My question is to the single women who are childfree. Whether you know it or not, you are really at a premium in the dating world. How do single men find single or divorced women who are also childfree? I know we can all relate to this. Always coming in last place is no fun at all! I'm darn tired of it. Could the single women give me some suggestions?
> —Pete (post on Childfree Network)

Ironically, several childfree women shot back with their belief that "childfree single men are at a premium too!" And it's true: Just because women have a "biological clock" and are often bred to nurture children, does not mean that men don't get the urge to procreate. My brother couldn't wait to have children once he hit his thirties, and even tried to talk his wife into having more than two. Perhaps the difference is, that men don't focus on it as early and often as women, until suddenly they're ready. The problem here is that a man may date or marry a childfree woman, only to later realize he wants kids:

> My ex-husband told me that he was about 90% sure that he didn't want children shortly after we got together. Unfortunately, he did eventually change his mind, probably because all his friends were becoming parents in their mid-30s. If a couple can't agree on this issue, the marriage is most likely doomed. —Helen, BC, Canada

> One fear I had prior to meeting my husband was whether or not I would find a man who felt as strongly as I did about not having children. A man who would take me seriously and not try to sway my decision. So many times I'd meet guys and they'd swear up and down they didn't want kids...only later did I find out they just didn't want them right away.
> —Tracy, 32, Iowa

Helen and Tracy are not alone, as more than 40% of those who took the CFD Survey ended a relationship because the partner wanted kids. In fact, 4.3% got divorced over it. This is why finding a like-minded partner is important to your future sanity. But again, how and where? I asked respondents for methods they used for finding a childfree partner, and here's a graph showing their responses:

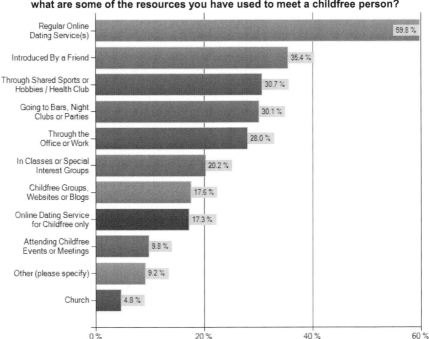

**If you have tried Childfree Dating (either now or in the past), what are some of the resources you have used to meet a childfree person?**

| Resource | Percentage |
|---|---|
| Regular Online Dating Service(s) | 59.8 % |
| Introduced By a Friend | 35.4 % |
| Through Shared Sports or Hobbies / Health Club | 30.7 % |
| Going to Bars, Night Clubs or Parties | 30.1 % |
| Through the Office or Work | 28.0 % |
| In Classes or Special Interest Groups | 20.2 % |
| Childfree Groups, Websites or Blogs | 17.6 % |
| Online Dating Service for Childfree only | 17.3 % |
| Attending Childfree Events or Meetings | 9.8 % |
| Other (please specify) | 9.2 % |
| Church | 4.8 % |

Take note all you available CFs: Online Dating Services are by far the most utilized resource for finding a childfree mate, followed by being "introduced by a friend." This brings me back to Pete who, when soliciting advice on how to meet CF women, was told this by a woman in our group:

> Pete, here is my two cents: My boyfriend, Dan, and I met on Match.com. Online dating is a great way to filter out those that definitely want to reproduce. If you decide to try the online dating thing I would suggest considering women who list their wanting children as a "maybe" or "not sure." Before Dan and I dated exclusively, I went on dates with men who were on the fence about being CF or were completely indifferent about the topic and they were waiting to meet someone and see what that person wanted to make their final decision about being CF. I would think it'd be the same for women. —Darla (post on Childfree Network)

Not everyone has the luck Darla had with online dating, however:

> Out of over 3,000 "matches" on a dating site about 20-50 stated they did not want kids. I broke up with more than one who changed his mind. I went out on dates with other men who I stopped seeing when I realized the only thing we shared in common was our childfree status.
> —Zoe, Washington

Zoe brings up an important point about childfree dating. To be compatible, a couple should have more in common than just the desire not to procreate. This is a common pitfall of joining a local childfree club in which you find you share few to none of the members' interests, including political views, sports or hobbies.

It behooves you to find a friend or mate who shares at least some of your views and interests in addition to your desire to remain kidfree, like these three women:

> I met my current boyfriend online because we shared some common interests. We debated a lot online and eventually discovered we were both bored with the whole family trend that seems to be peaking right now. It was only one of many ways we connected, though. Just being childfree doesn't make you have enough in common with another person to sustain a relationship, so it's important to just pursue your normal passions and interests and be open and find the gem. —Female in her 50s, Texas

> We met at a poetry festival and found out later that neither of us wanted children. —Margaret, Edmonton, Alberta, Canada

> My great success of meeting a childfree partner wasn't in the same office, but was work related. We were both attending the same training class, and we hit it off right away. I was living on the opposite side of the country at the time. We started a long distance relationship, and 10 months later, I was able to find a job and move to his state. —Alison, North Carolina

Since 20% of my CFD respondents are currently in a relationship after experiencing childfree dating (inferring success), and another 40% are still in the trenches looking, I thought I would ask people to rate their success with each technique in finding a childfree mate.

Of the ten resources listed, the one that brought "great success" to most who used it was the good old-fashioned "Introduction by Friend." This was closely followed by "Regular Online Dating."

As compiled from my Childfree Dating Survey, following is a list of techniques—from one to ten in descending order—that were reported to bring "great success" to the non-parents who tried them.

**Techniques that Brought Success in Childfree Dating (from most checked to least checked):**

1) Introduced by Friend
2) Regular Online Dating Service
3) Through Shared Sports or Hobbies
4) Through the Office or Work
5) Classes or Special Interest Groups
6) Going to Bars, Night Clubs or Parties
7) Childfree Groups, Websites and/or Blogs
8) Online Dating Service for Childfree only
9) Attending Childfree Events or Meetings
10) Church

I also let respondents write in their own techniques under "other," which rendered answers such as: school, chat rooms, my own website or blog; SecondLife; singles events; personal ads; common interests; word of mouth; and face-to-face dating. Today, the World Wide Web has become the most convenient tool to meet like-minded people who might be few and far between. It shrinks the world for the childfree.

I met my fiancé online. He had already had a vasectomy. We just celebrated 5 years together. The vasectomy was 10 years ago—best form of birth control ever! —JoAnna, Denver, CO

## Childfree Dating Issues

One of the advantages to using an online dating service is that you can clearly state in advance your desire not to have kids, saving you much time and embarrassment in the dating process. Traditional dating does not allow for this, with the big issue being "When do I pop the kid question?" Too early, and you look pushy or presumptuous. Too late, and there could be some hurt feelings and unnecessary drama.

I discovered that very little can truncate a first date faster than the answer "None" to the question, "How many kids do you want to have?" if the questioner wants children. Also, I found that my interest in any woman fizzled the moment I learned that she either had kids or planned to. After age thirty, it was next to impossible to find single women who didn't already have, or who didn't plan to have, children.
—Jerry Steinberg, Founding Non-Father Emeritus of No Kidding!

Although the childfree do not all agree on when to bring it up, the vast majority (91%) agree it's best before the relationship gets "serious," as shown in the following chart.

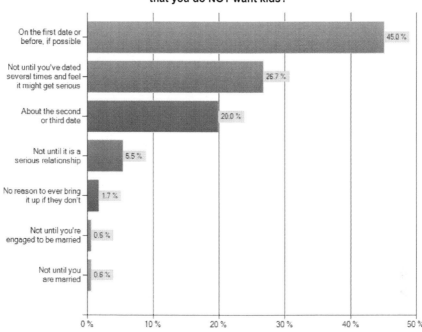

**When do you believe you should tell the person you're dating that you do NOT want kids?**

Nearly half the respondents polled believe the "kid issue" should be broached on the first date. One in five thought it should be brought up on the second or third date, and one in four said "Not until you've dated several times and feel it might get serious." Some reserve the first date to explore basic chemistry issues, while others want to cut to the chase.

I respectfully disagree, however, with those who checked off the bottom three. You don't discuss the huge issue of having children until *after* you're engaged or married, and maybe not even then? What if you don't agree? Look what happened when these two weren't open early on:

> I wasn't upfront about being CF, got involved to the point that we were talking "future" and the kid thing came up. I get called names like "monster" or "deranged"—we both get angry and hurt. That is why saying that you are CF right from the start can save so much heartache down the road. —Lori, Quincy, MA

> I seriously dated a man who wanted children. I had not articulated my CFness yet and I felt like a monster for not wanting kids. Something in my subconscious is much smarter than my conscious self, because I started having panic attacks. I didn't even know what they were because I had never had one. Once I broke off the relationship and embraced my CFness, I have never had another panic attack since.
> —Karen, North Carolina

Putting off voicing your position on procreation may save your relationship now, but all it does is postpone the inevitable to a future—and arguably more difficult—date. This woman took another approach and was adamant about her position early on, which worked for her:

> I was lucky. My husband and I worked together as teenagers, became friends and started dating. When things started to get serious, I made sure I told him how I felt—you need to accept this or move on. Luckily, he didn't want kids either and we've been together for 13 years. —Flame, Michigan

### Dating a Parent

There are people out there. Do NOT settle. If you know you don't want kids, don't ever opt for being a step-parent.
—Katie, Los Angeles, CA

It's no surprise that almost 70% of my CFD survey respondents were against the idea of dating a parent. Perhaps this is because—like me—they've tried this before and saw how difficult it is (whether you want kids or not!). I have dated childed men who were single and divorced, as well as single and widowed, and both presented challenges I had no control over. No matter how I tried, I was always the other woman and "not my mom." You can't blame the kids really, and it's hard on the single parent too.

If you are a confirmed childfree, dating a parent is a non sequitur, especially if the kids are around a lot. When asked, "Would you be willing to date someone who already has kids, but doesn't want more?" about 37% of the "childfree by choice" respondents said, "No never" and 35% said, "Probably not." Not surprisingly, only 6% would be willing to date a parent whose kids lived with them full-time.

Those numbers change noticeably for the "childfree by chance" (not choice) respondents, who are four times more likely to date a parent whose kids are living with them full-time. For these people, this may be an opportunity to parent a child that circumstances did not allow them to have themselves. It's noteworthy, however, that more than 70% of these folks are still not willing to date a full-time parent—perhaps fearing an experience like this man had:

> Actually lived with a woman with 3 kids for 3 months. (I know, I don't know what I was thinking.) She was great to me, but the kids turned into a nightmare. Would never do it again. I'm not saying I'm great or anything, but I would NEVER be with a woman with even one kid again.
> —"Anti-Dad," Pennsylvania

These experiences can be invaluable lessons, however. The difficulties of parenting I witnessed dating single dads were important eye-openers in my later decision not to have children. For those who prefer to learn from other's mistakes rather than attend the School of Hard Knocks, here are two more dating disaster stories:

> I became involved with a man who had 5 children but they didn't live with him. It was still a huge mistake because he got the kids on the weekends so I never had the weekends to myself—and he expected me to watch his youngest child, despite the fact he knew I didn't want children. I vowed never again. —Marci, Maryland

> I was engaged to a man who had one daughter from his previous marriage, and she was the key to destroying our relationship. She walked all over him, mooched off of him, got pregnant as a teenager, and it was just a disaster. My ex-fiancé was the one who ended things, but looking back, I'm glad he did. Otherwise, I'd be a step-grandma at the tender age of 34. —Angie, Maryland

You may be thinking, "It's better when the kids are grown and out of the house," and I agree. However, there will always be drama with offspring, no matter their age or whereabouts. And, as Michael wryly puts it:

> It doesn't count if the kids are grown and gone, because there is always the threat of grandsprogs. —Michael Pearce, Portland, OR

### The Silver Lining of Singlehood

Realize you are complete without a mate.
—GracieAllen, New York

It's not *all* bad being Single & Kidfree. In fact, there are several pluses singletons have over hitched non-parents. Besides being free and independent and owning your own identity, singles tend to be self-sufficient. Singles have fewer fears about not having kids, and almost 30% more singles than married respondents report having "no fears" about it.

Interestingly, only 23% of Singles in my Kidfree Survey fear "growing old with no one to care for me," versus 31% of married people. And while more than one in three married non-parents fear they'll "regret not having children," only one in five single non-parents share this fear.

For obvious reasons, single people are also less prodded about having children. While it seems to be one of the first things strangers like to ask a married couple, a single male or female is less likely to be asked, "Do you have kids?" or "Why don't you have kids?"

When survey respondents were asked, "Do your parents or siblings wish you had kids?" 40% more singles than marrieds answered "No."

Although people may falsely assume you plan to have them once you are hitched, they are at least not hounding you about it now.

Singles are also not quite as confused about not wanting children. Married people are 4% more unsure if they want kids or not (13% vs. 9%).

And lastly, single people have more time to cultivate good friends, and do not have to deal with the dating scene if they don't want to.

> Actually, I think being single is the best thing for me. I have a great life with a lot of male and female friends. Finally giving up the dating grind and just enjoying myself with friends has absolutely transformed my life.
> —Karen (in her 40s), North Carolina

## Success Stories

If you are one of the singles who wants to have a partner but not a child, never fear, success may be near! There are many resources in this book and online to help you in your search. And, of the dozens of success stories told by my CFD Survey respondents, here are four you might enjoy:

> Suffice to say that over the years I've had a great time with some fascinating men, and am now engaged to a loving, gentle, and alarmingly brilliant physicist [...], whose many interests are wonderfully diverse, whose passions are unbounded, who treats me like a queen, and is convinced that I'm the most wonderful thing that's ever happened to him. Needless to say, he's childfree. —Ayelet HaShahar, Oregon

> I dated a fantastic guy for three years, who also wanted to be childfree. I was not aware that he had not told his mother and happened to make a joke about us never having kids. She went pale and said, "Oh well, I will have to think of the dogs as the grandkids." A week later she started knitting the dogs jumpers!!! —Rebecca, Victoria, Australia

> Success: Met my current BF 4 years ago at a club, started dating, talked a lot, discovered he might want kids, asked him point blank, he said no, he didn't and we've been happy ever since with our 2 cats. —Sarah, Salt Lake City, UT

> My last three relationships were with childfree men and I wasn't even deliberately looking! The guys I dug just happened to be childfree. I wonder if they give off vibes? My current sweetie has told me he had no idea there was even a childfree movement; he just thought all women wanted kids. Just hang in there and keep being true to yourself. I've been with this magnificent man for five glorious years, and if I'd stuck with my first ex who wanted kids, I'd be so unhappy right now! —Artemis, Boise, ID

With all the studies showing single people as slightly unhappier than those in relationships, it should be noted that the Kidfree Survey found only a fraction of difference. When asked, "Are you happy being kidfree?" only 1% more singles answered "No" than couples. An impressive 96.1% of all singles said "Yes" they are happy being kidfree.

\*   \*   \*

I'll close this chapter with words of wisdom and support to single non-parents from ten non-parents who took my Childfree Dating Survey:

Don't be afraid to be single. —Lisa, Ontario, Canada

Good luck. Find happiness in yourself and in your friends & family first, and make yourself a stronger and better person in the meantime while you are waiting for that special person to come along. —Kathleen, Florida

Don't compromise. You will only make yourself and your partner miserable if you give in. There are CF people out there, so keep looking until you find one. —Erik, Jacksonville, FL

Stay true to yourself. —Alicia, New York

Never settle for a lifestyle you know doesn't fit you.
—Susan Banks, Dallas, TX

Be clear up front. Don't hope things will change.
—Colliehound, Queensland, Australia

Even if finding a childfree partner seems difficult, that is no reason to give up. Not everyone has, or wants, children. —Magickman, Minnesota

There are more of us out there than you might think; patience and perseverance are essential! —Amber, Portland, OR

Just enjoy your journey, and see where it takes you.
—Male, London, England

Be true to yourself, be honest from the beginning, and be grateful that you know exactly what you want in life! —Brit, Chicago, IL

Don't give up. It can be extremely frustrating when searching for someone who shares your desire for a childfree lifestyle, but rest assured they're out there and the numbers are only increasing!
—Tommy Blanks, New York

If I were to summarize the advice from fellow CFs, I would say first and foremost: Make yourself complete without a mate. Then if you choose to find a partner, be patient, don't compromise and don't give up—they are out there. Enjoy the journey.

And, if you *do* find someone, be honest up front with yourself and your partner. Because, if you're not, you may find yourself in a serious dilemma that we'll discuss right now...

# CHAPTER 22

## What If We Don't Agree?
### *When One Wants and One Doesn't*

Having children is a life-altering decision, and it is one decision
on which it is critical that a couple agree. I would never expect
someone who wanted children to sacrifice that dream for me,
just as I would never sacrifice my childfreedom for anyone.
~Julie Nisley, excerpt from "The K Word"

So you didn't discuss having kids before you got hitched, and now your significant other wants them and you don't? Or, worse yet, you did discuss it and both agreed—only to find that one changed his or her mind later? Of all the kidfree dilemmas, this could be the toughest. But if you are in this quandary, you are not alone, as more and more couples are facing it now that "childfreedom" is on the rise.

When one wants children and the other doesn't, there is no seemingly easy solution. This is an oft-discussed issue in childfree groups. In fact, many non-parents first discover the childfree movement when they are in this predicament and search online for a support group.

Dozens of new members have introduced themselves to the group by sharing their situation and seeking support and advice from veteran CFs. The advice given is not always warm and fuzzy, nor is it necessarily what they want to hear...

**Question posted on Childfree Network:**
I am in a long-term relationship and the issue of children is coming up again. My partner really wants kids. I do not. Has anyone come up with a way to deal with this and maintain the relationship? Thanks. —Lydia

**Response posted on Childfree Network:**
I'm afraid the kid issue is one of the few true deal-breakers, something that there really is no way to compromise on. You either have a kid and give up the life you want and get angry and resentful, or you don't have a kid and your partner gives up the life s/he wants and gets angry and resentful. Either way, it doesn't bode well for the relationship in the long term. Sorry there's not a better answer. —Maryellen, 48

I agree with Maryellen's advice above, with one caveat: that both partners have thoroughly thought through the issue, know what they want, and are positive of their positions. Don't just end a perfectly good relationship without first examining your means and motivations on the kid issue.

## What Are Your Motivations?

Self-help books proclaim, "You have the answer, just look inside you." However, it's not that easy to separate gut instincts from motivations ruled by fear and ego. Many people jump into parenthood for reasons based on fear and ego (i.e. they're afraid to buck the trend or fear growing old alone). Likewise, many childfree may shy away from parenthood due to fear and ego (i.e. the fear of commitment or the desire to stay young). But at least in the latter case, you are hurting no one but yourself.

One technique couples can use to explore their own inner truth is to make a list of "Why I Do or Don't Want to Be a Parent." Study these reasons. Are these good reasons? Let's say she thinks she wants to have children. Does she have a burning desire? Or is it because her best friend is begging her to join her in motherhood? Is she doing it to please her mom who wants grandkids? Or is it because she doesn't want to be the only one in her group without kids?

Likewise, if the husband wants them, is it because he wants to create a "mini-me" or carry on the family name? Is it because he fears he won't be seen as a "real man" until he's responsible for a wife and kids? Does he expect most of the childrearing to be done by his wife? Or, does he really love kids and want to spend time with his future children?

On the opposite page is a list of Shaky vs. Solid Motivations one might have for procreating. Check which ones apply to you and have your partner do the same.

**Shaky Motivations to Procreate:**

___ I want to carry on the family name (ego)

___ I want to have a mini-me (ego)

___ I want to fit in with my friends or siblings who have kids (ego)

___ I don't want to be the only one in my group without kids (fear)

___ I don't want to upset my parents or family (fear)

___ I don't want to be lonely when I grow older (fear)

___ I won't be seen as a *real* man or a *real* woman until I am a parent (fear/ego)

**Solid Motivations to Procreate:**

___ I have a strong urge or drive to be a parent

___ I love being around children for long periods of time

___ I am willing to work hard to be a good parent

___ I welcome going from a "couple" to a "group" situation at home

___ I embrace the lifestyle changes that raising children will bring

___ I accept that my child may be born with defects and/or not turn out the way I'd like

___ The sacrifices of being a parent are all worth it to me

You can check all seven shaky motivations ruled by fear and ego and still be a good parent. But, you must also check all seven solid motivations in order to be a good parent. Any unchecked on the lower half above? You might not truly want to parent.

## What Are Your Means?

Let's say one spouse has discovered his or her motivations are worthwhile, and he or she truly has a burning desire to have a child and be a parent. I suggest they make one more list: "Why I/We Would Make Good Parents." Then answer the following six questions:

- Can we afford them, or are we struggling now?
- Do we have the time for them, or would we have to put them in daycare?
- Is our home/neighborhood/school safe and adequate for raising a child?
- Is our relationship strong enough to withstand the test of parenthood?
- Are we each mentally and physically healthy enough to bear and raise children?
- Are we both young and energetic enough for the 18+ years of 24/7 responsibility?

I would bet the majority of parents never ask themselves these questions, nor consider their real motivations before popping out children. Yet, doesn't it seem basic that parents should have both the *means* and the *motivation* in order to be good parents?

Suppose one partner does all this inner searching, list making, book reading, etc., and his or her gut says, "Yes! I still want kids, no matter what!" Well, if their partner doesn't want them, the "no matter what" consists of ending the relationship. Period.

### "I Fear Losing my Spouse"

I fear that I will lose my partner/spouse because he wants them.
—Gala van Moskou, 29, Maryland

According to the Kidfree Survey, many childfree fear losing their spouse or significant other over the kid issue, because—while their partner may be undecided or leaning toward having them—they know they don't want them and are not willing to compromise on the issue. When asked, "What are your fears about not having children?" one non-parent answered:

The only fear I have regarding not having children is related to the problems it causes in relationships. I am seven years into a relationship with a man who, after being somewhat unsure on the subject (leaning more toward wanting them than not), has decided that he DOES want children and I worry that this will be the eventual end of us.
—Female, 24, Sedro Woolley, WA

And, it probably will be the end of them if he doesn't change his mind, because it doesn't sound like she's changing hers. And it sounds like she knows better than to sway him to suit her needs.

### The Rising Role Reversal

I fear that my partner will be disappointed that he never got
the opportunity to be a father or have a family like he had.
—Female, 25, Pittsburgh, PA

As cliché would have it, it is the woman who pines for marriage and babies, and the man who is dragged to the altar and ultimately concedes to starting a brood with her. Well, not so anymore, as this respondent attests:

I went out on a first date with a guy that knew I didn't want children. He proceeded throughout the night to tell me that I would make gorgeous babies and that he felt his job was to try and persuade me to have them. It was like he was trying to convert me like the door to door religious nuts!
—Tasha Mirone (in her 30s), New Jersey

Increasing numbers of women are favoring the life of career, travel and romance, over a life of drool, diapers and mini-vans—and for good reason. Career or not, women are still expected to be the primary caregivers, and studies have found (as we'll explore later) that the happiest group of women are those who are married and childfree.

Conversely, there are many men out there who love kids, and welcome the responsibilities and lifestyle changes that fatherhood brings. In a *Men's Health* essay, "Do You Want Kids? He wants kids. She doesn't," Larry Smith illustrates this increasingly common role reversal in his personal story of being a wannabe daddy:

> "You have it so good." This is what friends have been telling me for the past 7 years since I started dating Piper, the woman who recently became, for lack of a better term, my fiancée. Five seemingly innocuous words describing the evidently enviable situation surrounding my fiancée's views on spawning (as in: Let's not). Yet I promise you, I don't have it so good. When the love of your life isn't pushing you to impregnate her, your buddies declare her Woman of the Year. But you're left having to make some incredibly adult decisions that even a man who's lived and loved for more than 3 decades thought would be—somehow, some way, by somebody—made for him. Like: Am I willing to let the family name die on my watch? ~Larry Smith, *Men's Health*[1]

While it's good to know Smith is not willing to stay childless in order to be "cool" with his pals (ego), it's scary to see that one of his main desires for having children is to carry on his family name. The only other positive he mentions about having kids is "the fun of making goofy faces," which certainly won't last 18 years.

Motivations aside, Smith says, "I can't get this notion of daddy destiny out of my head," and he ponders the idea of one day leaving her to "find a younger woman who wanted kids." It's no wonder then that many women, when asked, "What are your fears of not having children?" answer either "That I will disappoint my husband," (Marlis, 32, Michigan) or "That my partner will change his mind and leave me to have kids with another woman" (Rebecca, 32, Alexandria, VA).

Some men choose to stay with their wives in spite of their desire to have kids, which can weigh on the wife's conscious:

> The only possible regret (not fear) I have is disappointing my husband, who wanted kids at one time when he was younger, but we both know I would have been a terrible mother and he's never pressured me to have kids. Otherwise, I have no personal regrets about my decision whatsoever and am very happy with it. —Juanita Marquez, 40, Cincinnati, OH

## What if One Changes His/Her Mind?

I worry about my husband changing his mind,
and us getting divorced over it.
—Janet, 29, Ledyard, CT

In addition to worrying that they will disappoint their spouse if they don't have kids, many survey respondents said they feared their spouse might change his or her mind. Even if you're emphatic up front that you don't want children, there is not much you can do to prevent a spouse from changing his or her mind *later* about having children.

People will often say what you want to hear in the beginning of a relationship, only to realize later they weren't being true to themselves. Or perhaps the issue didn't seem important at the time, so they hadn't completely thought it through yet. Here's a case where the woman fears her husband is simply "going along with her now" to appease her:

I worry that my husband is simply going along with me because he wants me to be happy. I fear he, at some level, still might want children and if he were to change his mind I would fear for the future of our relationship.
—Melissa Romsos, 32, Tucson, AZ

Apparently, changing one's mind about procreating is quite common, because many respondents to the survey had already experienced this roadblock in past relationships, leading them to divorce. Bridget even fears it will happen a second time:

I fear that my current spouse will (like my first husband) change his mind and want his own offspring, and leave me.
—Bridget, 37, Houston, TX

Although more women than men reported this fear on the Kidfree Survey, there are no statistics proving one gender more fickle than the other on the "kid issue." Some say men take longer to feel the urge to settle down and procreate, but more male than female respondents (45% vs. 39%) to my CFD Survey reported they had stopped dating, ended a relationship or divorced a partner because they wanted children.

Either way, when one does change his or her mind about procreating, it can have a devastating effect on the relationship. It must either come to a crashing halt, or one must compromise his or her own desires in order to fulfill the partner's. Neither option is ideal. The question is: Which is smarter? A painful break now, or a lifetime of compromise?

## The Consequence of Compromise

I fear making my wife sad, who wanted kids before we met and whom,
I believe, I have essentially talked into not having them.
—Josh Fost, 37, Salem, OR

Whoops, that's a no-no, Josh! Talking someone into or out of having kids could have serious repercussions. Have you ever resented somebody for trying to talk you out of something you really wanted, only to later think, "I never should have listened to them?"

It's one thing when a person comes to a realization on one's *own*, without coercion. But when a person goes against his or her own dreams to conciliate another, not only can it drive a wedge between them, there is the risk that the object denied will be magnified in importance. She may idealize what life *would have been* had she had children. Every TV ad showing a happy couple playing with their kids on the lawn—rolling around in sheer ecstasy—will remind her of what *could have been*.

The reality may be that family life is not the rosy picture painted by the life insurance ad, but she'll never know that. She'll always wonder what she's missing. And you'll always be the antagonist that kept her from it (if she doesn't leave you first).

Of course, there's a possibility that Josh's wife can transform into a true "kidfree"—by soul-searching, making lists, reading childfree books, observing unhappy parents—and will one day thank Josh for talking her out of motherhood. But it is a huge risk to take, and may not work out.

When Brian and I began exploring whether or not to have kids, the one thing we did not want the other to do was compromise their dreams. Clearly, if one of us truly wanted them and the other did not, we would have to go our separate ways. We knew it would not be fair—or prudent—for one of us to concede on the all-important issue of childbearing in order to please the other.

Having said that, a partner can act as an "instigator of revelation" by gently prodding the other to seek their own truth, which may already lie within them. For example, I had always thought I would have kids someday (but kept putting it off), and Brian was the first partner who—lukewarm at best about having kids—prompted me to soul search for the answer of whether I really wanted to be a parent or not.

Unlike the 53% of childfree in my survey who say they "never" wanted to have children, I am in the category of *thought I would some day, turned down many opportunities, and finally discovered my inner truth*: I don't have a strong desire to be a parent.

I have to credit both Brian and my "ticking biological clock" with finally reaching this discovery. Who knows, if Brian had pressured me to have kids, I might have either run for the hills like I did with those other wannabe papas, or I'd be barefoot, pregnant and anxiety-ridden! Here is the case of one frustrated mother who compromised for her husband:

> I have a childfree friend that went to visit her neighbor who has 3 small children. The neighbor had my friend hold her baby while she dealt with one of her other children. The neighbor asked my friend if holding her baby made her want one of her own. My friend flat out said "no." Then the mother started crying and pouring her heart out to my friend. The mother confessed to not wanting all these children; that her husband wanted to have children, not her. She said she wanted to have an abortion the first time she got pregnant as well as the third time.
> —Psylocke, 35, Houston, TX

Imagine being saddled with three children for eighteen years, when you didn't want even one to begin with! While I blame the husband for his selfish disregard for his wife's wishes, I also blame the wife for allowing herself to be put in that situation to begin with. She could have stood for what she believed in, rather than become a life-long martyr.

Then there's the "milquetoast man," like this CF woman's ambiguous husband whose words say one thing and actions say another:

> I fear that I may have to leave my current partner (as much as I love him) if he changes his mind and decides that he wants children. He would certainly make a good father. This is the one thought that makes me sick to my stomach with worry sometimes. I know I would have to leave him, and it would be very painful. Sometimes he says things without realising, like "If I were a dad..." Very blasé. It puts me on tenterhooks. He knows I don't want children, and he says he is fine with it. But deep down I have my doubts about him. So much so, that I think of getting a tubal so he knows there is not even a chance of kids happening with me.
> —Ann G., 29, Greater Manchester, England

That's actually not a bad idea Ann has. Why not make it permanent? At least it will force the issue to a head, instead of possibly drawing it out for years. The mere mention of getting a tubal could prod him into protest. If it does, you'll know where he stands on the issue. And if he waits until after you get it to leave you, at least you can move on with your life—with a surefire prevention of attracting any more wannabe dads!

## Making the Painful Break

I was married for a few years, so I was curious about other childfree marriages. Unfortunately my husband desperately wanted children, so we are divorced now.
—Pat, 41, Auckland, New Zealand

Although many people—probably more than we know of—give in to their partner's wish to procreate or not to procreate (perhaps seeing it as an altruistic move), it is arguably not the smartest decision. Childfree people are keenly aware that it is important to be fully committed to being a parent before having a child, and this is why many of us choose not to. This credo holds true for not just the mother, but for both parents.

Raising a child with a spouse who is neutral or disinterested in it could create an untold burden on you and/or resentment in them. Often the best solution for both parties—and the unborn child—is to dissolve the relationship instead.

I'm worried my husband may decide he really wants kids (his opinion on them is "definitely not now") and divorce me over it. We've been together 7 years. He never especially wanted kids before, but with his family nagging us about it all the time it's got him considering it.
—Charlotte, U.S. citizen living in Germany

Some are aware that they may lose their spouse over not having kids, but are resigned to the fact, as it beats the alternative of having an unwanted child:

I fear losing my husband, but I have dealt with that and would rather lose him than have a child. —"JustduckyCF," 24, Nebraska

If you are contemplating divorce or a painful breakup with someone who wants kids, there are those who can empathize. More than one in five of my CFD respondents say they have divorced and/or ended a serious relationship with a partner who wanted children.

My former wife and I promised each other to remain childfree permanently. We married and lived a happy childless life. But then my wife's biological clock struck, and she divorced me because I had a vasectomy. —arzamas70@yahoo.com (male in his late 30s), USA

Told my Ex Hubby for 3 years before we got married "no kids." He said OK. Three years AFTER my tubal ligation that (being military) he had to sign for, he asked me when we were going to have kids, begged me to untie or adopt. Turned out he was hoping I would change my mind. Nope, we divorced. I have been with my 10-year-younger CF man for 10 years. Met him through a common hobby. —DeeAnnR, 56, Atlanta, GA

As cliché would have it: *When one door shuts, another door opens...*

### There *Can* Be a Happy Ending

Although a relationship can end over the kid issue, it does not have to end in tragedy. In absence of illicit affairs and child custody battles, a relationship—like Jerry's below—can end on good terms for both parties:

**Question posted on Childfree Network:**
Would any of you who have been involved in otherwise wonderful romantic relationships, only to have them end because they wanted kids and you didn't—and then later went on to find someone even *better*—mind sharing your story? I need some cheering up, even though I walked into the aforementioned situation with what I *thought* were open eyes. Sigh... —Marina

**Response posted on Childfree Network:**
I was married for five years, until my wife decided that she wanted children after all, and we reluctantly went our separate ways. We respected each other enough not to try to prevail upon the other; we also knew that if one succeeded in convincing the other, it would probably result in dissatisfaction with the life that one had been forced into, and animosity against the other. She has since remarried and is the happy, but busy, mother of two; and we are still good friends. I, too, have remarried, and my wife and I have a cat and three dogs. I guess people who can't have pets have kids (hey, just kidding!). Sharon and I were able to find a compromise on every issue that arose—whether it was which restaurant we would go to, which car we would buy, or where we would live. Unfortunately, the issue of children offers no compromise. One would have been too many for me, and none wouldn't have been enough for her. —Jerry Steinberg, Founding Non-Father Emeritus of No Kidding!

\*     \*     \*

As Jerry's story proves, there can be a happy ending for both partners, even when they have to part ways. When both are honest with themselves and each other about what they truly want, and don't expect or allow the other person to compromise, they will both be happier in the long run.

She has now met a man who wanted kids and they are living happily as a family. He has met a childfree woman and they are living happily as a family (with their pets). They both have prevented a lifetime of resentment and living with the dreaded "Only if..."

You can't control whether your partner changes his or her mind down the road, but what you can do to prevent any future calamities is to:

Be honest with yourself and your partner. —Tilly, South Australia

And...

Don't give in. Don't back down. Stand up for your beliefs!
—Julie, California

# —PART III—

# THE GOOD STUFF
## *Purpose, Happiness and Kidfree Resources*

# CHAPTER 23

## Finding Purpose
### *Beyond Procreation*

Purpose is what gives life a meaning.
~Charles H. Parkhurst (1842-1933), social reformer

"What do you fear the most?" Larry King asked Oprah on his talk show in 2006. "I have a deep fear. I have a deep fear of not fulfilling my potential on earth," Oprah answered. I leaned forward and raised the volume to hear more:

KING: You don't think yet that you've fulfilled...

WINFREY: No, I definitely do not think I've fulfilled it.

KING: So you're a failure?

WINFREY: I'm not a failure, but I don't feel that I have used my life to the highest good. I feel like the television show was the foundation for doing other things in the world, and that, you know once—I'm 52, and something happens to you around 50, I think, when you realize you don't have as much time left as you had had. And so my fear is not using what I have to the greatest and highest order.[1]

While Larry might not have grasped Oprah's concern, I—being an able-bodied, kidfree woman near 50—knew exactly what she meant. I fear time will run out before I use what I have to the greatest and highest potential. It may sound abstruse to some, but finding and fulfilling my higher purpose in life is a very real and present goal of mine. The problem is: Unachieved goals turn into nagging burdens as we get older.

What is your life purpose? Do you have one? Do you care? Some believe that merely finding happiness is purpose enough in life. But others feel we are put on this earth for a greater purpose, beyond our own happiness and well-being. Whether from an inner knowing or a conscious sense of duty, we feel a need to—in one way or another—do our part to make the world a better place before we die.

While some may disagree, I believe that raising a child to be a happy and healthy human being in this world is not only a huge achievement, but is—in itself—an admirable purpose in life. This is partly why I struggle with the "purpose" issue. Some childfree know from a young age what their purpose is, and know that it is not to parent. These people are fortunate to have been more directed and focused in life. The rest of us have been defining—and redefining—ourselves as we go.

When asked about their fears of not having children, one in six survey respondents answered, "That I will lack purpose or fulfillment in life." I share this fear, not because I believe there are no worthy purposes beyond procreation, but to the contrary, because there are so many. It's a challenge to *find* one's own purpose and then actually *achieve* it before it's too late.

The fact that we non-parents don't have offspring soaking up our spare time and energy—I believe—puts an even greater onus on us to help others and our world, to the extent of our ability and resources. In addition to the proverbial "finding a cure for cancer"—purpose comes in many forms, from making people laugh to protecting the planet.

### Fretting Fulfilment

Fear: That I would not get to experience the fulfilment,
joy and love of having children.
—Dr. Laurie Bolt, 44, Montecito, CA

Although the above survey respondent reports she's "not sure" if she wants kids, I think even the confirmed childfree sometimes share the fear she expresses: that they are missing out on the joy, love and fulfillment of having children. The definition of "fulfillment" according to the Oxford American dictionary is: "satisfaction or happiness as a result of fully developing one's abilities or character."

Everyone's path to fulfillment is different. That's the beauty of being human. Not everyone needs to raise children to be fulfilled. In fact, not every parent I know is fulfilled. Some women I know are satisfied with the joys and rewards of motherhood. Others appear tired, frustrated or just plain bored with the arduous job.

Remember, it is not the simple having of kids that makes a parent fulfilled; it is the success in becoming a good parent who has reared a child who is happy and healthy. And the former does not always beget the latter, no matter how hard one tries.

Either way, "fulfillment" comes when one accomplishes a goal or achieves a purpose, so it is ultimately in our best interest to choose our goals wisely, and not be swayed by the convictions of others. Once we are on a path to fulfillment—be it through a higher purpose and/or a rewarding vocation—we will less likely feel the sense of lacking that this young woman from New York feels:

> I WISH I wanted to have kids and sometimes I do feel like I lack purpose. But that's because I have no life as it is. I feel like I should want to have kids and don't know why. —Casey, 27, Watertown, NY

### Finding One's Purpose
*(While Bucking the Bingos)*

> I have heard "It's just what humans do…It is the purpose for our existence." This makes me want to scream, because clearly if this is the purpose and I don't have a calling to do it, then I have no purpose, and I know that just can't be true!
> —Female, 31, Charlotte, NC

Purpose is defined as "the reason for which something is done or created or for which something exists." Let us first establish that just because society tells us it is our *purpose* to procreate does not make it so. Since the vast majority of people procreate (about 80% in the U.S.), this is a convenient and easily propagated credo. But it is nothing more than that—a credo, a belief that guides one's actions.

Those who intentionally choose not to procreate obviously don't follow this credo—they do not believe parenting is the reason for their existence. For those of us still looking for our purpose beyond parenting, two of the most painful comments we hear from parents are: "Parenting is the most important job in the world," and "It is human nature to procreate." Here are the two comebacks I give to these "bingos," respectively:

> 1) It may be the most important job for *you,* but it's not for me.
>
> 2) It's *animal* nature to procreate; humans are given the ability to *choose.*

That's all well and good if you *have*, in fact, chosen your most important "job" for this lifetime; but not all of us have.

The following female from North Carolina seems to be pondering her purpose without progeny:

> People with kids have an innate reason for living and that is to raise their kids and do the best they can. I can say I'm living for my cats, but truly, my purpose isn't one I can point to. I have to find it, pursue it, make it mine— and no matter what I say my purpose is, society (including my parents, friends, relatives) doesn't really respect anything as much as they respect having kids. It's the thing to do, after all—and the only thing that has any meaning. —"Childfree in Charlotte," 31, Charlotte, NC

It sounds as though this woman has been bombarded with baby bingoing from her friends and relatives. It's easier not to be defensive when one has her life purpose already mapped out. And, at 31, she's got plenty of time to do that. Some of us—on the other hand—don't.

I do have life goals that fall in the category of "purpose," I just haven't accomplished them all yet. I have always wanted to author books that inform and help others, and I would ultimately like to get out there and volunteer to help the elderly and dying and their relatives. Other goals that accompany this are: to bring joy and happiness to my significant other; to make my father's life more comfortable in old age; to be a loving aunt to my nieces and nephews; to respect the body I was given by keeping it in optimal health; and to be a good steward of the earth and its resources.

These are not earth-shattering goals, but we cannot all be Florence Nightingale. I'm sure Oprah has set the bar high for herself, given her resources as a celebrity, and I don't envy the burden she must place on herself. But with the goals she's already attained—including building schools in Africa and helping over a dozen causes for women, children and the less fortunate—she can die knowing she made the world a better place.

Although I still seek purpose, my significant other has no such compulsion. He is of the philosophy that, "aren't we here to enjoy life?" And who am I to repute that? Perhaps because he faced such loss and challenge early on (with the death of his parents), he is fortunate not to be carrying the burden of fulfilling his "highest order" today. Vanna Bonta, a witty writer-actor in her early 50s (who loves kids, but has none of her own) has a clever definition of "life" that might fit your philosophy:

> LIFE: Love, Intelligence, Fun, Evolution in that order.
> ~Vanna Bonta, novelist, poet, film actress

Lets now explore various life purposes that non-parents—from past to present—have found to both fulfill themselves and to enrich others' lives.

## Leaving Legacies Without Leaving Heirs

The way you get meaning into your life is to devote yourself to loving
others, devote yourself to your community around you, and devote
yourself to creating something that gives you purpose and meaning.
~Mitch Albom, author, journalist (kidfree)

Whether you believe you have a higher purpose and have found it or not, most cannot dispute the works and accomplishments left behind by the world's great female humanitarians, who chose to care for the children of the world, rather than children of their own.

Florence Nightingale is a stellar example of a childless woman with a powerful purpose and legacy. She chose—at the age of 17—to forgo motherhood and follow her "divine calling" to enter nursing and care for the impoverished. Nightingale rebelled against her parents' wishes and the expected role of a young affluent English woman to become a wife and mother. Although courted by men, she believed marriage (and the ensuing offspring) would interfere with her ability to follow her calling.

Needless to say, through a lifetime of aiding the ill and the war-wounded, and through her nurse training programs, books and essays, Nightingale contributed more to the improvement of nursing and hospital conditions throughout the world than any individual to date.

Born the same year as Nightingale (1820), Susan B. Anthony found her calling not in helping the sick and wounded, but in advancing the civil rights of women. Witnessing the inequalities toward the female gender throughout her life, Anthony started her career in speaking for women's rights at age 30, which she continued for 45 years, giving nearly 100 speeches per year throughout the U.S. and Europe.

Susan B. Anthony is best known for leading the Women's Suffrage movement in the U.S., which led to the legalization of women voting 14 years after her death. And interestingly—though her life purpose did not include motherhood—she helped secure rights for many mothers in her movement. When a leading publicist told Anthony he thought she'd make a wonderful mother, she commented as follows:

I thank you, sir, for what I take to be the highest compliment, but sweeter
even than to have had the joy of caring for children of my own has it been
to me to help bring about a better state of things for mothers generally, so
that their unborn little ones could not be willed away from them.
~Susan B. Anthony[2]

What Anthony was referring to here was her success in fighting for the right of a widowed mother to keep a child she birthed after the death of her husband. Previously, the child was considered part of the dead father's estate, and could be taken from the mother if so stated in the father's will.[3]

Born the same month Florence Nightingale died (August 1910), Mother Teresa knew at a young age that her calling was to *help* children, not *have* children. At age 18, she left home to become a missionary, and for 45 years she administered to the poor, sick, orphaned and dying in India and around the world. Although a controversial figure in the childfree community (due to her work against abortion and contraception), her tireless work to help thousands of poor people cannot be refuted. At her death, Mother Teresa's legacy included the expansion of over 600 missions in 123 countries, including: hospices for people with HIV/AIDS, leprosy and tuberculosis; soup kitchens; children's and family counseling programs, orphanages and schools.

These women—along with thousands of modern-day humanitarians who are far too busy helping the people of the world to properly raise their own—might take issue with the old adage that "Children are a woman's greatest achievement."

True, these are saintly cases of humanitarian accomplishments not all of us are capable of achieving. But many non-parents are helping mankind in their own corners of the world. Whether it's assisting needy children, the disabled, the mentally ill, the sick, the weak, the elderly or the dying, there are ways to help our fellow beings and fulfill a purpose at the same time.

## Helping Our Earth and Animals

I care for and rescue animals. I believe that there is a great need for
this and having kids would have restricted my ability to do this.
I find this lifestyle very satisfying. Animals are grateful.
Kids are rarely, and can turn out to be nothing but trouble!
—Houndwoman, 53, Birmingham, England

In a human-centric world, many kidfree are drawn to helping the more vulnerable amongst us: the earth and its animals. My friend, Lynn Adams, is a local gallery owner who devotes her extra time to rescuing animals. She and her hubby chose not to house children, but animals—of all shapes and sizes. If she hears about a group of unwanted stray peacocks, she gets to them before animal control can, so they can live out their lives at her home in the hills. Bird with a broken wing? Dog that's been abused?

Horses that are starving? Along comes Lynn Adams to the rescue! What a great feeling it must be to be animalkind's best friend.

Another childfree friend of mine, Karen Lee Stevens, has chosen to make *the betterment of animals' lives* her purpose in life. Her method is to educate humans to treat animals humanely starting at a young age. She runs her own nonprofit—All for Animals—to teach children compassion for critters through reading, storytelling and interaction with well-behaved dogs and other animals. Her children's book, *Animals Have Feelings, Too!* teaches kids that animals and people share many of the same feelings. If you've ever seen a child swing a helpless cat by its tail or treat an animal like an inanimate object, you know the value of Karen's life purpose.

The Kidfree Survey showed that non-parents are much more likely than parents to have pets, so it' no surprise that an inordinate number are animal lovers and caregivers. Several respondents to my survey commented that they chose not to have children in order to devote their time to animals. Here are two examples:

I am highly involved in animal welfare issues and don't want anything or anyone to take time away from that. —Ann, 39, Lynchburg, VA

I'm very devoted to animals and their welfare, and I do not want to have to shift my focus from that. —Female, 36, Gaithersburg, MD

One notable childfree who made a life out of helping our fine-feathered friends was ornithologist Florence Merriam Bailey. She dedicated her life to observing and protecting bird life, and did her part to end the killing of more than five million birds a year to supply the fashion industry's trend of feathers on hats in the late 19th century.

Another naturalist of note is E. O. Wilson who has won numerous awards for his discoveries and writings on the interrelations of plants, animals and humans. He's a non-parent who has dedicated his life to the study and conservation of Earth's environment.

If there's one common bond most of us kidfree share, it's the preservation of Earth's resources. We are all doing our part by not adding another carbon footprint to the earth, and some of us—like Bagfish below—have even made environmentalism our calling in this lifetime:

It [being kidfree] also means that I can concentrate on my career in nature conservation/biodiversity, which is more helpful to protecting the environment than pushing out kids.
—Bagfish (PhD), 34, Cumbria, England

## Bearing Books, Not Babies

The world might, perhaps, be considerably poorer if the great writers
had exchanged their books for children of flesh and blood.
~Virginia Woolf (1882-1941), novelist

As one who chose to leave us with literary works rather than her own bloodline, Virginia Woolf knew well what she spoke of above. In fact, one of her novels, *A Room of One's Own*, gave us her famous dictum, "A woman must have money and a room of her own if she is to write fiction."

I take personal interest in the issue of writing vs. parenting, because one of my life goals since I was a child was to be an author. In fact, as a six year old I enjoyed writing adventure stories far more than playing with dolls. But—as a young child—I assumed I could one day create babies and books at the same time without a conflict. Now, as an adult, I don't feel the writer's life lends itself to caring for children. Instead, I agree with American novelist Richard Ford's 2nd rule in his "Ten Rules for Writing Fiction," which is simply:

Rule #2. Don't have children. ~Richard Ford[4]

Perhaps Ford might not have won his Pulitzer Prize for *Independence Day* had he structured his life around kids and their activities. Although there are many writers who are mothers, I cringed when—at a recent writer's conference—a new author spoke about having to get used to writing her book at her "kids' favorite Chuck E. Cheese." I'm sorry, but I could never get used to writing a book at Chuck E. Cheese!

History points to dozens of foremost literary figures who chose writing over rearing children. You will find an impressive list of them in Chapter 25, but a few notables include: Jane Austen, Louisa May Alcott, Emily Dickinson, T. S. Eliot, Ayn Rand and Samuel Beckett.

In fact, Ayn Rand (*Fountainhead, Atlas Shrugged*) developed her own philosophy on life's purpose, which she called "Objectivism." Its essence:

The concept of man as a heroic being, with his own happiness as the moral purpose of his life, with productive achievement as his noblest activity, and reason as his only absolute. ~Ayn Rand[5]

If Rand's belief that our own happiness is the moral purpose of our life is correct, then Brian and I—along with many kidfrees—have already achieved our moral purpose. Furthermore, if one believes that they will be happier without children, isn't it their moral obligation to stay childfree? Yes.

However, Rand does add that "productive achievement" is our noblest activity, dashing any notions we had that it's fine to wile our lives away on a tropical isle, making love in the sun and sipping coconut milk all day...

Where was I? Oh yes, *purpose*. So, in Rand's theory (which I like), it's OK to focus on one's own happiness, provided we lead a productive life. In any case, it's often our productive achievements that add to our happiness and fulfillment in life, anyway.

By the way, it may please you to note that—although they never parented children—some of the most notable kidfree authors wrote for children. Included among this list of creative kiddie wordsmiths are: Hans Christian Andersen, Carlo Collodi (Pinocchio), and—my childhood favorite—Dr. Seuss. The latter was often told he would make a good parent, to which he would reply, "You have 'em, I'll entertain 'em."

Helping kids read and use their imaginations through creative rhymes, fairy tales and children's stories is both a valuable and fulfilling vocation. Likewise, furthering the knowledge and literacy of adults through informative or entertaining books is vital to our culture. As one childfree European novelist (who also fought for animal rights) once said:

> Leaving behind books is even more beautiful. There are far too many children. ~Marguerite Yourcenar (1903-1987), Belgian-born French author

## Begetting Beauty, Not Bodies
### *Making Art and Music*

Oh what a gift it would be to add beauty to the planet with the stroke of a hand or the strum of a chord! Even the great minds of the Renaissance saw the benefits of remaining childless when it comes to fulfilling one's creative potential. The famed English philosopher, Francis Bacon, did not father a child, but he is regarded as the *father of empiricism*, which jump-started modern science. In the following excerpt from one of his essays, Bacon alludes to the great legacies left by men who did not procreate:

> The perpetuity by generation is common to beasts; but memory, merit and works are proper to men. And surely a man shall see the noblest works and foundations have proceeded from childless men, which have sought to express the images of their minds, where those of their bodies have failed. So the care of posterity is most in them who have no posterity. ~Francis Bacon (1561-1626)

Perhaps it's no surprise, then, that some of the most prolific and celebrated artists and musicians throughout history did not have children.

Leonardo Da Vinci left outstanding works of art, rather than offspring, as his legacy. And American modernist Georgia O'Keeffe too dedicated her life to creating works of art rather than children. Known for her abstract paintings of flowers and the Southwest, she became one of the most famed artists of the 1920s when the art world was dominated by men.

The world's music heritage might be lacking had Ludwig van Beethoven and Franz Schubert been preoccupied with wives and offspring. Friends in the early 19th century, Beethoven and Schubert each composed hundreds of musical works to be enjoyed by listeners for centuries to come. It's important to note, however, that Beethoven's output dropped drastically during the five years he was embroiled in a battle with his deceased brother's wife to gain custody of her son (his nephew), and again during the seven tumultuous years in which he attempted to raise him.

\* \* \*

Obviously, there are more life purposes than can be mentioned here, and some of you are already in the midst of fulfilling yours. Just striving to make those around you—from strangers to spouses—*happier* is an admirable goal in life.

Chapter 25 lists hundreds of famous figures who share our non-parenting status, and shows the myriad vocations they chose. In addition to those mentioned here, there are: politicians and pioneers, scientists and inventors, philanthropists and philosophers, activists and athletes, and—of course—actors and entertainers who opt not to parent.

Whatever you find as your unique purpose in life, claim it as your own, and do not let the majority belittle you for not reproducing. Chances are, you will have oodles more time and energy to devote to your calling than a parent does, and may even find more success and fulfillment in the process. As one famous Scot once said:

> To know what you prefer instead of humbly saying Amen to what the world tells you you *ought* to prefer, is to have kept your soul alive.
> ~Robert Louis Stevenson (1850-1894), author

# CHAPTER 24

## Are We Happy Being Kidfree?
### *You Decide!*

I have a happy marriage, a teaching career, many friends and interests.
I have good relationships with my nieces and nephews. I also realize
that happiness comes in many forms and that having children isn't
the only path. I appreciate my life for what it is.
—Sandy, 43, Ashby, MA

Question: What is the path to happiness? Answer: There isn't one; there are many. The noun "happiness" is best defined by its many synonyms found in a thesaurus:

pleasure, contentment, satisfaction, cheerfulness, merriment, gaiety, joy, jollity, joviality, glee, delight, good spirits, light-heartedness, well-being, enjoyment, exuberance, exhilaration, elation, ecstasy, jubilation, rapture, bliss, euphoria...

These are all good feelings and, arguably, stuff we all want. But how do we achieve a sense of well-being and a life of contentment? For each of us, it is different. Do you know yet what your path to happiness is? Check out the items below in List A:

Baby's first step; kids laughing; a hug from your child; watching your child learn and grow; watching your child do sports and hobbies; family events and holidays; dining at kid-friendly restaurants; a lively, noisy household; kiddie shows and videos; trips to Disneyland; your teen's first prom; your child's graduation; your daughter's wedding.

Are you smiling? Does the above list make you feel content?

Now read the terms in List B:

Freedom; space; privacy; disposable income; successful career; a clean, quiet home; time to read; time to relax; spontaneous activities; romantic travel; fine dining; adult conversation; your favorite sports and/or hobbies; continuing education; no worries about the safety or well-being of a child; total attention to and from your spouse; earlier retirement.

Do you feel better now, or bored? Many people long for List A and would be bored with List B. Others might get nervous reading List A and calm reading List B. Of course, the two aren't mutually exclusive (non-parents can do a little of List A with other people's kids), but they are meant to trigger your gut feelings and lifestyle preferences.

Happy parents find the rewards in List A worth the sacrifices involved in parenting, while many non-parents would not even regard the events in List A as "rewards." The childfree definition of a rewarding lifestyle might align better with List B, and all the accouterments that come with it.

When asked, "Are you happy being kid-free?" almost 97% of my survey respondents said, "Yes" whereas only 3.1% said, "No." The results, shown in this pie chart, are what I call the *Kidfree Grin*:

**Are You Happy Being Kid-Free?**

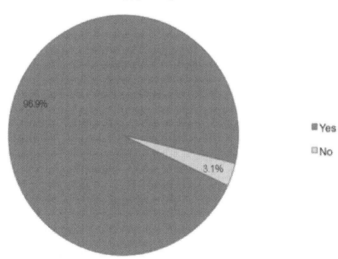

I have peppered this chapter with over four dozen quotes from survey respondents who are better equipped to describe—in their own words—their personal reasons why they are happy or unhappy being non-parents.

## First, the Bad News:
### *Some of Us* Are *Unhappy*

Not all non-parents are happy, as found in my survey when 3.2% answered "No" to being happy kid-free. This group might more accurately be called "childless" than "childfree." Let's take a look at these childless and why they are not content.

Do they all want kids but can't have them? No, it's a mixed bag. Of the unhappy non-parents: 39% want kids, 32% don't want kids, and 29% aren't sure. Interestingly, 95% of these respondents have at one time wanted children, removing them from the "confirmed childfree" who always knew. Only 20% of this unhappy group are not able to conceive and 28% are single. The, following three quotes from women who are unable to conceive each give different reasons for their discontent.

**Are you happy being kid-free?**

No, but it wasn't like I had a choice. It was just the way it was supposed to be. —"Itzok" (female), 46, Littleton, CO

I did want to have children, when I reached my late twenties and found a decent man. I was raised by an alcoholic mother and wanted to be the parent I never had. Unfortunately, my body didn't allow it. —Therese, 37, Boulder, CO

Living childfree has both positive and negative qualities. It means that you can live truly free. You don't have any responsibilities tying you down. However, I do feel a certain loneliness in not having any children of my own, and my husband was certainly disappointed when he found out that we could not have children. I think that was the hardest thing to bear of all that I have been through. —Penny, 41, Phoenix, AZ

But being unable to conceive does not preclude being happy, as only 11% of respondents who are "unable to conceive" report they are not happy being kidfree. Others—who can conceive and don't want children— are unhappy for reasons often relating to the issues discussed in Part II of this book, such as disappointing loved ones:

Right now at the age of 41, and my mother recently living in the same town as me, I feel I have let her down by not giving her grandchildren. Prior to her moving here, I felt great about not having kids. —Jade, Bothell, WA

I'm not happy because my wife does want children, and soon, and is devastated because I only recently admitted to myself that I don't want kids, whereas this is her life goal and we both thought I wanted kids before we got married. —Male, 25, BC, Canada

Although Jade can probably work through her guilt of not giving her mother grandkids, the above male from British Columbia has every right to be unhappy about the mess he's in, as does his wife. It appears he's the one that changed his mind (or rather found his mind), and now—as discussed in Chapter 22—he and his wife have got quite a predicament to work out.

Singles are only slightly less likely to be happy being kidfree, according to my survey. When broken down by relationship status: 4% of Singles, 3% of Married and 2.7% "In a Serious Relationship" report not being happy being kid-free. Some non-parents feel they might be missing out on something, like a close parent-child friendship:

> Feel I could be missing out on something. After all, I am MY mom's best pal. —Kathy Di Palma, 45, Santa Barbara, CA

Others feel somewhat like a social pariah—in this kid-centric world—for not wanting or even liking children:

> I know with every atom of my being that I shouldn't have kids. But I have to an extent interiorized the dominant social idea that there is something wrong with not wanting (and certainly with not liking!) children. I'm afraid to own up to it, and I'm afraid that maybe I am somehow deviant. And visiting with my parent friends is hard. I can only fake enjoying small children for a short time. I wish I could genuinely enjoy the kids, and be happy for my friends. —Female, 35, Seattle, WA

I hope this female from Seattle reads this book and discovers that—though not having children may be deviant—not everybody likes or wants to have children; and that's OK. The world is better off when people make brave choices, rather than giving in to fit in. The following Brit compares the non-parent status to that of being in the non-heterosexual minority:

> You do feel an outsider and a second-class citizen in too many situations. GLBT [gay, lesbian, bisexual, transgender] friends still say society is very hetero-centric. I think a similar line applies to gay or straight childless or childfree adults of any age. —Bev, Wolverhampton, England

Another English woman who is not happy being kidfree compares her feelings to that of American poet Molly Peacock, who continually revisits her decision not to parent:

> Like me, Molly Peacock had to make the "childfree" decision many times throughout her life. It is rarely a choice we make only once never to think about again. There are still times like Xmas, Halloween, family occasions, when I have to acknowledge what I am giving up, my role in that decision and the impact (both good and bad) on my life. Her words also portray the isolation and social stigma that those of us who go against "the norm" face. —Catgirl, 35, Warwickshire, England

Catgirl then quotes an excerpt from Peacock's memoir *Paradise, Piece by Piece* (see Peacock next chapter) where she explains her choice not to have children and the loneliness women often feel in dealing with the social pressures concerning motherhood.

Another respondent—who chose not to procreate due to genetic issues in her and her husband's family—answered "No" to being happy kidfree, due to a fear of the unknown:

My answer was no, because there are so many unknowns. I love my husband, we are happy, and we enjoy life. But there are still a lot of "what ifs." —"Nullipara69," 40, Frankfurt, KY

Still others in this 3% may not be "unhappy" at all, but were reluctant to call themselves "happy" as they are still assessing their situation:

I only put "no" because I'm not decidedly happy or unhappy being kidfree. I'm still assessing. —Female, 39, Maryland

If you let the challenges of non-parenting that we discussed earlier in the book—fear, stigma, status and pressure—get to you, it will weigh on your happiness. In any case, every group will have their percentage of unhappy members. But—as we will now explore—those who *parent* are even more likely to find themselves in a state of discontent.

## Studies Show Non-Parents *Are* Happier

I am just happy. My fiancé and I can now relax and keep our lifestyle. We can keep our hobbies, while being awesome aunt and uncle to our many older nieces and nephews.
—Kai Nimura, 27, Pittsburgh, PA

Ask any parent what their greatest joy in life is and they'll likely answer, "Oh, my kids!" But they might be fooling themselves, according to U.S. and European studies. Kids may bring a sense of purpose, but not the joy and blissfulness that Huggies and Pampers commercials portray.

In fact, studies over the past 25 years show that children actually have a negative impact on parents' happiness. One of the first such studies— "The Effects of Children on Adults' Psychological Well-Being: 1957-1976"—released in 1989 by sociologists Sara McLanahan and Julia Adams found that parenthood was perceived as more stressful in the 1970s than in the 1950s.[1] This is in part due to changes in the employment and marital status of parents, as well as the higher costs and complexities of raising children these days.

"Parents experience lower levels of emotional well-being, less frequent positive emotions and more frequent negative emotions than their childless peers," according to Robin W. Simon, PhD., a sociology professor who has conducted several parenting studies. In fact, one study she conducted in 2005 with Renae J. Evenson—based on the National Survey of Families and Households' data gathered from over 10,000 U.S. adults—found that parents report significantly more symptoms of depression (feelings of sadness, loneliness, restlessness and fear) than non-parents their own age. [2]

While happiness does spike when parents are *expecting* a baby, it sharply plummets after the first child is born, reaching its lowest point when the child is a teen. When are parents the happiest? When their children leave home. But data shows that even "empty nesters" are less happy than those who never had children. As a matter of fact, Evenson and Simon found "no group of parents that reports significantly greater emotional well-being than people who never had children."[3]

In his 2006 book *Stumbling on Happiness*, Harvard psychologist Daniel Gilbert offers more on this topic. In one graph he shows the results of four separate studies documenting the marital satisfaction of parents from pre-children to empty nest. All four studies show marital satisfaction decreases dramatically after the birth of the first child and increases only when the last child leaves home.[4]

Gilbert also cites a 2004 study of 909 women showing that as they go about their daily activities, "they are less happy when taking care of their children than when eating, exercising, shopping, napping or watching television."[5] This probably doesn't surprise most of you childfree who observe the harried lives of your childed friends and relatives, but it is still something most mothers don't divulge to their daughters.

One reason parents erringly point to their children as their greatest source of happiness is: selective memory. Unless they are forced to analyze their daily activities and hourly feelings, parents will recall mostly the fun activities they have with their kids—i.e. playing in the yard, reading a book—which make up only a small portion of the day with them. But when asked to specifically describe their daily routine for a study, they report the laborious hours spent trying to get their child bathed, dressed or ready for bed.

Some childfree speculate that another reason parents name their kids as their "greatest source of happiness" is because they are too busy parenting to develop other interests; hence their kids may be their *only* source of happiness.

But what about the axiom that kids are the key to a good marriage? Well, not so anymore. Remember the Pew Research chart shown in Chapter 13? The 2007 survey on marriage and parenting of 2,020 adults nationwide found that children had fallen to eighth place out of nine on a list factors that people associate with successful marriages.

The National Marriage Project's 2006 "State of Our Unions" report says that parents have significantly lower marital satisfaction than non-parents, partly because they experienced more single and childfree years than previous generations. Due to this delay of marriage and childbearing, "life with children is experienced as a disruption in the life course rather than as one of it's defining purposes."[6]

And if you don't believe the slew of studies and experts, why not take it from a mother herself? In her essay, "I love my kids, but I admit it—I'm happier on my own!" Lucy Cavendish bravely confesses:

> I know I may be lambasted for saying it, but it's true. I realised all my happy moments revolved around freedom from being a mummy—freedom from the endless rounds of sock-finding, washing, dressing, cooking, breaking up fights, getting the children to school, putting them to bed, etc., etc. —Lucy Cavendish, *Daily Mail, U.K.*[7]

Cavendish first realized she was happier away from her kids when she took a holiday from them and could actually do the things she wanted to do—such as listen to her own music, dine at adult restaurants, converse on her own level, etc. But when she came home to her kids, her self-described euphoria ended abruptly:

> I had such a blissful time that it was a terrible shock to go home. I came in through the door and the mayhem and chaos started almost instantaneously. The calm I had felt on holiday dissipated in a matter of minutes, which I found rather depressing.[8]

Cavendish says it's not that she doesn't love her kids, "it's the endless minutiae of looking after them that pales somewhat. [...] In many ways, you cease to be you." She says that many women are frightened to admit this lest it make them sound like a bad mother.

> They worry that if they say it is other people, or other things, that make them happy, they are somehow letting their children down.[9]

The good news is: More and more parents are bravely coming out to write books and essays that reveal the long-held secret that having—and spending time with—offspring does not make you a happier person.

## Why Are We Happier?
*Freedom is Foremost*

I have freedom! I have none of the restrictions that parents are
burdened with, and can have an infinitely flexible lifestyle.
—Heather, 33, Scotland

When I asked non-parents why they are happy, I received more write-in
responses than any other question on my survey—over 3,000! An entire
anthology could be compiled from all the truly positive and inspiring
comments on why people are happy with their lives.

More than 80% of my survey respondents rattled off comments
containing verbs like: live, love, give, grow, help, create, dine, desire,
enjoy, celebrate and accomplish; and adjectives like: exclusive, exotic,
romantic, relaxing, spontaneous, flexible and blissful.

But most telling were the frequently used nouns to describe kidfree
happiness: independence, wealth, opportunity, money, time, travel,
privacy, peace, pleasure, intimacy, quiet, home, sleep, sex, spouse,
satisfaction, cats, dogs, pets, hobbies, career, choice, energy, nieces,
nephews, liberty, and, drumroll please…freedom!

This last word was by far the most used word on my survey. Freedom
of Choice, Freedom of Lifestyle, Freedom from Demands, Freedom from
Worry and Freedom from Financial Burden—all were themes addressed by
non-parents as to why they are happy.

Not only were the vast majority of reasons for being happy related to
freedom, almost half of all respondents actually used the word "free" or
"freedom" in their responses. Here's a sampling from around the world:

**Why are you happy being kid-free?**

I am free. —Dolly, 37, Venice, Italy

I enjoy my freedom! —Usha Rags, 38, San Francisco, CA

Total freedom of time, finances, self indulgence.
—Weldon Middlebrooks, Arlington, TX

Because I have the freedom to make the choice and do whatever I want,
whenever I want. —Lee Hopkins, 30, Cardiff, Wales, UK

Because I am free, and I can dedicate myself to the things I like.
—Chiara, 41, Napoli, Italy

I have more freedom to travel, go to school, and pursue personal
interests. —Swearbear, 29, Washington, DC

I have freedom and peace in my life. —Alice, 31, Dallas, TX

Freedom, more money, no screaming kids nipping at my heels.
—Paul H., 57, Riorges, France

**Why are you happy being kid-free? (cont.)**

Freedom and more alone time with my wife.
—Richard Keller Butkus, 36, Chicago, IL

Love having the freedom (both personally and financially) to do what I want. —Melissa D., 39, Little River, SC

Freedom from crushing responsibility. Simplicity of life and choice. Harmony and constancy. —Sandhya, 32, Chennai, India

Freedom to be, and Freedom to try new things. Just FREEDOM in general. —Janine, 43, Beacon Falls, CT

I absolutely cherish my freedom. Freedom to take a job that is extremely enjoyable and rewarding, even if it doesn't pay enough to support a family of four, five, six, or more. Freedom to work part time. Freedom to come home to a quiet or a noisy house—of my choosing. Freedom to watch what I want on TV [...]
—Jerry Steinberg, Founding Non-Father Emeritus of No Kidding!

This last quote—by Jerry Steinberg, the founder of the childfree group No Kidding!—is just a snippet of a 350-word survey response he wrote on the freedoms of being a non-parent. His "freedoms" all equate to a better lifestyle. We saw how important "lifestyle" is to us in Chapter 5, and we can thank spontaneity and flexibility for bringing joy to our lives:

My husband and I enjoy staying up late and sleeping in. We love spontaneous trips and traveling in general. —Carolyn, 35, Woodstock, GA

I'm perfectly content with my life and the choices I've made thus far. I love to travel. I love to be spontaneous. I love to avoid as much responsibility as I can (half joke/half serious). —Melanie, 38, Brooklyn, NY

It allows us the flexibility to get up and go. To take off at the last minute for a weekend trip without a lot of hassle. We love to travel and see culturally exciting places like Italy or Spain and we can enjoy these places without having to pack a kid along. —"Babs6987," 37, Seattle, WA

While a free, spontaneous and flexible lifestyle were core themes of happiness in non-parents, peace, quiet, privacy and alone time with spouse were strong sub-themes:

I enjoy peace and quiet...I enjoy financial freedom...I enjoy my exclusive relationship with my husband. —Barbara, 59, Oregon

After being around children, it is always a relief to go home to peace, quiet, and cleanliness and to spend time alone with my wife. I am entirely devoted to her and would never want to split my attention between her and another human being. —James Kyle, 37, Mason, MI

Being childfree gives me all the liberty in the world to accomplish things I like to do. Plus I have privacy. I also don't have to share my spouse with a child. —Jesenia, 29, Brooklyn, NY

I have all the freedom, quiet, privacy and space that I want. No child could ever match the happiness that those things bring me.
—Stacey C., 39, Philadelphia, PA

For some it's about the ability to *choose*. Many kidfree revel in the wealth of choices they have without offspring in tow, while others are just happy they have the choice not to procreate and are exercising it.

> Actually complete choice in what I do. Not selfish really, just real simple. —Jeromeo, 50, California
>
> My husband and I have the choice to do whatever we want to do at any time. —Lauren Wallett, 27, Johannesburg, South Africa
>
> I'm so thankful that I have the choice. I don't see anything about childrearing that looks the least bit interesting to me. —Jez, 37, Ohio
>
> It's my choice, and I enjoy all my life as it is. —Yoda, 40, Melbourne, Australia

As government chips away at our individual freedoms by adding laws and taxes for things we don't believe in, it is good to know they can't (knock on wood) take away our choice not to procreate.

When asked why they are happy, these respondents from Italy say:

> I'm free to be myself. —Morgenstern, 34, Piacenza, Italy
>
> I am who I want to be. —Giusi, 40, Rome, Italy

### We Have *Other* Interests

> I have a wonderful husband, a home with a dog and cat,
> and I have hobbies and friends I enjoy.
> —Melissa C., 33, Raleigh, NC

What can be greater than having the free time and energy to focus on what we love most? As explored throughout this book, there are many things in life—creating, writing, learning, traveling, competing, helping, rescuing—that bring us joy and meaning. Parents have to curb—if not forgo—their hobbies and interests while raising their kids. Non-parents have the extra time, money and energy to jump right in for life:

> Freedom to read, travel, focus on dog rescue, dance, date, spend time with adults, write, move a lot... —Female, 38, Virginia
>
> My husband and I have a very fulfilling life together. We travel the world, enjoy spending money on ourselves, focus on our careers without guilt and enjoy our clean, quiet and clutter-free home. —Suzanne Rea, 36, Tulsa, OK
>
> I take great pleasure in the personal freedoms I enjoy as a non-parent. Traveling, pursuing higher education and a meaningful career, adult hobbies, and having a fit body are just some of the aspects of my life I can devote greater attention to by choosing not to become a mother. I love the intimacy I share with my husband that isn't marred by the day-to-day drudgery of caring for a child. —Leslie Feeny, 24, Colorado Springs, CO

By the way, not all of our special interests need be lofty goals of career, fitness, education, travel and helping the world. Some of us are content using our spare time and energy to focus on our loved ones, including our significant other, pets, family or friends:

All I have to focus on is my husband and cats. —Char, 33, Indiana

I love that it is just my wife and me. We are so closely bonded that I couldn't imagine having to give that up. Every time we make love it is an uninterrupted celebration of our life being kid-free. We have our freedom, we can travel, go out for dinner, the list is endless.
—Lance, 39, Orlando, FL

I am in a loving, stable relationship and enjoy my job and the company of friends. —Finlay, 42, Manchester, England

I love my work, my fiancé, my family, and my animals. Having a child would take my time and energy away from these. I feel fulfilled right now, and don't need to do anything different.
—Jessica Donahoe, 25, Columbia, MO

My husband and I are SO happily in love, and have a very relatively stress-free life compared to our married w/children friends. We enjoy our freedom and our lifestyle!! —Angelica Kibler, 27, Tucson, AZ (yes email)

Other survey respondents defined their happiness not by what they are gaining, but by what they are *missing*. Dozens of non-parents said they were glad to be avoiding the stress, worry, responsibility and demands that caring for offspring would bring:

I don't have to worry about being completely responsible for another human life. —Jane Thomas, 26, Pensacola, FL

I have none of the down side to having children (finances, worry, intrusion into my chosen life style and living standard) and I don't miss the "up side" (whatever that is). —John Robinson, 45, Minnesota

I love not having the mess, noise, and constant drain on my time and money that kids involve. —Denise, 47, Clearfield, UT

I don't have a responsibility that will last the rest of my life, and our life as a couple is ours. —Sharloe, 34, California

No restrictions, no whinging, no telling me how to raise them.
—Phoenvix, 28, Blackpool, England

Besides the obvious benefits of a free and unburdened lifestyle and the ability to focus on our favorite people and interests, many non-parents are happy for philosophical reasons. Some are happy that they are not adding another being to this crowded planet. Some do not believe in the propagation of the human species. Still others are just pleased to be dodging the consumer culture so ingrained in parenting today.

*   *   *

A 2008 Gallup poll showed that 14% of Americans are dissatisfied with their lives, and yet just over 3% of my respondents report not being happy being kidfree. That's almost 97% who checked "Yes" they are Happy!

So to the question, "Are non-parents—as a whole—a happy group?" we can safely answer, "Yes."

Although there are many parents out there who are unhappy with the lifestyle they were (perhaps unwittingly) thrown into, there will always be those who—rightly or wrongly—tell us we are "missing out." But thank goodness that the vast majority of non-parents are quite content knowing what they are missing out on, and quite happily living the life they choose.

# CHAPTER 25

## You Are Not Alone
### *Prominent People Who Passed On Procreating*

"Where is it written that you have to have kids?
You can easily borrow other people's and give them back later." [1]
~George Clooney, actor

In a culture where pregnancy is portrayed as the latest Hollywood trend and celebrity "bumpwatches" are a weekly bombardment, it's easy to feel alone in our non-parent status. But we are not alone. There is a countertrend seeping into the lifestyles of the rich and famous, and the über-talented the world over. Many are questioning the wisdom in attempting to "have it all" (career, fame, power and progeny), as well as the logic of bearing children just because one can *afford* them.

My research uncovered hundreds of notable non-parents worldwide, dating back to the Renaissance and beyond. From A to Z—Jane Austen to Renee Zellweger—there are famous people in history who have chosen not to procreate. Some of the most prolific writers, composers, scientists, philosophers, artists and actors have lived complete—and arguably admirable—lives without taking on the role of "parent."

I thought it would be both fun and enlightening to end this book with a list of prominent people who passed on procreating, and sprinkle in some of their quotes on the matter. I've also listed some of their works and/or accomplishments, though the descriptions are only partial. *Please note the obvious:* Those on the list who are still alive and kicking can change their non-parent status at any moment after printing this book. Also note that some may not have *chosen* the life of non-parent as much as it chose *them.*

The following list of over 260 notable non-parents is a labor of love, as it was compiled over several years and required tedious fact checking. While you read, I hope you will be as giddy with surprise as I when discovering these—mostly familiar some not so familiar—kidfree gems...

## ACTORS / CELEBRITIES

**Marty Allen** – Stand-up comedian, actor (*The Big Valley*)

**Dame Judith Anderson** (1897-1992) – Australian actress (*Rebecca*)

**Jennifer Aniston** – Actress (*Friends, Marley & Me*), director, producer

**Max Baer Jr.** – Actor ("Jethro" on *Beverly Hillbillies*), producer, director

**Tallulah Bankhead** (1902-1968) – Actress, talk show host

**Bob Barker** – Former TV game show host *(The Price is Right)*, animal rights activist, philanthropist

**Kathy Bates** – Actress (*Misery*), director

**Jacqueline Bisset** – English actress *(Airport, The Deep, Nip/Tuck)*

"I don't regret not having children. I am very much at peace with that. Perhaps I do have that occasional twinge, but you can't do everything."[2]

**Lara Flynn Boyle** – Actress (*Twin Peaks, The Practice*)

"I had such a great mom and I know that I'd never be that mom. I wouldn't want to bring a child into this world unless I could be. And I don't believe that women can successfully have it all. I really don't."[3]

**Delta Burke** – Actress (*Designing Women*), producer, clothing designer, author

**Raymond Burr** (1917-1993) – Canadian-born actor (*Perry Mason, Ironside*)

**Brett Butler** – Actress (*Grace Under Fire*), comedian, author

**Kim Cattrall** – English-Canadian actress (*Sex and the City, Mannequin*)

"When I answered those questions regarding having children, I realized that so much of the pressure I was feeling was from outside sources, and I knew I wasn't ready to take that step into motherhood...Since then I've found other ways to fulfill my maternal instincts—when a young actress comes to me for advice about her career, or when I give a talk at a school, babysit my friends' kids, or work with children's charities or organizations. And even though I'm now married, my decision still stands...My newest projects sometimes feel like my children. Being a biological mother just isn't part of my experience this time around."[4]

**Stockard Channing** – Actress (*The West Wing, Grease*)

**Julia Child** (1912-2004) – Chef, author, TV personality

**Margaret Cho** – Comedian, actress, author, humanitarian

"I do not want children. When I see children, I feel nothing. I have no maternal instinct. I am barren. I ovulate sand...I look at children and feel no pull toward them, no desire whatsoever."[5]

**Julie Christie** – British actress (*Fahrenheit 451, Doctor Zhivago*)

Beatty told his friends he had asked Christie to marry him, but she refused as she did not want children.[6]

**Patricia Clarkson** – Actress *(HBO Series *Six Feet Under, Pieces of April)*

**George Clooney** – Actor (*Ocean's Eleven*) director, producer, screenwriter

"Even one kid running around my villa makes me nervous, so I'm definitely not a candidate for father of the year. If I need to surround myself with children and feel like I have this big extended family, I can always call Brad and Angelina and ask them to stay with me, just to remind myself why I'm so happy."[7]

**Imogene Coca** (1908-2001) – Comic actress, philanthropist

**John Corbett** – Actor (*Northern Exposure*), country music singer

The 49-year-old actor, who reprises his role as Aidan Shaw in "Sex and the City 2" says he and his 53-year-old partner [Bo Derek] are now too old to conceive a child but the couple would consider opening their home to a disadvantaged child.[8]

**Simon Cowell** – British music executive, TV personality, producer

**Mary Crosby** – Actress (*Dallas, Knots Landing)*

**John Cusack** – Actor *(Say Anything, Con Air),* screenwriter

**Patti Reagan Davis** – Actress, author, daughter of former president Ronald Reagan and First Lady Nancy Reagan

**Ellen DeGeneres** – Talk show host (*The Ellen DeGeneres Show*), stand-up comedian, actress (married to Portia de Rossi)

"We have a niece, so that's good, because we play with her, then she cries and we hand her back."[9]

**Dana Delany** – Actress *(Desperate Housewives)*

"I have tried hard all my life not to be a desperate housewife. My mother is 80 years old and still works as an interior designer, so I was raised with a very strong work ethic. I didn't think that being a wife and mother made her happy, so I remember saying to her when I was 16: 'I'm never going to have kids.' She said, 'Oh, you'll change your mind,' but I never did."[10]

**Bo Derek** – Actress (*10, Bolero*), model, producer, horse activist

**Loretta Devine** – Actress *(Boston Public, Grey's Anatomy)*

**Cameron Diaz** – Actress *(There's Something About Mary),* former model

I think women are afraid to say that they don't want children because they're going to get shunned. But I think that's changing too now. I have more girlfriends who don't have kids than those that do. And honestly? We don't need any more kids. We have plenty of people on this planet."[11]

**Leonardo DiCaprio** – Actor (*J. Edgar, The Aviator, Titanic*), producer

At 35, DiCaprio told the *Inquisitr*, "I'm not that old, my biological clock isn't ticking yet. I'd like to leave it to fate if and when I'm going to be a father. A part of me has too many professional plans to even seriously consider it."[12]

**Matt Dillon** – Actor (*Crash, There's something About Mary*)

**Tamara Dobson** (1944-2006) – Actress (*Cleopatra Jones*), fashion model

**Richard Donner** – Film director (*Lethal Weapon, Superman, The Omen*)

"I was lucky because I never had kids. I never wanted kids. I wanted dogs."[13]

**Shelley Duvall** – Actress (*Popeye, The Shining*), producer

**Bonnie Erbé** – Journalist, TV host (*To the Contrary with Bonnie Erbe*)

From her article "Why Non-Parents Are Happier Than Parents":

"I am child-free by choice and have honestly never looked back and wished I'd had children. I've seen too many of my friends stressed out by their own work-life juggles to have wanted that for myself. They all love their children and say they wouldn't have it any other way. But I've also seen a lot of women (it's almost always the mother, not the father) give up promising careers for motherhood and never being quite able to fight their way back into the workforce. That's a sacrifice I could not have made. I wanted to follow my own dreams, not spend my life helping someone else follow his or hers. Very few women succeed at doing both."[14]

**Linda Evans** – Actress *(Dynasty, The Big Valley)*

At one time, Linda did want a child, as long as the circumstances were correct, including love and marriage. Unlike some of her colleagues, Evans considers having a husband a prerequisite for having a baby. "I could easily adopt a child on my own right now, but I think it is real important for the child to have a father as well as a mother," she says.[15]

**Rupert Everett** – English actor (*My Best Friend's Wedding*)

Openly gay actor Rupert Everett won't be signing adoption papers any time soon—he told Britain's *Daily Express*, "Oh God, I could never do that to a child. Can you imagine what it would be like, having your two dads coming to school speech days? And hearing those awful queeny rows while you are trying to get to sleep?"[16]

**Barbara Feldon** – Actress (*Get Smart*), model, TV host, author (*Living Alone and Loving It*)

**Ralph Fiennes** – English actor (*Schindler's List, The English Patient*)

"Children? Ewww!"[17]

**Lynn Fontanne** (1887-1983) – British-born actress, stage star (the most acclaimed acting team in American theater with husband Alfred Lunt)

**Tanya Franks** – British actress (*Family Affairs*), writer, producer

"I don't have children and I don't see children in my future life. I like my nieces and nephews, but I don't think I'm a natural mum. I don't have plans for it, that's for sure!"[18]

**William Frawley** (1887-1966) – Actor ("Fred Mertz" in *I Love Lucy*)

**Eva Gabor** (1919-1995) – Hungarian-born actress (*Green Acres*), voice actor (she and sister, Magda, had a string of marriages but no children)

**Magda Gabor** (1918-1997) – Hungarian-born actress (Eva Gabor's sister)

**Greta Garbo** (1905-1990) – Swedish-born actress in Hollywood's silent film era

**Ava Gardner** (1922-1990) – Actress (*Mogambo, The Night of the Iguana*)

During her marriage to Frank Sinatra, Gardner became pregnant twice, but she had two abortions. She said years later, "We couldn't even take care of ourselves. How were we going to take care of a baby?"[19]

**Janeane Garofalo** – Comedian, actress, political activist

Funny girl Janeane Garofalo doesn't plan on becoming a parent, though she thought she wanted to at one point. "I thought that I did," she said. "Now I realize that I don't. People think that you are a nasty, selfish person if you don't want to have children."[20]

**Ricky Gervais** – English comedian, actor, writer, producer, director

He and girlfriend, Jane Fallon (the TV producer and writer whom he met at college) decided not to have children as a "life-style choice," he says, because "we wanted to work on our careers."[21]

**Lillian Gish** (1893-1993) – Actress, silent films (*Birth of a Nation*), named 17th among the "greatest female stars of all time" by the American Film Institute

**Crispin Glover** – Actor (*Back to the Future*), director, screenwriter, author

**Jeff Goldblum** – Actor (*Jurassic Park, The Fly*), producer

**Heather Graham** – Actress (*Austin Powers: The Spy Who Shagged Me*), producer

**Kathy Griffin** – Actress (*Suddenly Susan, Kathy Griffin: My Life on the D-List*), comedian, TV personality, producer, author

**Terry Gross** – National radio host, producer (*Fresh Air* on NPR)

**Jon Hamm** – Actor (*Mad Men, Friends With Kids*), director, producer

When asked by Mark Malkin if playing fathers in his TV shows has compelled the 40 year old to start his own family, Hamm replied: Ïl have a lot of friends with kids and a lot of family members with kids. I'm like a six time uncle. I have enough kids in my life.Ó[22]

**Chelsea Handler** – Comedian, TV host, actress, author

Chelsea to Larry King, on *Larry King Live*:
"You know, I have a lot of nieces and nephews. [....] I love them so much, and they give me a lot of joy and happiness. A lot of that joy and happiness comes from walking away when they are in a bad mood. You know, you get the best of them when you're their aunt and I get the best of them. [...] I would rescue a child. If there was one that needed a better home, I would totally take a child in. But procreating doesn't sound appealing to me."[23]

**Daryl Hannah** – Actress (*Blade Runner, Splash, Wall Street*), environmentalist

**Katherine Hepburn** (1907-2003) – Actress (*The African Queen, Guess Who's Coming to Dinner, On Golden Pond*), four-time Academy Award winner

Only when a woman decides not to have children, can a woman live like a man. That's what I've done.[24]

**Bonnie Hunt** – Actress (*Cheaper by the Dozen*), comedienne, producer, TV host (*The Bonnie Hunt Show*)

**Anjelica Huston** – Actress *(Prizzi's Honor)*

"There have been times when I wanted children and other times I've been grateful not to have them." I am a mess if I have to say goodbye to my dog for longer than five days. I don't know how I would deal with kissing my children as I left for work. I know there are women who are able to do that. I don't know if I could."[25]

**Lauren Hutton** – Model, actress *(American Gigolo, Lassiter)*

**Carolyn Jones** (1930-1983) – Actress ("Morticia" in *The Addams Family*)

**Ashley Judd** – Actress *(De-Lovely)*, humanitarian, political activist

"It's unconscionable to breed with the number of children who are starving to death in impoverished countries."[26]

**Madeline Kahn** (1942-1999) – Actress *(Blazing Saddles)*

**Vincent Kartheiser** – Actor *(Angel, Mad Men, Money)*

"I've been a vegetarian for four years and I have chosen not to have children, which are both green choices in my life."[27]

**Julie Kavner** – Actress, comedian, voice artist ("Marge" on *The Simpsons*)

**Dan Lauria** – Actor *(The Wonder Years, Independence Day)*

**Jay Leno** – TV host *(The Tonight Show)*, comedian

Although talk show host Jay Leno has written a children's book, *If Roast Beef Could Fly*, he's said that he and wife since 1980, Mavis Nicholson Leno, never wanted children.[28]

**Laura Linney** – Actress *(The Big C, John Adams, The Savages, Kinsey)*

**Carole Lombard** (1908-1942) – Actress *(Twentieth Century, My Man Godfrey)*, 1930s classic film star

She tried to have children with husband Clark Gable, but did not succeed. They proceeded to happily raise chickens and horses on their ranch.

**Bill Maher** – TV host *(Politically Incorrect)*, comedian, author

"I don't dislike children, I just don't particularly want to be around them a lot. Problem is, neither do their parents."[29]

**Steve Martin** – Actor *(Father of the Bride, L.A. Story)*, comedian, writer, producer, musician, composer

**Eva Mendes** – Actress *(Training Day, Hitch, We Own the Night)*

"I was joking the other day that everywhere you look there is a celebrity having a baby—and I said I hoped I didn't catch it. There are just so many things I want to do."[30]

**Alyssa Milano** – Actress *(Charmed, Who's the Boss)*, former singer

**Alley Mills** – Actress *(The Wonder Years, The Bold and the Beautiful)*

**Helen Mirren** – English actress *(The Queen, Elizabeth I, The Last Station)*

Asked if she regrets never having had children, Mirren says, "No. Absolutely not. Absolutely not. I am so happy that I didn't have children. Well, you know because I've had freedom."[31]

**Marilyn Monroe** (1926-1962) – Actress (*The Misfits, Some Like it Hot, Gentlemen Prefer Blondes*), model, film producer, singer, showgirl

**Diana Muldaur** – Actress (*L.A. Law*), first woman to serve as president of the Academy of Television Arts & Sciences (1983-1985), dog trainer

**Judd Nelson** – Actor *(The Breakfast Club, St. Elmo's Fire)*

**Lisa Niemi** – Finnish-American actress (*One Last Dance*), dancer, writer (widow of Patrick Swayze)

**Annie Oakley** (1860-1926) – Famous sharpshooter, exhibition shooter, lead star in traveling show *Buffalo Bill's Wild West*

**Suze Orman** – TV host, financial advisor, motivational speaker

**Alexandra Paul** – Actress *(Baywatch)*, triathlete, activist

"I am childless by choice. It was a choice I made when I was a kid, after seeing the UNICEF commercials of hungry, thirsty children in crowded cities, swollen bellied with stick legs, black flies on their faces. At 9, I told my friend Susie Hollander, "I am not going to have my own kids because there are too many children in the world."[32]

**Joaquin Phoenix** – Actor *(Walk the Line)*, musician, rapper

**Parker Posey** – Actress (*Inside Out, Broken English, The House of Yes*)

**Rachael Ray** – TV personality (*Rachael Ray*), celebrity chef, author

"I don't have time. I work too much to be an appropriate parent. I feel like a bad mom to my dog some days because I'm just not here enough. I just feel like I would do a bad job if I took the time to literally give birth to a kid right now and try and juggle everything I'm doing."[33]

**Keanu Reeves** – Canadian actor (*Bill & Ted's Excellent Adventure, Speed, The Matrix, Point Break*)

**Portia De Rossi** – Actress (*Ally Mcbeal, Arrested Development, Nip/Tuck*), author (married to Ellen DeGeneres)

**Mickey Rourke** – Actor (*Angel Heart, Barfly, 9 ½ Weeks*), screenwriter, professional boxer, PETA spokesperson

**Winona Ryder** – Actress, producer (*Girl Interrupted*)

**Diane Sawyer** – TV journalist, news anchor (has 3 grown stepchildren)

**Kevin Spacey** – Actor (*The Usual Suspects, American Beauty*), director, screenwriter, producer

**Patrick Swayze** (1952-2009) – Actor (*Dirty Dancing, Ghost*), dancer, singer-songwriter

**Quentin Tarantino** – Film director, screenwriter, producer (*Inglourious Basterds, Pulp Fiction, Reservoir Dogs*), cinematographer, actor

Tarantino tells GQ, "I'm not saying that I'll never get married or have a kid before I'm 60. But I've made a choice, so far, to go on this road alone. Because this is my time to make movies."[34]

**Marlo Thomas** – Actress (*That Girl*), producer, social activist (has 5 grown stepchildren)

**Marisa Tomei** – Actress *(My Cousin Vinny, The Wrestler)*

When asked why she's not married and without children, she says, "I really hate those questions. Let me tell you that up front. I'm not that big a fan of marriage as an institution and I don't know why women need to have children to be seen as complete human beings."[35]

**Lily Tomlin** – Actress *(Laugh-in)*, comedian, writer, producer

In 1973, when *Tonight Show* host Johnny Carson asked actress Lily Tomlin about having children, she answered "I like children but I don't really want to have any children and raise them." Now, she tells *Metro Weekly* that she doesn't regret not having kids with partner Jane Wagner, confiding, "God only knows what I would have done with them, poor things. I really do like kids, but there wouldn't have been room in my life to raise children."[36]

**Christopher Walken** – Actor *(Joe Dirt, Annie Hall, The Deer Hunter)*, film director (he has appeared in more than 100 movies and TV shows)

Walken has stated in interviews that not having children is one of the reasons he has had such a prolific career.[37]

**Betty White** – Actress *(The Mary Tyler Moore Show, The Golden Girls, Hot in Cleveland)*, comedian, writer

**Oprah Winfrey** – TV host *(The Oprah Winfrey Show)*, actress *(The Color Purple)*, producer, philanthropist, founder of *O, The Oprah Magazine*

Excerpt from interview in *O, The Oprah Magazine*, May 2010:
**Barbara:** How do you feel about not having children?
**Oprah:** Really good. No regrets whatsoever. Gayle grew up writing the names of her would-be children, making little hearts and putting children's names in them. Never occurred to me to do that. I never had a desire. And I don't think I could have this life *and* have children. One of the lessons I've learned from doing the show is just how much sacrifice and attention is required to do the job of mothering well. Nothing in my background prepared or trained me to do that. So I don't have any regrets about it at all. And I do feel like I am a mother in a broader sense—to a generation of viewers who've grown up with me.[38]

**James Woods** – Actor *(Once Upon a Time in America, Salvador, Nixon, Ghosts of Mississippi, Shark)*

**Chow Yun-fat** – Hong Kong–born actor *(Crouching Tiger, Hidden Dragon, A Better Tomorrow)*

**Billy Zane** – Actor *(Titanic, The Phantom, Twin Peaks)*, producer, director

**Renée Zellweger** – Actress *(Bridget Jones's Diary, Chicago)*, producer

"My brother has two children now, so I've been playing aunt Renee. They're two and four. It's chaos. Moms out there, kudos to you. The cool thing about being an aunt is like, I can leave. No offence to my big brother Drew, but that is slavery. I dare you to take a shower. You can't do anything unless they let you. It's a dictatorship. They're little dictators in their crib."[39]

**Daphne Zuniga** – Actress *(Melrose Place)*, environmentalist

## MUSICIANS

**Louis Andriessen** – Dutch composer, pianist, teacher of composition

Born in 1939, Andriessen was married to the late Jeanette Yanikan for 40 years. Having decided not to have children, they were devoted to their work and their cats.[40]

**Louis Armstrong** (1901-1971) – Jazz trumpeter, singer

"Satchmo" loved to play to the neighborhood kids, but never had his own.

**Ludwig van Beethoven** (1770-1827) – German composer and pianist (gained custody of his nephew upon his brother's death)

**Eubie Blake** (1887-1983) – Jazz and ragtime composer, pianist, lyricist

**Susan Boyle** – Scottish singer, 2nd place winner on *American Idol* (2008)

**Captain & Tennille** (Daryl Dragon and Toni Tennille) – 1970s pop singing duo

They agree on two important issues: vegetarianism and no children. "Because of the kind of life we lead," Toni explains, "it would be worse for us to have children than not. I can't even get Daryl to feed the dogs."[41]

**Mary Chapin Carpenter** – Folk and country singer-songwriter, guitarist

**Kelly Clarkson** – Pop rock singer-songwriter, actress

"Oh, my God, I have no desire. I would not be a good mother. I mean, I love being an aunt to my niece and nephew. And I used to want to, like, adopt 10 kids—because I had friends who were adopted, and I thought that was the coolest thing, to be chosen. But again, my job is too selfish."[42]

**Robert Fripp** – British guitarist (King Crimson), composer, producer

**Gloria Gaynor** – Singer-songwriter (#1 disco hit "I Will Survive"), actress

**Lionel Hampton** (1908-2002) – Jazz vibraphonist, pianist, percussionist, bandleader, singer, actor

**Georg Friedrich Handel** (1685-1759) – German-British Baroque composer, famous for his operas, oratorios and concertos

**Debbie Harry ("Blondie")** – Singer-songwriter, actress

**Franz Joseph Haydn** (1732-1809) – Austrian composer, "Father of the Symphony"

**Janet Jackson** – Singer-songwriter, dancer, record producer, actress

**Wendy Matthews** – Australian adult alternative pop singer-songwriter from Canada (Models, Absent Friends, and as a solo artist)

**Christine McVie** – British singer-songwriter, keyboardist (Fleetwood Mac)

**Stevie Nicks** – Singer-songwriter (Fleetwood Mac)

"I made a conscious decision that I was not going to have children. I didn't want others raising them, and looking after them myself would get in the way of being a musician and writer."[43]

**Dolly Parton** – Country singer-songwriter, record producer, actress, author

**Bonnie Raitt** – Blues-rock singer-songwriter, guitarist, political activist

**Franz Schubert** (1797-1828) – Austrian composer (almost 1,000 works)

**Robert Smith** – Singer-songwriter (lead singer of The Cure)

> "I have 25 nephews and nieces, so I have the pleasure of lots of children around when want them. But I can shut the door on them," Smith says. "My wife and I decided at a very early age that we would not have children. I don't feel responsible enough to bring a child into the world."[44]

**Robbie Williams** – British singer-songwriter (Take That), vocal coach

> "I don't believe that to be fulfilled as a human being, you have to have kids. I maintain the right to change my opinion at any time, but what's the point of having kids? I can't guarantee that I won't father a child that won't be in pain, cos that kid's going to be in pain at some point in their life, and I don't want to see that."[45]

**Yanni** – Pianist, keyboardist, composer (*Dare to Dream* album)

**Dwight Yoakum** – Country singer-songwriter, actor, film director

## ARTISTS

**Scott Adams** – Cartoonist, creator of *Dilbert* comic strip, author

**Charles Addams** (1912-1988) – Cartoonist for *The New Yorker*, creator of the Addams Family characters

> Their marriage broke up after Mr. Addams, an inveterate hater of small children, balked at the prospect of adopting one.[46]

**Lynda Barry** – Cartoonist (*Ernie Pook's Comeek*), author

**William Blake** (1757-1827) – English poet, painter, printmaker

**Pierre Bonnard** (1867-1947) – French painter and printmaker

**Judy Chicago** – Feminist, artist, author, educator, animal rights activist

**Leonardo Da Vinci** (1452-1519) – Italian painter, sculptor, scientist, mathematician, engineer, inventor, writer

**Steve Ditko** – Comic book artist, co-creator of Spider-Man and Doctor Strange

**Frida Kahlo** (1907-1954) – Mexican painter (surrealism), known for self-portraits

**Lee Krasner** (1908-1984) – Abstract expressionist painter, wife of Jackson Pollock

**Mary Ellen Mark** – Internationally acclaimed photographer and photojournalist

**Georgia O'Keeffe** (1887-1986) – Painter (abstract, American modernism), awarded the Presidential Medal of Freedom

**Jackson Pollock** (1912-1956) – Influential abstract expressionist painter

**Bill Watterson** – Cartoonist (creator of *Calvin and Hobbes* comic strip)

**Margaret Ely Webb** (1877-1965) – Children's book illustrator, writer

> She never had children, but had a "special affinity for youngsters" and was known for her children's book illustrations.[47]

## WRITERS

**Mitch Albom** – Author (*Tuesdays with Morrie, The Five People You Meet in Heaven*), journalist, screenwriter, dramatist, broadcaster, musician, philanthropist

**Louisa May Alcott** (1832-1888) – Novelist (*Little Women*), abolitionist, feminist (took in her niece upon her sister's death)

**Hans Christian Andersen** (1805-1875) – Danish novelist, fairy tale author (*The Snow Queen, The Little Mermaid*)

**Jane Austen** (1775-1817) – English novelist (*Sense and Sensibility*)

**Samuel Beckett** (1906-1989) – Irish novelist, playwright, poet, essayist (Nobel Prize in Literature)

**Baroness Karen Blixen** (1885-1962) – Danish author (*Out of Africa*)

**Nathaniel Branden** – Canadian author, psychotherapist (former student and romantic partner of Ayn Rand)

"I cannot regret not having children of my own because I am so work-focused; I always knew that it would be a major achievement to integrate and do right by my career and my marriage, and that children would spread me too thin and I did not want to be the father who wasn't there."[48]

**James Burke** – British author, broadcaster, creator of PBS Series *Connections*

**Leo Buscaglia, PhD** (1924-1998) – Author (*The Fall of Freddie the Leaf*), motivational speaker, professor, known as "Dr. Love" for his work on love

"I think we have to make choices in life, and the choice for me was to embrace all person-kind rather than concentrate on one single individual... The universal is what I've selected."[49]

**Raymond Chandler** (1888-1959) – Novelist, screenwriter (*The Big Sleep*)

**Sir Arthur C. Clarke, CBE** (1917-2008) – British science fiction author (*2001: A Space Odyssey*), inventor, futurist

**Dorothy Clewes** (1907-2003) – English author of children and teen books

**Carlo Collodi** (1826-1890) – Italian children's book author (*Pinocchio*)

**Charlotte Curtis** (1928-1987) – News reporter, society editor, first female journalist to head *The New York Times*

**Emily Dickinson** (1830-1886) – American poet

**George Eliot** (born Mary Ann Evans) (1819-1880) – English novelist

**T.S. Eliot** (1888-1965) – American-born English poet and playwright

**Jane Fallon** – English producer (*Teachers, This Life, EastEnders*), novelist

In an interview last year, Jane Fallon, wife of Ricky Gervais, said: "It's a difficult world and you shouldn't have kids unless you really want them. I've seen people go broody in a physical way that I've never experienced. Luckily, Ricky feels the same way."[50]

**Richard Ford** – American novelist (*The Sportswriter, Independence Day*)

His 2nd rule in writing fiction: "Don't have children."[51]

**Theodor Seuss Geisel "Dr. Seuss"** (1904-1991) – Children's book author, cartoonist, animator, book publisher

> Though he devoted most of his life to writing children's books, Geisel (Dr. Seuss) never had any children. He would say, when asked about this, "You have 'em; I'll entertain 'em."[52]

**Elizabeth Gilbert** – Novelist, memoirist (*Eat, Pray, Love*)

> "I also know that I won't go forth and have children just in case I might regret missing it later in life; I don't think this is a strong enough motivation to bring more babies onto the earth."[53]

**W. S. Gilbert** (1836-1911) – English dramatist, librettist, composer (Gilbert & Sullivan)

**Jan Goodwin** – Award-winning journalist, author (*The Price of Honor*), concerned with social justice and human rights

**Marguerite Henry** (1902-1997) – Children's book author (esp. horse stories)

> During their sixty-four years of marriage she didn't have children, but instead had many pets that inspired some of her stories.[54]

**Dean Koontz** – Novelist (suspense thrillers), short story writer, screenwriter

**Charles Lamb** (1775-1834) – English essayist, author

> "When I consider how little of a rarity children are—that every street and blind alley swarms with them—that the poorest people commonly have them in most abundance—that there are few marriages that are not blest with at least one of these bargains—how often they turn out ill, and defeat the fond hopes of their parents, taking to vicious courses, which end in poverty, disgrace, the gallows, etc.—I cannot for my life tell what cause for pride there can possibly be in having them. If they were young phoenixes, indeed, that were born but one in a year, there might be a pretext. But when they are so common."[55]

**Philip Larkin** (1922-1985) – British poet, librarian, novelist

> "Man hands on misery to man. It deepens like a coastal shelf. Get out as early as you can, and don't have any kids yourself."[56]

**Harper Lee** – Author (Pulitzer Prize for *To Kill a Mockingbird*)

**H. L. Mencken** (1880-1956) – American journalist, essayist, satirist

**Margaret Mitchell** (1900-1949) – Pulitzer Prize novelist (*Gone with the Wind*)

**Flannery O'Connor** (1925-1964) – Novelist, short story writer, essayist

**Sheila O'Flanagan** – Irish novelist (*Stand by Me*), journalist

> "A company interviewing me for a job asked me what my circumstances were and I told them I had no intention of having children. It was the first time I had ever verbalised it, but I was always sure. I suppose it's a lack of a maternal instinct. I'm just not sure everyone has it. Some people are forced into having it, though." She adds, "I've been told that I can 'write good children,' but it's just the rearing of them I didn't fancy."[57]

**Dorothy Parker** (1893-1967) – Author, poet, critic, screenwriter, satirist

**Molly Peacock** – American-Canadian poet, essayist, writer

"As it turns out, my choice not to have children has defined my adult life. It's been like hacking through undergrowth while walking down a hardly used, perfectly paved way...In fact, on that path my choice not to be a Mother became more of a *discovery* of a decision...It took insight to see it and release it—an insight I didn't always have. For this is a decision you do not make once, but many times. I would leave the idea of not having children behind only to face it again and again as I went on."[58]

**Ayn Rand** (1905-1982) – Russian-American novelist (*The Fountainhead, Atlas Shrugged*), philosopher, playwright, screenwriter

**George Bernard Shaw** (1856-1950) – Irish playwright (*Pygmalion*), critic, political activist, Nobel Prize in Literature (1925)

"Life isn't about finding yourself. Life is about creating yourself."[59]

**Lionel Shriver** (born Margaret Ann Shriver) – Journalist, novelist (*We Need To Talk About Kevin, So Much for That*)

**Lynn Truss** – English author (*Eats, Shoots & Leaves),* writer, journalist

**Kate Douglas Wiggin** (1856-1953) – Children's book author (*Rebecca of Sunnybrook Farm*), educator

While she had had no children of her own, she left behind a legacy of devotion and commitment to bettering the lives of children everywhere in her stories and life's work.[60]

**Virginia Woolf** (1882-1941) – English novelist, essayist, publisher, critic

**Marguerite Yourcenar** (1903-1987) – Belgian-born French novelist, essayist, poet, animal rights activist

## POLITICOS / GOVERNMENT OFFICIALS

**James Buchanan** (1791-1868) – 15th President of the U.S. (1857-1861)

**Pat Buchanan** – Political commentator, writer, conservative politician

**Barbara Castle** (1910-2002) – British Labour Party politician, longtime Member of Parliament, the only woman to have held the office of First Secretary of State

**Helen Clark** – Former New Zealand Prime Minister, Administrator of the U.N. Development Program, ranked 38th most powerful woman in world (*Forbes* 2007)

**Anne Cools** – Canadian Senator (born in Barbados), first black woman to be appointed to Canada's upper house

**Gray Davis** – California's 37th Governor, Democrat politician, attorney

**Edward VIII, later Duke of Windsor** (1894-1972) – King of the United Kingdom (Jan.-Dec. 1936), Duke of Windsor (1937-death)

**Elizabeth Dole** – Politician, former Secretary of Transportation, former Secretary of Labor (has one adult stepchild)

**Warren G. Harding** (1865-1923) – 29th U.S. President, advocated civil rights for African-Americans (had one stepson who did not live with him)

**Elena Kagan** – U.S. Supreme Court Justice, former Dean of Harvard Law School

**APJ Abdul Kalam** – 11th President of India (2002-2007), aerospace engineer

**William Lyon Mackenzie King** (1874-1950) – 10th Prime Minister of Canada

**William Rufus King** (1786-1853) – 13th U.S. Vice President

**Giuseppe Mazzini** (1805-1872) – Italian patriot, philosopher, politician, journalist (known as the "Soul of Italy")

**Angela Merkel** – Chancellor of Germany (2005-present), physical chemist (named the most powerful woman in the world by *Forbes* in 2011)

**Harriet Miers** – 31st U.S. White House Counsel 2005-2007, attorney

**Marjorie "Mo" Mowlam** (1949-2005) – British Labour Party politician, former Member of Parliament (1987-2001), former Secretary of State for Northern Ireland

**Janet Napolitano** – 3rd U.S. Secretary of Homeland Security (Obama Administration), ranked 51st most powerful woman by *Forbes* in 2009

**Queen Elizabeth I** (1533-1603) – Queen of England and Ireland (1558 'til death)

**Jeanette Rankin** (1880-1973) – First woman in U.S. Congress (Republican), known for her anti-war stance, founding member of Women's International League for Peace and Freedom

**Condaleeza Rice** – 66th U.S. Secretary of State, first African-American woman to be secretary of state, professor, diplomat, author

**Sonia Sotomayor** – U.S. Supreme Court Justice (first Hispanic justice)

**David Souter** – Former U.S. Supreme Court Justice (1990-2009), once named "one of Washington's 10 Most Eligible Bachelors" by *The Washington Post*

**Atal Bihari Vajpayee** – 10th Prime Minister of India, former Member of Parliament for over four decades, gifted orator, poet

**George Washington** (1732-1799) – First U.S. President (1789-1797), had no kids of his own, but helped raise two of Martha's children from her first marriage.

## BUSINESS PHILANTHROPISTS / ENTREPRENEURS

**Cecil Howard Green** (1900-2003) – British-born American geophysicist, founder of Texas Instruments, philanthropist (gave over $200 million to education and medicine)

**Milton S. Hershey** (1857-1945) – Founder of Hershey Chocolate Company, philanthropist (since he and his wife could not have children, they chose to benefit others by establishing the Hershey Industrial School with a Deed of Trust in 1909)

**Howard Hughes** (1905-1976) – Industrialist, aviator, engineer, film producer, director, philanthropist, chairman of Hughes Aircraft

**John A. "Jack" Jackson** (1913-2003) – Geologist, oilman, philanthropist (he and his wife left their estate worth over $150 million to University of Texas at Austin)

**Raymond Albert "Ray" Kroc** (1902-1984) – Entrepreneur (developed McDonald's into the world's most successful fast food operation), philanthropist

## SCIENTISTS / PHILOSOPHERS / THEORISTS

**Francis Bacon** (1561-1626) – English philosopher, statesman, scientist, author

**Simone de Beauvoir** (1908-1986) – French existential philosopher, author (*The Second Sex*), feminist (long-term open relationship with Jean-Paul Sartre)

**Nicolaus Copernicus** (1473-1543) – Polish astronomer, mathematician, physician, scholar, economist (formulated "Heliocentrism")

**Grace Hopper** (1906-1992) – Computer scientist (the "mother of the computer"), United State Naval Officer, Rear Admiral

**Immanuel Kant** (1724-1804) – 18th-century German philosopher

**Plato** (427 BC-347 BC) – Classical Greek philosopher, founder of the Academy in Athens (the first institution of higher learning in the Western world), teacher of Aristotle

**E. O. Wilson** – Biologist, researcher, theorist, naturalist, environmental advocate, author (*The Ants, Human Nature*), two-time Pulitzer Prize winner for nonfiction

**Sir Isaac Newton** (1642-1727) – English physicist, mathematician, astronomer, natural philosopher, alchemist, theologian, author of the monograph *Principia*, considered by many to be the greatest and most influential scientist who ever lived

## HUMANITARIANS / ACTIVISTS / CIVIL RIGHTS PIONEERS

**Susan B. Anthony** (1820-1906) – Civil rights leader, Suffragist, 19th-century women's rights advocate (fought for women's voting rights), anti-slavery activist

**Rosamond Carr** (1912-2006) – Humanitarian (Rwanda's orphanage), author

**Carrie Chapman Catt** (1859-1947) – Women's suffrage leader, founder of the League of Women Voters and the International Alliance of Women, campaigned for the 19th Amendment to the U.S. Constitution that gave U.S. women the right to vote in 1920

**Eugene Victor Debs** (1855-1926) – American union and socialist leader

**Bessie Delany** (1891-1995) – Civil rights pioneer, second African-American female dentist in New York State, author, lived to the age of 104

**Sadie Delany** (1889-1999) – Civil rights pioneer, first African-American allowed to teach domestic science in New York State, author (co-authored *Having Our Say: The Delany Sisters' First 100 Years*), lived to the age of 109

**Margaretta Forten** (b. early 1800s, death unknown) – Black abolitionist, fought against slavery in mid-1800s, founded Philadelphia Female Anti-Slavery Society

**Emma Goldman** (1869-1940) – Political activist, anarchist, feminist
"Women need not always keep their mouths shut and their wombs open."[61]

**Patricia Ireland** – Feminist, social activist, lawyer, former president of National Organization of Women (1991-2001)

**Florence Nightingale** (1820-1910) – English nurse, writer, statistician, pioneer of modern nursing, founded the first secular nursing school in the world (London)

## RELIGIOUS FIGURES

**Tenzin Gyatso "Dalai Lama"** – 14th and current Dalai Lama (1950 to present), most influential figure in Tibetan Buddhism

**Jesus of Nazareth "Jesus Christ"** (c. 3 BC – c. 30 AD) – Central figure in Christianity which views him as the Messiah and the Son of God

It should be noted that some historians believe he *did* father a child.

**Joan of Arc** (1412-1431) – Catholic saint and national heroine of France

**Mother Teresa** (1910-1997) – Catholic nun, humanitarian, Christian missionary

## SPORTS FIGURES

**Grover Cleveland Alexander** (1887-1950) – Major League Baseball pitcher (Phillies, Cubs, Cardinals), Baseball Hall of Famer

**Marcus Allen** – Former NFL football running back (Raiders, Chiefs), Football Hall of Famer, former TV football analyst

**Dario Franchitti** – Scottish race car driver, won 2010 Indy 500 (married to Ashley Judd)

**Lou Gehrig** (1903-1941) – Major League Baseball player first baseman (New York Yankees), Baseball Hall of Famer

**Althea Gibson** (1927-2003) – Tennis Pro, first Black to win a Grand Slam title (1956) and break the color barrier on the tennis circuit

**Deacon Jones** – Former NFL football defensive end (Rams, Chargers, Redskins), Football Hall of Famer

**Billy Jean King** – Tennis Pro (39 Grand Slam titles), founder of Women's Tennis Association, Women's Sports Foundation and World Team Tennis, feminist

**Martina Navratilova** – Former World No. 1 Tennis Pro (record for most career titles men or women), author, political and animal rights activist

**Bill Parcells** – NFL team consultant (Miami Dolphins), former NFL coach (most recently with Dallas Cowboys), winner of two Super Bowl rings

**Danica Patrick** – Auto racing driver, model, advertising spokeswoman

Danica told reporters that, although she always knew she wanted to be a wife, she's still not sold on motherhood. "I never worried about kids. But I always wanted to get married."[62]

**Serena Williams** – Tennis Pro (27 Grand Slam titles), ranked World No. 1 five times since 2002, Olympic gold medalist, fashion designer, author

Serena tells *Black Celebrity Kids* that she wants to start a family but fears her forgetfulness will make her a bad mom (citing forgetting her two little dogs now and then). In addition, she says, "Every time I see a woman walking around pregnant, I'm like, 'Oh my god, I could never do that.' How are you walking? I look at them and my back starts hurting!"[63]

**Venus Williams** – Tennis Pro (21 Grand Slam titles), ranked World No. 1 three times since 2002, Olympic gold medalist, designer, entrepreneur

## OTHER NOTABLES

**Dr. Robert C. Atkins** (1930-2003) – Physician, cardiologist, creator of the "Atkins Diet"

**Helen Gurley Brown** (1922-2012) – Magazine editor, editor-in-chief of *Cosmopolitan* for 32 years, author, publisher, businesswoman

> "My sister, Mary, had polio and was in a wheelchair all her life," Brown said. "I know what it is to care for somebody. I didn't want the responsibility for any other little creatures. I have never regretted that decision."[64]

**Gabrielle Bonheur "Coco" Chanel** (1883-1971) – French fashion designer, entrepreneur, founder of the Chanel brand

**Ann Coulter** – Conservative political commentator, lawyer, syndicated columnist, author (*Slander: Liberal Lies About the American Right*)

**Sir Francis Drake** (1540-1596) – English sea captain, privateer, Vice Admiral of the English fleet, led the first English circumnavigation of the globe

**Amelia Earhart** (1897-1937) – Aviation pioneer, author, first woman to fly solo across the Atlantic Ocean (had two stepchildren)

**Martha Graham** (1894-1991) – Choreographer, dancer, pioneer of modern dance

**Susan Helms** – NASA astronaut, U.S. Air Force Major General, engineer

**Helen Keller** (1880-1968) – Author, political activist, lecturer, first deaf-blind person to graduate from college, Presidential Medal of Freedom

**John F. Kennedy, Jr.** (1960-1999) – Journalist, magazine publisher, lawyer, son of President John F. Kennedy

**T. E. Lawrence "Lawrence of Arabia"** (1888-1935) – British Army officer (renowned for his role during the Arab Revolt)

**Gloria Steinem** – Feminist, journalist, writer (*Ms. Magazine*), activist

## YOUR OWN ADDITIONS

_____

_____

_____

_____

_____

_____

*    *    *

The preceding list of notable non-parents is far from complete, as there are hundreds I did not include in the interest of brevity—and certainly thousands more I don't know of around the world. In addition to yourself, do you know of any to add to the list? Since the childfree trend is growing, there will likely be new names to add monthly.

It's interesting that three U.S. presidents were non-parents, as it seems today a spouse and offspring are social prerequisites for running for office.

I'm not surprised, however, that some of my favorite people—from past and present—are non-parents. Some of the most talented entertainers, writers and thinkers did not procreate.

And look at the humanitarians and pioneers that adorn this list—men and women who improved our world by giving to others, starting movements and founding organizations. Quite an impressive group!

I wonder how many of these folks could have touched our lives or changed our world as they did, had they offspring to care for? Surely—had they parented—they could not have devoted themselves to their life's calling with such vigor and success.

We are not alone. We are in good company!

# KIDFREE RESOURCES
## *A Potpourri for Non-Parents*

I would like to say that it was a big relief when I finally found
child-free resources, and began to read about other child-free women
and couples who share similar issues and experiences!
—Joy, 44, Mammoth Lakes, CA

**KIDFREE TERMS**

Most of the following terms have been bantered around among childfree groups for years. Some I found on childfree websites; others I coined myself. While many may be offensive to parents, they are meant for use among non-parents (not over dinner with our childed friends please!).

**Baby Rabies** – Obsession with having or conceiving a child.

**Bingo** – A cliché statement made by a parent to a childfree, questioning their decision not to have kids.

**BNP** – "Breeder, Not Parent." (See Breeder below)

**Breeder** – A bad parent. One who is careless at raising their children.

**Breeder Entitlement** – Breeders' belief that because they have kids they are entitled to special treatment, more time off, tax breaks and baby bonuses.

**Childfree (CF)** – One who is childless by choice.

**Childless** – One who has no children, but wishes they did.

**Diaperwhipped** – Parents who are controlled by their child's every want and whim.

**DINK** – "Double Income, No Kids."

**DINKER** – "Double Income, No Kids, Early Retirement."

**Fence-sitter** – One who has not decided whether or not to have kids.

**Freemale** – A woman who chooses freedom over both marriage and motherhood.

**GINK** – "Green Inclinations, No Kids."

**Kid-centric** – Unnaturally centered around kids.

**Kidfree** – A term I coined to mean "free of kids" whether by choice, chance or circumstance.

**KIDFREE TERMS cont...**
**Misopedist** – One who strongly abhors children.
**MOO** – "Mother Operating Offensively." A publicly rude mother.
**Non-parent** – An adult without children, regardless of reason.
**PANK** – "Professional Aunt with No Kids" who enjoys nieces & nephews.
**PNB** – "Parent, Not Breeder." A good parent. One who is raising their kids well, and who behaves in a non-obnoxious manner regarding their children.
**SITCOM** – "Single Income, Two Children, Oppressive Mortgage."
**Sprog** – A slang term from the British word for "child."
**THINKER** – "Two Healthy Incomes, No Kids, Early Retirement."
**Tokophobia** – The fear of childbirth and/or pregnancy.

## KIDFREE READING

Here is a list of nine books with nine different angles on parenting and non-parenting. See my website for an updated list of reading on the subject. (Listed in descending order from most recently released):

*Two is Enough: A Couple's Guide to Living Childless by Choice* by Laura S. Scott (2009). The author interviews couples who have opted out of parenthood; and explores their reasons and the lives they lead.

*NO KIDS: 40 Reasons Not to Have Children* by Corinne Maier (2009). A mother of two gives her 40 pithy reasons not to have kids.

*Blindsided by a Diaper* by Dana Bedford Hilmer (2007). More than 30 men and women reveal how parenthood changes a relationship.

*Pride and Joy: The Lives and Passions of Women Without Children* by Terri Casey (2007). Interviews with 25 women who have chosen not to have children.

*I Hate Other People's Kids* by Adrianne Frost (2006). A wry look from a comedian/actor at why kids today are such terrors.

*Baby Not On Board: A Celebration of Life Without Kids* by Jennifer L. Shawne (2005). A humorous account of the world of "unparenting."

*Childfree After Infertility: Moving from Childlessness to a Joyous Life* by Heather Wardell (2003). Stories of how infertile people have moved from "childlessness" to creating happy kidfree lives.

*The Baby Boon: How Family-Friendly America Cheats the Childless* by Elinor Burkett (2002). How government and employers cheat the childless by giving parents special treatment.

*The Childless Revolution: What it Means to be Childless Today* by Madelyn Cain (2001). Cain divides childless women into three subsets and explores their issues.

## KIDFREE GROUPS, BLOGS AND WEBSITES

Because new sites come and go frequently, I recommend an internet search of "childfree websites" or "childfree blogs" for a current selection.

**Childfree.net** – www.childfree.net
An active childfree discussion list, to which I've referred throughout this book. Through a moderator, list members send and receive emails daily on childfree topics including: issues we face, opinions about kids and parenting, and off-topic items ranging from pet care to politics.

**The Childfree Life** – www.thechildfreelife.com
A site featuring a blog for the childfree, as well as childfree books, films, products, articles, quotations, links and more.

**Childfree Meetup Groups** – www.childfree.meetup.com
These are groups of childfree couples and singles that hold social meetings in towns around the world. As of this publication, there were more than 10,000 members in 72 groups in four countries.

**Child Free Zone** – www.child-free-zone.blogspot.com
Launched by David and Susan Moore of Australia (authors of *Child-Free Zone),* this site is chock-full of stories, social events, articles, links, childfree products and an active blog.

**Childfree Christians** – www.cf-christians.livejournal.com
Launched in 2005, this blogsite ponders the life and issues of being a childfree Christian, with hundreds of journal entries and comments.

**Childless by Choice Yahoo Groups** –
www.groups.yahoo.com/group/childlesschoice
A yahoo blog for the childless by choice, with nearly 500 members. This group's active blog stays mostly on-topic.

**Happily Childfree** – www.happilychildfree.com
Launched by Phoena in 2001, this site is a complete resource for the childfree, including childfree book reviews, "breeder bingo" responses, a lengthy childfree lingo list and a rant journal.

**Kidding Aside** – www.kiddingaside.net
The site of The British Childfree Association, which was founded in 2000 to campaign for the rights of childless British people. This group works to promote the childfree lifestyle as a legitimate alternative to parenthood, and campaigns for equal opportunity for non-parents.

**Kidfree & Lovin' It!** – www.kidfreeandlovinit.com
An online resource center for all non-parents, whether single, coupled, male or female, kidfree, childfree or on the fence. Includes lists and links to childfree resorts, websites, TV interviews, books and articles, as well as findings from the Kidfree and Childfree Dating surveys.

**Married No Kids** – http://marriednokids.bellaonline.com
Part of the BellaOnline forum, it caters to childfree married women. The editor routinely publishes articles and essays on non-parenting, which she emails to her members through an online newsletter. The site also offers an online forum of topics for discussion.

**No Kidding!** – www.nokidding.net
Founded in 1984 by Jerry Steinberg, this is one of the oldest and largest childfree organizations. An international social club for childfree couples and singles, there are dozens of chapters in the U.S., Canada and New Zealand that hold local meetings and events regularly. You can start a chapter in your own town.

**We Kid You Not** – www.wekidyounot.org
This discussion forum is a place for childfree to meet, greet and chat. Fence-sitters are welcome as are members of the GLBT community.

## KIDFREE DATING & SINGLES SITES

**Dink Link** – www.dinklink.com (DINK=Dual Income, No Kids) Started in 2011, this website is dedicated to helping childless singles who don't have and don't want kids, to meet, mingle or date.

**I Do NOT Want Kids** – www.puzzele.com/datingsite
Dating site launched in 2008 to match childfree singles. The site is free, interactive and includes photos and a personal questionnaire.

**No Kids Passions** – www.nokidspassions.com
A childless social networking and dating site, which is 100% free. Its "No Interest in Having Children" group boasts over 2,600 members.

**Yahoo Childfree Singles Group** –
www.groups.yahoo.com/group/Childfree_Singles
Yahoo group created in 2001 for meeting singles with an interest in remaining childfree. Hosts more than 700 members and growing.

## KIDFREE TRAVEL

Exciting new trends abound in the travel world, including a buzz about potential childfree airline flights. Keep an eye out for my future project, *Kidfree Travel*, which will reveal and explore resorts, airlines and destinations around the world that offer sanctuary from the sights and sounds of young children.

In the meantime, you'll find a partial list of age-restricted resorts and their links on my Kidfree website: **www.kidfreeandlovinit.com**

For an agency that specializes in vacation travel free from noisy children, visit ChildFree Travel: **www.childfreetravel.net**

# AFTERWORD

They say you write your first book about yourself or the things you know. In hindsight, I wrote this book about myself and the things I *didn't* know, but wanted to. When I launched this project, I knew I wasn't going to have kids, but I didn't know what that meant.

Conducting my research and writing these past six years has been the best way to find the answers I sought long ago. In my explorations, I have become more than familiar with the childfree, kidfree and childless. I have heard the issues we contend with—many of which I share myself. And I have heard the hundreds of good reasons not to procreate—many of which I've added to my *own* list along the way.

When I was about halfway into this project, a friend of mine said, "How much can there *be* to say about not having kids?" (Hinting it was taking *far* too long to write, which it was!) I told her that I was learning and reading new things daily about non-parenting. My book was growing larger by the week as I found more aspects of the subject to explore. Three years later, I had a book I had to whittle down from over 400 pages!

As I could not reveal all the findings of my Childfree Dating Survey in one chapter, I plan to write a separate treatment on the Single & Kidfree in the future. The Kidfree Survey will also remain open to include new quotes and findings in future editions of *Kidfree & Lovin' It*. Go to my website, if you have not yet taken either of these two surveys.

As the first part of my journey ends, I now know—more than ever—that I made the right choice to be kidfree. And, as you finish this book, I hope *you* know that you have made—or will make—the choice that is uniquely right for you.

# ACKNOWLEDGEMENTS

This project has been both a labor of love and a labor of learning. I would first like to thank the Childfree Network for giving me my first experience of connecting with others in the childfree community. Since 2006, this online group has given me great insight into the issues concerning non-parents today—some of which I knew firsthand, much of which I was unaware until joining the group, and *all* of which helped me to better structure the questions for my two international surveys.

A big thanks to Cork Millner—my writing mentor who has authored more than a dozen books—for not only sharing his nuggets of writing wisdom with me, but also for believing early on (probably more than anyone) in the potential success of *Kidfree & Lovin' It!*

A special thanks goes to my editor, Denise Iest, for imparting both her wisdom and her attention to detail, as well as offering me her invaluable opinions as a fellow childfree.

Of course, this entire project would not have been complete without the 4,500+ survey respondents from 55 countries worldwide who made this "tome" the most complete and fact-based of its kind. I am grateful to those who took my Kidfree Survey and/or Childfree Dating Survey for giving me thoughtful answers and clever quotes to share throughout this book.

I would also like to thank my father for supporting both my decision to remain kidfree as well as my decision to write a book about it. I know I've stretched the bounds of traditional upbringing he gave me, but we had many good talks over lunch about how parenting has changed these days.

As much as I know my sister Denny and brother Dave would have liked me to raise children alongside them and give their kids cousins to play with, I thank them for not prodding me to do so, and for giving me five fabulous nieces and nephews—Chelsea, Tanner, Braydon, Max and Claire—without whom I would miss the joys of watching children grow!

Thanks to my late mom, Sue, who never made me feel a need to follow the norm, and who told me more than once that women today are more free to choose not to marry or have kids than they were in her day.

I am also grateful to my friends who have made it easier to be kidfree, either because they are non-parents themselves or because their kids are grown and they don't harp about them daily. To my friend "Charles" (you know who you are), thank you for allowing me to share with my readers your wise letter to your daughter (page 106), and for warning me away from parenting years ago.

Finally, a big thank you to my partner and best friend, Brian, who never stopped believing in me and supporting me throughout this laborious Kidfree Project, and who makes it a joy to be...kidfree!

## ABOUT THE AUTHOR

Kaye Walters has enjoyed a career in the magazine industry for more than 25 years. She has worked as an international advertising executive for such publications as *ISLANDS* and *Unique Homes* magazine. Most recently, she was publisher of *Passport Gateway Magazine of Santa Barbara*—a visitor publication she co-launched in 1995—before stepping down to pursue the Kidfree Project.

Walters lives on the beach in Santa Barbara with her soul mate, Brian. Together they like to play beach volleyball, kayak, stand-up paddleboard, snorkel, ski, scuba, hike, bike, tennis, travel, garden, read, and hunt for sea glass on the beach—you got it—kidfree!

# KIDFREE BINGO CARD

| When are you going to have kids? | It's Human Nature to Procreate | What if your parents never had children? | Don't You Like Kids? | Who will take care of you when you're older? |
|---|---|---|---|---|
| You're Not a Family Without Children | You Were a Child Once Too | Your child could grow up to cure cancer | Aren't you curious what they would look like? | What about carrying on the family name? |
| You'll Change Your Mind! | Don't you want to give your parents grand-children? | **P** KIDFREE PARKING | Your Biological Clock is Ticking! | You aren't a real adult until you have kids |
| It's Selfish Not to Have Kids | You would make such a good parent | The only reason to get married is to have children | If everyone chose not to procreate, the human race would die out | Parenthood is the most important job in the world |
| It's All Worth it! | My kids are the most important thing in my life | It's Different When They're Your Own | You aren't a real woman until you experience childbirth | You'll Regret it Later! |

| WHY | DON'T | YOU | HAVE | KIDS? |
|---|---|---|---|---|
| B | I | N | G | O |

©2012 *Kidfree & Lovin' It*

(Your copy to tear out and take with you)

# KIDFREE BINGO CARD

**WHY** **DON'T** **YOU** **HAVE** **KIDS?**

**B** **I** **N** **G** **O**

©2012 *Kidfree & Lovin' It*

(Blank copy to create your own "Bingos")

# NOTES

## Chapter 1: Kidfree? Childfree? Who Are We?

[1] *The World Factbook*, CIA, "Country Comparison: Total Fertility Rate" (accessed April 11, 2012), https://www.cia.gov/library/publications/the-world-factbook/rankorder/2127rank.html

[2] Jane Lawler Dye, U.S. Census Bureau, "Fertility of American Women: 2006," http://www.census.gov/prod/2008pubs/p20-558.pdf

[3] *The World Factbook*, CIA, "Country Comparison: Total Fertility Rate" (accessed April 11, 2012), https://www.cia.gov/library/publications/the-world-factbook/rankorder/2127rank.html

[4] According to the National Center for Health Statistics of the Centers for Disease Control and Prevention, United States, 2002.

[5] Susan Stobert and Anna Kemeny, "Childless by Choice" 2003 study, *Statistics Canada.*

[6] Ethel Colquhoun, "Quarterly Review," July 1913, as quoted in the *American Journal of Sociology*, vol. 19, no. 3 (November 1913), p. 422.

[7] Kristin Park, "Choosing Childlessness: Weber's Typology of Action and Motives of the Voluntarily Childless," *Sociological Inquiry,* Volume 75 (3): 372. August 2005 (Wiley Online Library).

[8] Ibid.

[9] U.S. Census Bureau, "Educational Attainment of the Population 18 Years and Over: 2007."

## Chapter 2: Why People Have Kids

[1] curlylib, reply to blog post, "Do all women have a 'biological urge' to have children?," *NaturallyCurly.com*, May 2009 (accessed May 18, 2011), www.naturallycurly.com/curltalk/non-hair-discussion/91410-do-all-women-have-biological-urge-have-children.html

[2] Ceci Connolly, "More Women Opting Against Birth Control, Study Finds," *Washington Post,* January 4, 2005

[3] Ibid.

## Chapter 3: Why We Don't Want Kids

[1] Baby Center's "Cost of Raising Your Child" calculator; based on average of all 4 regions of the U.S., city or suburb, $57,260-$99,150 income, two-parent home, including public college (accessed April 13, 2012), http://www.babycenter.com/cost-of-raising-child-calculator

## Chapter 4: "I Have No Urge or Drive to Parent"

[1] Catherine Guthrie, "The male biological clock—it's tick-tick-ticking too," July 2006, *BabyCenter.com*, http://www.babycenter.com/0_the-male-biological-clock-its-tick-tick-ticking-too_1490614.bc?page=1
[2] Loren G. Yamamoto, MD, MPH, MBA, *Tidbits On Raising Children: Making Our Most Important Job Easier by Doing It Better, Version 1* (1st Book Library, June 2000), http://www.hawaii.edu/medicine/pediatrics/parenting/c22.html
[3] BabyCenter Medical Advisory Board, "Will you be a good mother? Demystifying the maternal instinct," 2007, http://www.babycenter.com/0_will-you-be-a-good-mother-demystifying-the-maternal-instinct_9897.bc

## Chapter 5: "I Like My Lifestyle"

[1] Sam De Brito, "The Hidden Truth About Parenthood," *The Sydney Morning Herald*, November 28, 2007, http://www.smh.com.au/news/opinion/hidden-side-of-parenthood/2007/11/27/1196036887502.html
[2] Ibid.
[3] Julie Scelfo, "Parent Shock: Children Are Not Décor," *New York Times*, February 14, 2008, http://www.nytimes.com/2008/02/14/garden/14kids.html?pagewanted=1&_r=4
[4] Ibid.
[5] Better Sleep Council and Mental Health Assoc., "Sleep and Mental Health," Better Sleep Series #3, www.sleepdisorders.about.com/od/sleepdeprivation/
[6] Dr. Amy Wolson, "Better Sleep Series #3: Q&A with Dr. Amy Wolson," http://sleepdisorders.about.com/od/sleepdeprivation/a/bettersleep3_2.htm

## Chapter 6: It is Financially Restricting

[1] *BabyCenter.com*, "Cost of Raising a Child Calculator;" Figures are average estimates based on city or suburb, two-parent home with $57,260-$99,150 income, and were calculated on this website on April 13, 2012, http://www.babycenter.com/cost-of-raising-child-calculator
[2] Ibid.
[3] Michelle Singletary, "Spare the IPod, Unspoil the Child," *Washingtonpost.com*, April 16, 2006, www.washingtonpost.com/wp-dyn/content/article/2006/04/15/AR2006041500165_pf.html
[4] Ibid.
[5] Center on Media and Child Health, Children's Hospital Boston, "Cell Phones" (accessed May 25, 2011), http://www.cmch.tv/mentors/hottopic.asp?id=70
[6] Mark Morford, "American kids, dumber than dirt. Warning: The next generation might just be the biggest pile of idiots in U.S. history," *SFGate* (*San Francisco Chronicle*), October 24, 2007, http://www.sfgate.com/cgi-bin/article.cgi?file=/g/a/2007/10/24/notes102407.DTL
[7] Ibid.
[8] The National Assessment of Educational Progress (NAEP) Report Cards, the Council for American Private Education (CAPE), http://www.capenet.org/facts.html
[9] Council for American Private Education, "Indicators of School Crime and Safety, 2006," http://www.capenet.org/facts.html

[10] U.S. Department of Education, National Center for Education Statistics, Schools and Staffing Survey (SASS), "Digest of Education Statistics," http://nces.ed.gov/programs/digest/d05/tables/dt05_071.asp

[11] Council for American Private Education, "Average Private School Tuition 1999-2000," http://www.capenet.org/facts.html

[12] Mike Males, "Wild in Deceit: Why 'Teen Violence' is Poverty Violence in Disguise," *Extra* March/April 1996, http://www.fair.org/index.php?page=1351

[13] Center for Disease Control and Prevention, "National Birth Defects Prevention Month and National Folic Acid Awareness Week," *Morbidity and Mortality Weekly Report (MMWR)*, January 5, 2007, http://www.cdc.gov/mmwr/preview/mmwrhtml/mm5551a1.htm

[14] Center for Disease Control and Prevention, "Economic Costs of Birth Defects and Cerebral Palsy—United States, 1992," *Morbidity and Mortality Weekly Report (MMWR)*, September 22, 1995, http://www.cdc.gov/mmwr/preview/mmwrhtml/00038946.htm

[15] Vincent Ciaccio, "Kids Are Worth the Cost—Pro or Con?" Con: "Thanks, But No Thanks," *Business Week Debate Room*, Businessweek.com, http://www.businessweek.com/debateroom/archives/2007/08/kids_are_worth.html

## *Chapter 7: Earth Doesn't Need More Humans*

[1] Live World Population Growth Chart, *Health24* (accessed May 27, 2011), http://www.health24.com/Graphics/Graphics_World_Population/3561-3604,36539.asp

[2] U.S. Census Bureau, Current Population Projections (accessed October 17, 2011), http://www.npg.org/facts/world_pop_year.htm

[3] Ibid.

[4] Olivia Rose-Innes, Enviro Health editor, "6.8 Billion and Counting," *Health24*, updated July 8, 2010, http://www.health24.com/medical/Condition_centres/777-792-1461-1671,36531.asp

[5] Rosamund McDougall, Optimum Population Trust, "Too Many People: Earth's Population Problem," updated in 2010 (accessed May 27, 2011), http://populationmatters.org/wp-content/uploads/population_problem.pdf

[6] Carl Lehrburger, "The Disposable Diaper Myth," *Whole Earth Review*, Fall 1988.

[7] Craig Freudenrich, PhD, "How Landfills Work," *HowStuffWorks.com*, October 16, 2000 (accessed May 27, 2011), http://science.howstuffworks.com/landfill.htm

[8] Dr. Patrick Moore, "Landfill Issue Isn't Lack of Space," *SensibleEnvironmentalist.com*, http://www.napsnet.com/pdf_archive/34/65003.pdf

[9] Oceana organization, "Protect Our Oceans: Stop Cruise Ship Pollution," *Oceana.org* (accessed May 27, 2011), http://na.oceana.org/sites/default/files/o/uploads/cruiseshippollution_abigproblem.pdf

[10] Oracle Education Foundation, "The Greenhouse Effect," *ThinkQuest.org* (accessed May 27, 2011), http://library.thinkquest.org/11353/greenhouse.htm.

[11] E.O. Wilson, *The Future of Life* (Knopf, 2002).

[12] Don Hinrichsen and Bryant Robey, "Population and the Environment: The Global Challenge," *Actionbioscience.org*, http://www.actionbioscience.org/environment/hinrichsen_robey.html.

[13] Elisabeth Rosenthal, "World Food Stocks Dwindling Rapidly, UN Warns," *International Herald Tribune*, December 18, 2007, http://www.commondreams.org/archive/2007/12/18/5885

[14] Julian Cribb, Professor, FTSE, "The Coming Famine; Constraints to global food production in an overpopulated, affluent and resource-scarce world: the scientific challenge of the era," May 2008, UTA Foundation (accessed May 27, 2011), http://www.utafoundation.org/cribb.htm

[15] Bob Doppelt, "Population, Consumption Key to Climate Solutions," *The Register Guard*, February 9, 2009, www.registerguard.com

[16] John Feeny, "Population: The Elephant in the Room," *BBC News*, February 2, 2009 (accessed May 27, 2011), http://news.bbc.co.uk/2/hi/science/nature/7865332.stm

[17] RT Wolf, "The One Problem Causing Almost All the Others," December 5, 2008, *Mind-Manual.com* (accessed May 27, 2011), http://www.mind-manual.com/blog/index.php/2008/12/05/the-one-problem-causing-almost-all-the-others/

### Chapter 8: "I Don't Particularly Like Kids"

[1] Adrianne Frost, *I Hate Other People's Kids* (New York: Simon Spotlight Entertainment, 2006).

### Chapter 9: Parenting: The Good, The Bad and the Inept

[1] ThinkExist.com, excerpt by John Lennon, accessed May 1, 2012

[2] Tom McGrath, "Bad Parents: We give our kids everything and ask for nothing in return. Is it a shock that they're clueless and entitled? How a generation of well-intentioned Philadelphians has screwed up its children," *Philadelphia Magazine*, September 2007, http://www.phillymag.com/articles/bad_parents/

[3] Wikipedia 2007, http://en.wikipedia.org/wiki/Spanking#Legal_situation

[4] "Bill Making it Illegal to Spank Your Kids Going to the Legislature," *Digg.com*, January 18, 2007.

[5] *The Associated Press*, "The pitfalls of parenting: If it's not toys, it's something else to fear," August 26, 2007.

[6] Jackie Donaldson, "Take a Child Outside Week Starts Monday," *That'sFit.com*, September 21, 2007, http://www.thatsfit.com/2007/09/21/take-a-child-outside-week-begins-september-24/

[7] Rick Wolff, *The Sports Parenting Edge* (Running Press 2003).

[8] Ibid.

[9] Kevin Osborn, "The Future of Helicopter Parenting: The trend is gathering speed in the U.S.," report for Social Technologies, September 23, 2007.

[10] Cheryl Wetzstein, "SSI reforms drive drug users, drunks to faith-based welfare," January 26, 1998, *Insight on the News*

[11] U.S. Census Bureau, "12.2 million single parents," Internet Release Date September 2004, http://www.census.gov/population/socdemo/hh-fam/tabFM-2.pdf

[12] Office for National Statistics UK, July 7, 2005, Sources: Census, 2001, Office for National Statistics; General Register Office for Scotland; Northern Ireland Statistics and Research Agency, www.statistics.gov.uk/cci/nugget.asp?id=1166

[13] Australian Bureau of Statistics, "Australian Social Trends, 2004," June 15, 2004, www.abs.gov.au/Ausstats/abs@.nsf/94713ad445ff1425ca 25682000192af2/2f6217fec4a8fa37ca256ea70082b950!OpenDocument
[14] Sara McLanahan and Gary Sandefur, *Growing Up with a Single Parent: What Hurts, What Helps* (Cambridge: Harvard University Press, 1994).
[15] Cynthia Harper and Sara McLanahan, "Father Absence and Youth Incarceration," *Journal of Research on Adolescence,* 2004.
[16] Department of Health and Human Services (HHS), quoted in *ParentingTime.net* (accessed June 2, 2011), http://www.parentingtime.net/parents.htm
[17] U.S. Census Bureau, "Special Edition: Unmarried and Single Americans Week," July 19, 2004, http://www.census.gov/Press-Release/www/releases/archives/facts_for_features_special_editions/002265.html
[18] The National Council for One Parent Families, London, UK, "Lone Parent Facts," 4/10/07, http://www.oneparentfamilies.org.uk/1/lx3x1olx
[19] Beverly Engel, M.F.C.C., *The Parenthood Decision: Discovering Whether You Are Ready and Willing to Become a Parent* (Main Street Books, 1998).
[20] *TheSite.org*, "Should I have a baby?," *YouthNet UK*, April 23, 2010, http://www.thesite.org/sexandrelationships/safersex/unplannedpregnancy/shouldih aveababy

## Chapter 10: "I Fear Childbirth"

[1] *BabyCenter.com*, "Abdominal pain during pregnancy," October 2006, http://www.babycenter.com/0_abdominal-pain-during-pregnancy_204.bc
[2] Kate Snow and Sarah Amos, "Maternal Mortality Rates Rising in California," March 4, 2010, *ABC News,* http://abcnews.go.com/WN/changing-life-preventing-maternal-mortality/story?id=9914009#.T7GQXa4RXCk
[3] National Center for Health Statistics Data Brief, "Infant Mortality in the United States," October 2008 (6.71 deaths per 1,000 births in 2006), http://www.cdc.gov/nchs/data/databriefs/db09.htm
[44] American Academy of Financial Physicians, "Postpartum Depression and the Baby Blues," *FamilyDoctor.org*, updated February 2008, familydoctor.org/online/famdocen/home/women/pregnancy/ppd/general/379.html

## Chapter 11: "I Don't Want To Bring Them Into This World"

[1] EPE Research Center, "Cities in Crisis 2009: Closing the Graduation Gap," April 2009, http://www.edweek.org/media/cities_in_crisis_2009.pdf
[2] Clint Van Zandt, MSNBC analyst, "Beware of Cyber Stalkers," MSNBC TV, http://www.msnbc.msn.com/id/11101454/
[3] Crimes Against Children Research Center, "1 in 7 Youth: The statistics about Online Sexual Solicitations," http://www.unh.edu/ccrc/internet-crimes/factsheet_1in7.html
[4] MyKidsBrowser, "Internet Pornography Statistics" (accessed June 6, 2011), MyKidsBrowser.com, http://www.mykidsbrowser.com/pornography_stats.php
[5] Anti-Bullying Alliance Research, November 16, 2009, http://www.antibullyingalliance.org.uk/press_centre/latest_news/new_research_on _cyberbullying.aspx

[6] Amanda Lenhart, "Teens and Sexting," Pew Internet and American Life Project, December 15, 2009 (accessed January 22, 2010), http://www.pewinternet.org/Reports/2009/Teens-and-Sexting.aspx
[7] KlaasKids Foundation, "Missing Child Statistics" (accessed June 6, 2011), http://www.klaaskids.org/pg-mc-mcstatistics.html
[8] Siddharth Kara, *Sex Trafficking: Inside the Business of Modern Slavery* (Columbia University Press, 2008), 17.
[9] The National Center on Addiction and Substance Abuse at Columbia University, "National Survey of American Attitudes on Substance Abuse VI: Teens," report February 2001, p. iii.
[10] Partnership/MetLife Foundation Attitude Tracking Study (PATS) 2009, released March 2, 2010, http://www.drugfree.org/Files/PATS_Full_Report_2009_PDF
[11] National Center on Addiction and Substance Abuse at Columbia University, "Wasting the Best and the Brightest: Substance Abuse at America's Colleges and Universities," March 2007, http://www.casacolumbia.org/articlefiles/380-Wasting%20the%20Best%20and%20the%20Brightest.pdf
[12] British Medical Association (BMA), "Alcohol and Young People," *Prevention Alert,* Vol. 5, No. 6, May 10, 2002.
[13] Suicide Prevention Resource Center (SPRC), "Promoting Mental Health and Preventing Suicide in College and University Settings," October 21, 2004, 13-year study of 13,000 Kansas State University students, http://www.sprc.org/library/college_sp_whitepaper.pdf
[14] Alex Johnson of msnbc.com, NBC affiliate KXAN of Austin, Texas, contributed to this report. "Half of College Students Consider Suicide," *msnbc.com* and NBC, August 18, 2008, http://www.msnbc.msn.com/id/26272639/
[15] The Disaster Center, "United States Crime Rates 1960-2010," Source: FBI, Uniform Crime Reports, http://www.disastercenter.com/crime/uscrime.htm
[16] The Disaster Center, "United States Crime Index Rates Per 100,000 Inhabitants," Source: FBI, Uniform Crime Reports, www.disastercenter.com/crime

### Chapter 12: *"I Would Have to Give Up My Career"*

[1] Penelope Trunk, "Your family would be better off with a housewife (so would mine)," August 27, 2006, *blog.penelopetrunk.com,* http://blog.penelopetrunk.com/2006/08/27/your-family-would-be-better-off-with-a-housewife-so-would-mine/
[2] Michael Noer, "Don't Marry Career Women," opinion piece, *Forbes.com,* Career and Marriage, Aug. 23, 2006, http://www.forbes.com/home/2006/08/23/Marriage-Careers-Divorce_cx_mn_land.html
[3] Penelope Trunk, "Your family would be better off with a housewife (so would mine)," August 27, 2006, *blog.penelopetrunk.com,* http://blog.penelopetrunk.com/2006/08/27/your-family-would-be-better-off-with-a-housewife-so-would-mine/
[4] Sharon R. Cohany and Emy Sok, "Trends in labor force participation of married mothers of infants," February 2007, Monthly Labor Review Online, Bureau of Labor Statistics, http://www.bls.gov/opub/mlr/2007/02/art2exc.htm

[5] John Espinosa, comment to "A Downside to Daycare?" *Newsweek*, Health News, March 27, 2007.

[6] "The Negative Effects of Childcare? Studies: Longer Stays in Childcare Can Lead to Aggressive Child Behavior," *CBS News.com*, New York, July 17, 2003, http://www.cbsnews.com/stories/2003/07/16/earlyshow/living/parenting/main5636 39.shtml

[7] Online response from "Dan" to *Daycares Don't Care* (website), February 3, 2005, http://www.daycaresdontcare.org/PeopleSay/PeopleSay_page_15.htm

[8] Trent Hamm, "The Costs of Having Children," *The Simple Dollar*, January 2008, http://www.thesimpledollar.com/2008/01/16/the-costs-of-having-children/#comment-189035

[9] Sarah Achenbach, "Waving the Long Goodbye: After six years of struggling to be a full-time worker and a full-time mother, our writer bids farewell to her vision of career mom," *Style Magazine* of Baltimore, http://www.baltimorestyle.com/index.php/style/features_article/fe_mother_nd03/

[10] Carolyn Hax, syndicated columnist, "Tell Me About It: New mom putting on a performance," *Santa Barbara News Press*, February 17, 2008.

## Chapter 13: "We Like Our Relationship"

[1] Anonymous mother, "I wanted to be a full-time mother, but I hadn't reckoned on falling out of love with my husband," *Times Online UK*, July 15, 2007, http://women.timesonline.co.uk/tol/life_and_style/women/families/article2044495.ece

[2] Ibid.

[3] Drs. Les and Leslie Parrott, Real Relationships, "When Husband and Wife Become Mom and Dad," Families Northwest, (accessed December 29, 2008), http://www.familiesnorthwest.org/pages/page.asp?page_id=12238

[4] Ibid.

[5] Joe Sindoni, "Can Having a Baby Save Your Marriage?," May 1, 2007, http://www.authorsden.com/visit/viewnews.asp?AuthorID=57046&id=17066

[6] Coreen Beth Gray, "Living a Childfree Lifestyle: A Hermeneutical Analysis of Couples Who Choose Not to Have Children," Masters Thesis, CSUF, Spring 2003.

[7] Hilary Rich and Helaina Laks Kravitz, MD, *The Complete Idiot's Guide to the Perfect Marriage* (Alpha, June 2001).

[8] Joe Sindoni, "Can Having a Baby Save Your Marriage?," May 1, 2007, http://www.authorsden.com/visit/viewnews.asp?AuthorID=57046&id=17066

[9] Ibid.

[10] "Poll: Fewer People See Kids as Key to a Good Marriage," by David Crary, Associated Press, published in *Santa Barbara News-Press*, July 1, 2007

[11] Pew Research Center Publications, "Generation Gap in Values, Behaviors: As Marriage and Parenthood Drift Apart, Public is Concerned About Social Impact," Report July 1, 2007, http://pewresearch.org/pubs/526/marriage-parenthood

[12] Ibid.

[13] Kelly Sons, "Why Some Mothers Kill Their Children," December 2005, http://www.associatedcontent.com/article/14935/why_some_mothers_kill_their_c hildren.html

[14] Kathleen M. Heide, "Why Kids Kill Parents. Tragedy in the family: When kids murder their parents," *Psychology Today*, September 1, 1992 (accessed October 2, 2009), http://psychologytoday.com/articles/pto-19920901-000027.html%20/

[15] *Splash News*, "Ellen Degeneres and Portia De Rossi don't want a baby," July 18, 2010, *MSN.com* Celebrity UK, http://celebrity.uk.msn.com/news/gossip/articles.aspx?cp-documentid=154159095

### Chapter 14: Pets & Surrogates Are More Fun

[1] Australian Companion Animal Council, "Australians and Their Pets, The Facts," (accessed June 13, 2011), http://www.acac.org.au/pdf/PetFactBook_June-6.pdf
[2] American Veteran Medical Association, "U.S. Pet Ownership 2007," National pet ownership 57.4%, http://www.avma.org/reference/marketstats/ownership.asp
[3] Leger Marketing, "Canadians and their Pets," 2002 report (accessed February 22, 2011), http://www.legermarketing.com/documents/spclm/020617eng.pdf
[4] Pet Food Manufacturers' Association (PFMA) research, "Facts on Pet Ownership," *Pet Doctors,* August 22, 2008, http://www.petdoctors.co.uk/news-and-events/facts-on-pet-ownership/
[5] The WillaWoman blog (WillaWoman is disabled and a wheelchair service dog trainer), May 5, 2008, http://willawoman.blogspot.com/2008_05_01_archive.html
[6] Matthew Moore, "Cat owners more educated than dog owners," *The Telegraph,* February 6, 2010, http://www.telegraph.co.uk/science/science-news/7165164/Cat-owners-more-educated-than-dog-owners.html

### Chapter 15: Our Four Biggest Fears

[1] National Survey of Families and Households, "Study shows moms, dads more depressed than other adults," May 15, 2006 (Study of 13,000 U.S. Adults), Freedom News Service, http://www.eastvalleytribune.com/story/65616

### Chapter 16: Pressures to Procreate

[1] Karyn Johnson, "Childfree in a Military Community," *UnscriptedLife.net,* April 2007 (accessed October 2008).

### Chapter 17: "Breeder Bingo"—and Creative Comebacks

[1] Happily Childfree, "Quick Responses to Breeder Bingo," *happilychildfree.com*, (accessed June 15, 2011), http://www.happilychildfree.com/bingo.htm

### Chapter 18: "Stunted Souls"—and other Childfree Myths

[1] Study sponsored by four groups: Institute for American Values, Institute for Marriage and Public Policy, Families Northwest of Redmond, WA, the Georgia Family Council, April 15, 2008, http://www.americanvalues.org/coff/media/time.pdf
[2] *Huffington Post,* "'Octomom' Nadya Suleman Has Bankruptcy Case Thrown Out Of Court," May 12, 2012, http://www.huffingtonpost.com/2012/05/16/octomom-bankruptcy-thrown-out_n_1520521.html
[3] Betsy Hart, "Ain't this America…The kid trap," June 16, 2006, *Capitol Hill Blue*, http://www.capitolhillblue.com/artman/publish/printer_8884.shtml

## Chapter 19: Stigma and Status in a Kid-Centric World

[1] Laura Clark, "Childless women 'vilified by bosses': Why NOT having a family can ruin your career," *Daily Mail*, May 18, 2009, http://www.dailymail.co.uk/femail/article-1183895/Childless-women-vilified-bosses-Why-NOT-having-family-ruin-career.html

[2] Robin Cooper, "Child-free isn't too risky," Philadelphia Sex Examiner, *Examiner.com*, August 15, 2009, http://www.examiner.com/article/child-free-isn-t-too-risky

[3] Dr. Martee Hensley, "Childless Women and Cancer Risks," *Everyday Health*, October 21, 2008, http://www.everydayhealth.com/womens-health-specialist/childless-women-and-cancer.aspx

[4] Karyn Johnson, "Childfree in a Military Community," *UnscriptedLife.net*, April 2007, http://unscriptedlife.net/articles/childfree-in-a-military-community

[5] J.D. Griffloen, "Against babies in bars: the Brooklyn 'Stroller Manifesto,'" *parentdish (Aol Lifestyle)*, December 27, 2005, http://www.parentdish.com/2005/12/27/against-babies-in-bars-the-brooklyn-stroller-manifesto/

[6] Ramona Creel, "Celebrating Christmas the Child-Free Way," *RamonaCreel.com*, December 23, 2009, http://www.ramonacreel.com/BlogEntry.asp?Entry=852

[7] Elle Halliwell, "$2,500 cakes being made for kids' parties," *News.com.au*, March 9, 2008, http://www.news.com.au/cakes-being-made-for-kids-parties/story-e6frfkp9-1111115750155

[8] Alison Sandy, "Parents fear units pose spying threat to Wynnum school," *Courier Mail*, December 11, 2008, http://www.couriermail.com.au/lifestyle/parenting/units-a-haven-for-pedophiles/comments-e6frer7o-1111118284836

[9] "Park attendants ordered to interrogate adults spotted without children," *Mail Online*, September 10, 2008, http://www.dailymail.co.uk/news/article-1053863/Park-attendants-ordered-interrogate-adults-spotted-children.html#

## Chapter 20: Breeder Entitlement

[1] Elinor Burkett, The Baby Boon: How Family-Friendly America Cheats the Childless (New York: The Free Press, 2000), p. 216.

[2] Harvey Wallop, "Women without children should be allowed maternity leave, survey says," Telegraph.co.uk, October 16, 2009, http://www.telegraph.co.uk/news/uknews/6243019/Women-without-children-should-be-allowed-maternity-leave-survey-says.html

[3] Martin Beckford, "New fathers should get eight months paid paternity leave," Telegraph.co.uk, March 30, 2009, www.telegraph.co.uk/news/uknews/5070951/New-fathers-should-get-eight-months-paid-paternity-leave.html

[4] "Flexible Working Arrangements," Fair Work Online (accessed April 23, 2010), http://www.fairwork.gov.au/Pay-Leave-and-conditions/Conditions-of-employment/Pages/Flexible-working-arrangements.aspx?role=employers

[5] Elinor Burkett, The Baby Boon: How Family-Friendly America Cheats the Childless (New York: The Free Press, 2000).

[6] Ibid, 8.

[7] Martin Vaughan, "House Plan Targets Child-Care Tax Credit," The Wall Street Journal, May 11, 2010, http://online.wsj.com/home-page

[8] D. Day, Andrew Fisher: prime minister of Australia (Harper Collins Publishers, 2008), p. 258.

[9] Sandra Van Eyk, "Penalising The Deliberately Barren: An Evaluation of Australia's Pronatalist Policy," an unpublished post-graduate paper, 2010

[10] Ministry of Community Development, Youth and Sports, "Baby Bonus Scheme Brochure," Singapore, November 2010, http://www.babybonus.gov.sg/bbss/html/English2008.pdf

[11] Jeremy P. Meyer, "Birth leave sought for girls," The Denver Post, January 7, 2008, http://www.denverpost.com/news/ci_7899096

## Chapter 21: Single & Kidfree (For Better or Worse)

[1] U.S. Census Bureau, America's Families and Living Arrangements: 2011, "Marital Status of People 15 Years and Over, 2011" (accessed April 13, 2012), http://www.census.gov/population/www/socdemo/hh-fam/cps2011.html

[2] Calculated by multiplying the Total Unmarried Adults (47.2% in 2010) by the Childless Women Age 40-44 (18.8% in 2010), for a total of 8.9%.

[3] Gwyneth Rees, "Rise of the Freemale," June 8, 2008, FMWF (Daily Mail) http://www.fmwf.com/features/2008/06/rise-of-the-freemale/

[4] 2010 State of our Unions, "Social Indicators of Marital Health & Well-Being," report by The National Marriage Project (University of Virginia) and the Institute for American Values (accessed November 20, 2011), http://stateofourunions.org/2010/si-cohabitation.php

[5] Bella DePaulo, "Single and Happy: It's the norm, not the exception" (accessed July 20, 2010), http://www.mysinglespace.org/images/Bella_DePaulo-Single_and_Happy.pdf

[6] Ibid.

[7] Arthur C. Brooks, Gross National Happiness (New York: Basic Books, 2008), pp. 60-61.

## Chapter 22: What if We Don't Agree?

[1] Larry Smith, "Do You Want Kids? He wants kids. She doesn't," Men's Health, August 17, 2004, http://www.menshealth.com/best-life/fatherhood-and-your-family-tree

## Chapter 23: Finding Purpose—Beyond Procreation

[1] Larry King Live, CNN, September 30, 2006, quoted from the transcript of the show, http://transcripts.cnn.com/TRANSCRIPTS/0609/30/lkl.01.html

[2] President, Woman's Christian Temperance Union (1907), "President's annual address," National Woman's Christian Temperance Union, 37th (accessed March 2, 2010), http://pds.lib.harvard.edu/pds/viewtext/2580740?op=t&n=3

[3] Feminists for Life of America (FFLA), "Herstory: Susan B. Anthony," Mary Krane Derr, reprinted from "The American Feminist," Spring 1998, p. 19 http://www.feministsforlife.org/history/herstory/sbanthon.htm

[4] Richard Ford, "Ten Rules for Writing Fiction," guardian.co.uk, February 20, 2010, http://www.guardian.co.uk/books/2010/feb/20/ten-rules-for-writing-fiction-part-one

[5] Ayn Rand, "About the Author," *Atlas Shrugged* (Penguin Group USA Incorporated, 1992), pp. 1170-1171.

## Chapter 24: Are We Happy Being Kidfree? You Decide!

[1] Sara McLanahan and Julia Adams, "The Effects of Children on Adults' Psychological Well-Being: 1957-1976," *Social Forces* 68 (1989): 124-146.
[2] Robin W. Simon, "The Joys of Parenthood, Reconsidered," *Contexts,* Spring 2008: 40-45.
[3] Ibid, 43.
[4] Daniel Gilbert, *Stumbling on Happiness* (New York: Vintage Books, 2007), 243.
[5] D. Kahneman et al., "A Survey Method for Characterizing Daily Life Experience: The Day Reconstruction Method," *Science* 306 (2004): 1776-1780.
[6] "The State of Our Unions: The Social Health of Marriage in America, 2006," The National Marriage Project, Rutgers, State University of New Jersey, July 2006, http://www.virginia.edu/marriageproject/annualreports.html
[7] Lucy Cavendish, "I love my kids, but I admit it—I'm happier on my own!" March 2010, *Daily Mail,* http://www.dailymail.co.uk/femail/article-1255282/I-love-kids-I-admit--Im-happier-own.html
[8] Ibid.
[9] Ibid.

## Chapter 25: You Are Not Alone

[1] *Childfreebychoice.com*, "The Long List of Childfree (and Childless) in History" (accessed September 3, 2008), http://www.childfreebychoice.com/history.htm
[2] *Daily Mail Weekend* magazine, "I want to marry my toy boy," June 14, 2008, http://www.jacquelinebissetfans.org/dailymail.html
[3] Diana Vilbert, "Child-Free Celebrities," *Marie Claire*, August 11, 2010, http://www.marieclaire.com/sex-love/relationship-issues/articles/child-free-celebs
[4] *O, The Oprah Magazine*, "Kim Cattrall's Aha! Moment," March 2003, excerpts from article, http://www.oprah.com/spirit/Kim-Cattralls-Aha-Moment
[5] Diana Vilbert, "Child-Free Celebrities," *Marie Claire*, August 11, 2010, http://www.marieclaire.com/sex-love/relationship-issues/articles/child-free-celebs
[6] IMDb, "Biography for Julie Christie" (accessed June 2012) http://www.imdb.com/name/nm0001046/bio
[7] *Heat* magazine, "George offers to adopt Brad's kids," October 17, 2009, http://heat.co.za/celebrity-news/george-offers-adopt-brads-kids/3125/
[8] *The Inquisitr,* "John Corbett and Bo Derek 'Beyond' Having Biological Children," June 10, 2010, http://www.inquisitr.com/75360/john-corbett-and-bo-derek-beyond-having-biological-children/
[9] *Splash News,* "Ellen DeGeneres and Portia De Rossi Don't Want a Baby," July 18, 2010, http://celebrity.uk.msn.com/news/gossip/articles.aspx?cp-documentid=154159095
[10] Maureen Paton, "Dana Delany: I've tried hard all my life not to be a desperate housewife," *Daily Mail,* October 16, 2008, www.dailymail.co.uk/home/you/article-1073291/8216-I-8217-ve-tried-hard-life-desperate-housewife-8217.html#ixzz0vrwD9mRL

[11] *Woman's Day,* "Cameron: It's natural to not want children," June 15, 2009, http://womansday.ninemsn.com.au/celebrity/celebrityheadlines/997497/cameron-its-natural-to-not-want-children
[12] *The Inquisitr,* "Leonardo DiCaprio Too Busy for Children," February 3, 2010, http://www.inquisitr.com/60353/leonardo-dicaprio-too-busy-for-children/
[13] *Childfreebychoice.com,* "The Long List of Childfree (and Childless) in History" (accessed September 3, 2008), http://www.childfreebychoice.com/history.htm
[14] Bonnie Erbe, "Why Non-Parents are Happier than Parents," *U.S. News & World Report,* July 9, 2010, http://www.usnews.com/opinion/blogs/erbe
[15] Scot Haller, "Bringing Up Baby: For *Dynasty's* Linda Evans, Playing Mom Is the Next Best Thing to Being One," *People Magazine,* December 17, 1984, http://www.people.com/people/archive/article/0,,20089412,00.html
[16] Diana Vilbert, "Child-Free Celebrities," *Marie Claire,* August 11, 2010, http://www.marieclaire.com/sex-love/relationship-issues/articles/child-free-celebs
[17] *Childfreebychoice.com,* "The Long List of Childfree (and Childless) in History" (accessed September 3, 2008), http://www.childfreebychoice.com/history.htm
[18] *OK!* Magazine, "Tanya Franks and Jennifer Hennessey," August 19, 2008, http://www.ok.co.uk/food/view/2612/Tanya-Franks-and-Jennifer-Hennessy/
[19] Wikipedia, "Ava Gardner" (accessed October 1, 2010), http://en.wikipedia.org/wiki/Ava_Gardner
[20] Diana Vilbert, "Child-Free Celebrities," *Marie Claire,* August 11, 2010, http://www.marieclaire.com/sex-love/relationship-issues/articles/child-free-celebs
[21] Rosie Millard, "News Review Interview: Ricky Gervais," November 2, 2008, *Times Online,* http://entertainment.timesonline.co.uk/tol/arts_and_entertainment/tv_and_radio/article5061421.ece
[22] Marc Malkin, "Is *Mad Men's* Jon Hamm Ready to Have Kids?," *E! Online,* February 24, 2012, www.eonline.com/news/296610/is-mad-men-s-jon-hamm-ready-to-have-kids
[23] Transcript from CNN's *Larry King Live,* interview with Chelsea Handler, April 1, 2010, http://transcripts.cnn.com/TRANSCRIPTS/1004/01/lkl.01.html
[24] *Fixster.com,* Katharine Hepburn Quotes (accessed October 7, 2010), http://www.flixster.com/actor/katharine-hepburn/katharine-hepburn-quotes
[25] *Cinema.com,* "Angelica Huston: I Don't Want Children," November 11, 2000, http://www.cinema.com/news/item/1450/angelica-huston-i-dont-want-children.phtml
[26] *ContactMusic.com,* "No Kids for Judd," January 29, 2006, http://www.contactmusic.com/new/xmlfeed.nsf/story/no-kids-for-judd_29_01_2006
[27] Katy Hall, "Vincent Kartheiser: I Won't Have Kids For Environmental Reasons," *The Huffington Post,* November 17, 2010, TheHuffingtonPost.com, Inc., http://www.huffingtonpost.com/2010/11/17/vincent-kartheiser-i-wont_n_785053.html
[28] Diana Vilbert, "Child-Free Celebrities," *Marie Claire,* August 11, 2010, http://www.marieclaire.com/sex-love/relationship-issues/articles/child-free-celebs
[29] *TV.com,* "Bill Maher Trivia and Quotes" (accessed October 11, 2010), http://www.tv.com/bill-maher/person/22299/trivia.html

[30] *TheBosh.com*, "Eva Mendes in 'no rush' to have children," December 20, 2008, http://thebosh.com/archives/2008/12/eva_mendes_in_no_rush_to_have_children.php

[31] Daniel Schom, "Nudity No 'Big Deal' for Dame Helen," *CBSNews.com*, August 3, 2007, (on Morley Safer's interview with Helen Mirren), http://www.cbsnews.com/stories/2007/01/04/60minutes/main2330675_page3.shtml?tag=contentMain;contentBody

[32] Alexandra Paul, "Married Without Children," *Huffington Post*, February 17, 2010, http://www.huffingtonpost.com/alexandra-paul/married-without-children_b_465517.html

[33] Liza Hamm and Michelle Tauber, "Rachael Ray's Recipe for Marriage," May 2, 2007, *People*, http://www.people.com/people/article/0,,20037511,00.html

[34] *PR-Inside.com*, "Tarantino Sacrificed Love for His Career," July 28, 2009, *http://www.pr-inside.com/entertainment-blog/2009/07/28/tarantino-sacrificed-love-for-his-career/*

[35] David Hochman, "Girl! Girl! Girl!," January 2009, *Angelino* magazine, p. 72.

[36] Diana Vilbert, "Child-Free Celebrities," *Marie Claire*, August 11, 2010, http://www.marieclaire.com/sex-love/relationship-issues/articles/child-free-celebs

[37] Dixie Reed, "'Bend' it like Walken: Actor has more to say about food and hair than acting," *The Sacramento Bee*, October 24, 2004 (accessed October 12, 2010) http://www.sacticket.com/static/movies/news/1024walken.html

[38] *O, The Oprah Magazine*, "Oparah Talks To You," May 2009, p. 254

[39] *Contactmusic.com*, "Zellweger Re-Evaluates Motherhood," August 21, 2009, http://www.contactmusic.com/news.nsf/story/zellweger-re-evaluates-motherhood_1113603

[40] Wikipedia, "Louis Andriessen" (accessed October 13, 2010), http://en.wikipedia.org/wiki/Louis_Andriessen

[41] David Sheff, "The Captain & Tennille Go Out on a Limb with a New Image," *People*, March 17, 1980, http://www.people.com/people/archive/article/0,,20076054,00.html

[42] Elysa Gardner, "Former 'Idol' Kelly Clarkson has all she ever wanted," *USA TODAY*, March 8, 2009, http://www.usatoday.com/life/music/news/2009-03-08-clarkson-album_N.htm

[43] *Brainy Quote*, http://www.brainyquote.com/quotes/authors/s/stevie_nicks.html

[44] *Contactmusic.com*, "The Cure-Robert Smith Happy Without Children," July 23, 2004, http://www.contactmusic.com/news-article/robert-smith-happy-without-children

[45] *RobbieWilliams.com*, "Robbie Talks to the Big Issue," Interview by Hattie Collins reprinted courtesy of *The Big Issue*, December 18, 2006, http://www.robbiewilliams.com/discography/interviews/robbie-talks-to-the-big-issue

[46] Janet Maslin, "In Search of the Dark Muse of a Master of the Macabre," *The New York Times*, October 6, 2006, http://www.nytimes.com/2006/10/26/books/26masl.html?_r=2&oref=slogin&ref=arts&pagewanted=print

[47] Michael Redmon, "History 101: Margaret Ely Webb," *Santa Barbara Independent*, April 3, 2008, http://www.independent.com/news/2008/apr/03/i-am-interested-artist-margaret-webb-who-i-think-l/

[48] *Childfreebychoice.com*, "The Long List of Childfree (and Childless) in History" (accessed September 3, 2008), http://www.childfreebychoice.com/history.htm

[49] Ibid.

[50] Diana Vilbert, "Child-Free Celebrities," *Marie Claire*, August 11, 2010, http://www.marieclaire.com/sex-love/relationship-issues/articles/child-free-celebs

[51] *The Guardian*, "Ten Rules for Writing Fiction," February 20, 2010, Guardian News and Media Limited, http://www.guardian.co.uk/books/2010/feb/20/ten-rules-for-writing-fiction-part-one

[52] Wikipedia, "Dr. Seuss" (accessed October 12, 2010), http://en.wikipedia.org/wiki/Dr._Seuss

[53] Elizabeth Gilbert, *Eat, Pray, Love* (New York: Penguin Books, 2006), p. 92.

[54] Wikipedia, "Marguerite Henry," (accessed October 12, 2010), http://en.wikipedia.org/wiki/Marguerite_Henry

[55] Charles Lamb, "A Bachelor's Complaint of the Behaviour of Married People," (excerpt), from Essays of Elia, *London Magazine* (1823), http://www.ucs.louisiana.edu/~jer6616/elia(1823).htm#MARRIED

[56] Philip Larkin, excerpt from a poem, *Goodreads.com* "author quotes," http://www.goodreads.com/author/quotes/64716.Philip_Larkin

[57] Aine Nugent, "Childfree and happy...no kidding," *Independent Woman*, (excerpt), June 27, 2008, http://www.independent.ie/lifestyle/independent-woman/love-sex/childfree-and-happy--no-kidding-1421760.html

[58] Molly Peacock, *Paradise, Piece by Piece*, (New York: Riverhead Books, 1998), excerpt from Chapter 1.

[59] George Bernard Shaw, *ThinkExist.com Quotations* (accessed March 14, 2012), http://en.thinkexist.com/quotes/George_Bernard_Shaw/

[60] The Literature Network, accessed 10/13/10, http://www.online-literature.com/kate-wiggin/

[61] Emma Goldman, *Thinkexist.com Quotations* (accessed 3/13/12), http://en.thinkexist.com/quotes/Emma_Goldman/

[62] *People*, "Danica Patrick says motherhood isn't on the horizon," May 26, 2008, Time Inc., http://celebritybabies.people.com/2008/05/26/danica-patrick/

[63] *Blackcelebkids.com*, "Serena Williams: I Want To Have Kids But Am Too Forgetful," *BKM*, February 9, 2010, http://www.blackcelebkids.com/2010/02/09/serena-williams-i-want-to-have-kids-but-am-too-forgetful/

[64] Caroline Overington, "All Work and No Play? No Way," *The Age*, July 3, 2004, http://www.theage.com.au/articles/2004/07/02/1088488153788.html?from=storyrhs

Made in the USA
Charleston, SC
19 December 2013